TERRORISM RESEARCH

AND

PUBLIC POLICY

Is terrorism the work of crazies and misfits? Recent research has turned away from this idea and focuses instead on understanding how normal people – perhaps especially idealistic people – can become capable of terrorist acts. This book includes several contributions to the new look in terrorism research, including a history of terrorism that reaches back two thousand years, an examination of the life-cycle of terrorist groups that have come and gone since World War II, and a new theory of the stages by which political protest becomes political violence and terrorism.

Is terrorism a research category or a political statement? Many in traditional academic disciplines believe that 'terrorism' is a pejorative label that does not identify any coherent set of behaviors. From this point of view, terrorism research makes no more sense than the now-discredited studies of 'witchcraft'. This book puts the critique into print for the first time, together with recent terrorism research that offers at least the beginnings of an answer to the critique.

How is terrorism research communicated to policy makers who have to deal with terrorist threats? Poorly and with considerable difficulty, according to the contributors to this book, and the reasons for the failures of communication are addressed both by those who would have closer relations with government and those who would keep government at a distance. Conferences and books about terrorism research have been numerous, but this book is unusual in giving explicit consideration to the problems of communicating and applying the results of such research.

Clark McCauley is Professor of Psychology at Bryn Mawr College, Pennsylvania. He has chaired Harry Guggenheim Foundation conferences on violence and his previously published research concentrates on the psychology of terrorist groups and individuals.

First published 1991 in Great Britain by
FRANK CASS AND COMPANY LIMITED
Gainsborough House, 11 Gainsborough Road,
London E11 1 RS, England

and in the United States by
FRANK CASS
c/o International Specialized Book Services Ltd.
5602 N.E. Hassalo Street
Portland, OR 97213–3640

British Library Cataloguing in Publication Data

Terrorism research and public policy.
1. Terrorism
I. McCauley, Clark   II. Series
322.42

ISBN 0-7146-3429-8

Library of Congress Cataloging-in-Publication Data

Terrorism research and public policy / edited by Clark McCauley.
    p.   cm.
'This group of studies first appears in a special issue terrorism
and public policy in Terrorism and political violence, vol. 3, no.
1' – T.p. verso.
Includes bibliographical references and index.
ISBN 0-7146-3429-8
    1. Terrorism—Psychological aspects. 2. Terrorists—Psychology.
3. Terrorism—Government policy. I. McCauley, Clark.
HV6431.T495   1991
3634'5—dc20   91-12424
                                                                            CIP

This group of studies first appeared in a Special Issue on Terrorism
Research and Public Policy in *Terrorism and Political Violence*, Vol. 3,
No. 1, (Spring 1991) published by Frank Cass & Co. Ltd.

Printed and bound in Great Britain by
Antony Rowe Ltd, Chippenham

TERRORISM RESEARCH
AND
PUBLIC POLICY

Edited by

CLARK McCAULEY

FRANK CASS

Contents

Notes on Contributors

Clark McCauley is a social psychologist whose research interests include stereotyping and group dynamics. He is Professor of Psychology at Bryn Mawr College, Bryn Mawr, Pennsylvania 19010.

Everett L. Wheeler, an ancient historian specializing in Graeco-Roman military affairs and the history of military theory, is author of *Stratagem and the Vocabulary of Military Trickery* (1988) and translator with W. J. Renfore of Hans Delbrück, *History of the Art of War*, Vols. II–IV (1980–1985). He is currently Scholar in Residence at Duke University, Durham, NC 27706.

Joseba Zulaika teaches Anthropology in the Basque Studies Program and the Department of Anthropology at the University of Nevada, Reno. He has written on fishermen, hunters and soldiers. His most recent ethnographic study is *Basque Violence: Metaphor and Sacrament* (1988). He is currently completing an essay on terrorism as ritual warfare.

Ehud Sprinzak teaches Political Science at the Hebrew University of Jerusalem. He is presently a Visiting Professor of Government at Georgetown University. He is the author of *Illegalism in Israel Society, The Ascendence of the Israeli Radical Right*, and numerous other monographs and essays on political extremism, violence and terrorism.

Martha Crenshaw is Professor of Government at Wesleyan University, Middletown, Connecticut 06457.

Ariel Merari is an Associate Professor at the Department of Psychology, Tel Aviv University, and Director of the Political Violence Research Project.

Gustavo Gorriti is a journalist and the author of *Sendero: Historia de la guerra milenaria en el Peru* (Lima, Peru: Apoyo ASA, 1990), the first of a three-volume series about the Shining Path insurrection. He lives in Lima, where hs is now investigating the impact of the Sendero war and the drug trade on indigenous Indian groups in Peru. An abbreviated English version of his three volumes will be published by Princeton University Press.

Raphael S. Ezekiel, Associate Professor in Psychology at the University of Michigan, holds a Berkeley doctorate and has worked for some years under grants from the Harry Frank Guggenheim Foundation and the Carnegie Corporation of New York in field-based studies of racist extremists. His in-depth interviews and field observations will be incorporated in a forthcoming book *Hitler's Stepchildren*. His previous book, *Voices from the Corner*, examined similar in-depth research among poor Blacks in Detroit.

Jerrold M. Post, MD is Professor of Psychiatry, Political Psychology and International Affairs at The George Washington University. He founded and directed the US government's Center for the Analysis of Personality and Political Behavior. Research interests include: the psychology of leadership and leader-follower relations, crisis decision-making, and the psychology of terrorism. *The Captive King* (co-authored by R. Robins), a study of the effects of illness and disability on leadership, will be published by Yale University Press.

Editor's Introduction:
Terrorism Research and Public Policy

Clark McCauley

There have been in recent years a number of conferences, national and international, to examine the problems governments face in dealing with terrorism. Such conferences usually bring together the relatively small number of those who study terrorist groups, who present their most recent studies of terrorist behavior and debate the implications of their research in relation to potential responses to terrorism. The seminar at the School of American Research in Santa Fe, New Mexico, from 12 to 16 October 1987, was notably different in going beyond discussion of research to focus on the problems and prospects of putting research on terrorism to work in the formation of public policy. The seminar brought together an international group of investigators who, after three days of discussion, were joined by representatives of three US government agencies with operational responsibilities for combatting terrorism: Larry Ropka from the Defense Department, David Long from the State Department, and Richard Marquize from the FBI. The result was a very lively treatment of both research issues and the nature of the relation between terrorism researchers and policy-makers who might profit from their work.

The ten scholars who participated in the seminar were themselves a very diverse group, both with regard to their backgrounds and with regard to their views of terrorism research in relation to policy. Included were an anthropologist (Joseba Zulaika), an historian (Everett Wheeler), a journalist (Gustavo Gorriti), three political scientists (Martha Crenshaw, Ehud Sprinzak, John Thompson), three psychologists (Ariel Merari, Clark McCauley, Raphael Ezekiel), and a psychiatrist (Jerrold Post). They agreed generally that they were all interested in terrorism 'from below' – violence by groups outside of government – as opposed to violence 'from above' – violence visited by governments upon their own or other citizens. But beyond this agreement lay a multiplicity of views represented in the different papers prepared for the seminar.

Six of those papers have been revised in the light of seminar discussion and are presented in this volume in an ordering designed to highlight the two major issues raised.[1] The first issue concerns the value of terrorism as a category for research, and the first four papers offer two kinds of challenge and two kinds of response on this issue. Of course scholars like

1

to begin with definitions, and of course policy-makers are impatient with academic hair-splitting. But there are important practical implications in the definition of terrorism, not least in affecting what research policy-makers will support or even attend to in trying to cope with terrorism. The second issue concerns the practical problems associated with terrorism research, and especially the problems of communication between academic researchers and policy-makers. Three papers address this second issue, again representing important differences in opinion and perspective. Finally, the last paper is the editor's effort to convey an overview of seminar papers and discussions in relation to these issues.

The difficulty of defining terrorism is introduced in the first article as Everett Wheeler puts modern terrorism in the context of two thousand years of history of unconventional warfare. Those who seek to distinguish guerrilla warfare from terrorism will find scant support in this history, which suggests rather that terrorism may be best understood as the warfare of the weak. Similarly, those who think of terrorism as a modern problem, for which some new social or technological solution must be sought, will be challenged to see both terrorism and guerrilla war traced to a common origin in primitive war.

In the second contribution, Joseba Zulaika goes still further in raising doubts about terrorism as a category. His study is a critique – as a Basque and as an anthropologist – of the report of an international commission of terrorism researchers who were brought in by the Spanish government for advice about how to deal with Basque terrorism. Zulaika raises the question of whether the category 'terrorist' is anything more than evaluative label and whether, in particular, there is sufficient coherence in the instances thus labeled to be a useful category for understanding behavior. He points to totem and witchcraft as categories that once seemed obviously useful but which have been left behind by the progress of anthropological research. The article is also valuable in raising to our attention the problematic moral status of 'the state'. There is no easy answer to the question of when a government is legitimate, when it is worth fighting for or worth fighting against.

The third paper, by Ehud Sprinzak, introduces a theory of the origins of terrorist groups in normal opposition politics. The theory describes a trajectory from opposition to particular policies or policy-makers, through opposition to the whole system of government in terms of an alternative ideology or culture, to a culminating opposition to every individual associated with government. It is the last stage that supports and requires terrorist violence against noncombatants, and, in response to Zulaika, it may be the indiscriminate violence of the last stage that finally gives the state moral superiority over its opposition. Sprinzak's theory offers a promising way of thinking about the commonality beneath the diversity of terrorist groups and terrorist individuals: their common trajectory from non-terrorist beginnings in political opposition.

The fourth paper, by Martha Crenshaw, examines a neglected area of terrorism research: when and how do terrorist movements come to an end? It is not easy to know whether a movement is dead or only temporarily exhausted, or changing tactics, or fissioned into new groups. Even allowing for some uncertainty about details of particular groups, however, Crenshaw's review of 77 post-Second World War terrorist groups represents a major scholarly accomplishment. The good news is that 46 of these groups seem now no longer a threat: 11 of these lasted five years or less, 18 lasted five to ten years, and 17 lasted more than ten years. The bad news is that 28 groups continue in terrorism, 24 of these having lasted already ten years or more. Further, the review indicates that explanations of terrorist decline appear to be various and complex in ways that do not lead to easy prescriptions for policy makers. Still, it is clear that government forces seldom have been able to inflict decisive defeat even on domestic terrorists, much less on terrorists with international bases or support. The interaction of government and terrorist actions, especially in determining the sympathies of the governed, appears to be more important in determining the decline of terrorism than any simple effect of government policy.

It is worth noting that Sprinzak's theory about the beginnings of terrorism can complement rather than compete with Crenshaw's findings about how terrorism ends. The understanding of origin does not logically entail understanding of end. This is a distinction commonly recognized in arguments about both biological and social evolution, where the present function of a structure or a behavior cannot explain its origin (cf. Zulaika, this volume). Rather the existence of a variation is necessary before selection can operate for or against it. Similarly, the rise of a terrorist group at a particular time and place may be the result of factors very different from the conditions that make the group more or less successful. The evolutionary perspective shared by Sprinzak and Crenshaw is at least the beginning of an answer to the questions raised by Wheeler and Zulaika about terrorism as a category. A trajectory of terrorist psychology and life-cycle pressures on terrorist organization may offer sufficient commonality across groups to make terrorism a useful analytic category.

The next three contributions move to the issue of the proper relation between terrorist researchers and policy-makers.

The fifth paper, by Ariel Merari, draws on the author's extensive experience as both researcher and consultant on problems of terrorism. On the research side, he acknowledges considerable doubt about whether terrorism is one pheonomenon or many, considerable difficulty in getting good data on the characteristics of individual terrorists and terrorist

groups, and considerable amateurism in a proliferating literature interpreting the few data available. On the consulting side he suspects that
academic research has thus far produced little that can be useful to policy-
makers, and, at the same time, he finds major problems in getting that
little to the attention of policy-makers. The problems of communication
between academics and policy makers are probably greater in larger
nations, so Merari's experience in Israel can be taken as a minimal
estimate of these difficulties. Perhaps the best advice for academic
researchers in this chapter is to concentrate on what they can do better
than government specialists with access to the latest classified cables, that
is, the work that requires long application to the same problem. The
weakness of government specialists is that their attention to a problem is
usually measured in days and their tenure in the same job seldom more
than a year or two.

The sixth paper, by Gustavo Gorriti, represents a strong contrast with
the previous one. Where Merari is concerned with how to get better
attention from policy-makers for better research, Gorriti's experience as
a journalist inclines him to share Zulaika's concern about the dangers of
too close a relation between researcher and policy-maker. Reporting on
Peru's Shining Path insurrection for the Lima weekly *Caretas*, Gorriti
found that objective research required criticizing the terrorism of government security forces as well as Shining Path terrorism. Peru is a shaky and
fallible democracy for which the Shining Path is at least as threatening as
any terrorist threat to Israel, so the contrast in the views of Gorriti and
Merari is all the more striking. If Gorriti is correct, the government
agencies closely assisted by academic researchers will get a product less
objective, less creative, and less useful than if academics were to keep
their distance.

The seventh was written after the seminar was over by two of the
seminar participants, Raphael Ezekiel and Jerrold Post. They bring
together here much of the seminar discussion about how researchers –
those who desire to – can contribute to government efforts against
terrorism. The study suggests that the difficulties of communication
between researchers and policy-makers are perhaps best understood as
the clash of two cultures defined by different priorities, different assumptions, and different languages. In light of the difficulties, a number of
different models of communicating research results are explored; these
range from the careful distance of writing for publication what policy-
makers among others may read, to personal participation in the rough-
and-tumble of policy-making.

The eighth paper is the editor's overview of some of the discussion and
debate of the seminar that did not get specifically into any of the previous
articles. This contribution attempts to pull together some of the implications

of the work of the seminar, both for future research toward understanding terrorist groups and for policy-making in the light of recent research.

As noted at the beginning of this introduction, there have been in recent years a number of conferences aimed at clarifying and updating terrorism research for policy-makers with responsibilities for combatting terrorism. The Santa Fe seminar represented in the contributions to this volume did some of this kind of work, but went beyond it to raise questions about how or even whether researchers should try to contribute to policy. Both kinds of question bring researchers up against their differences with policy-makers.

One answer to the clash of cultures is more acquaintance of each side with the culture of the other. The opportunity for this kind of broadening acquaintance is not easy to come by for busy people in or out of government, and the Santa Fe seminar was a conspicuous success in providing just this rare opportunity. Thanks are owed to the Harry Frank Guggenheim Foundation, and in particular to the directing enthusiasm of the Foundation's Program Officer, Karen Colvard, for supporting the seminar. Since the seminar, the Foundation has continued a generous sponsorship of occasional meetings between policy-makers and scholars whose work can illuminate problems of terrorist behavior. In this way the work of the seminar continues.

NOTE

1. Thompson's paper has been published elsewhere: see Thompson [*1989*].

Terrorism and Military Theory: An Historical Perspective

Everett L. Wheeler

Late twentieth-century terrorism should be viewed as a form of war and falls within the framework of military theory. Terrorism, like guerrilla warfare a form of unconventional warfare, represents a revival of primitive (or pre-state) warfare. Distinctions of terrorism from guerrilla warfare are formalistic and ignore options to conduct and actual practice. The historical roots of contemporary terrorism are examined. Besides Classical doctrine on tyrannicide and terrorism in Jewish and Islamic traditions, modern terrorist and guerrilla theory also derives from the Graeco-Roman military doctrine of stratagem, which influenced the Islamic idea of *jihad* and has a demonstrable record in Western military thought from antiquity to modern guerrilla theorists. Terrorism as an offshoot of stratagem stresses psychological warfare, avoidance of direct confrontation, and a test of moral endurance. Terrorism is a strategy prone to appear under favorable conditions, not a societal problem with a definite solution.

For two decades before the cold war's thaw (1989–90), terrorism probably gained the most media attention of any aspect of international affairs, although the annual carnage on American highways greatly exceeded terrorist fatalities. Taking a bath may actually be more dangerous.[1] But the shock value of unexpected savagery toward innocent victims creates the impression of civilization teetering on the brink of anarchy, as governments seem (and frequently are) helpless to protect either their own citizens or foreigners within their territorial domains. Hence frantic cries that something must be done and responses by policy-makers and academic experts. Terrorism's multiple forms, however, defy facile generalizations, and an immense literature attests scholars' groping efforts to understand this phenomenon.[2] Without claim to mastery of this vast literature (a growth industry of the 1980s), I venture an historian's perspective.

A general question of this essay must be: what does history offer the policy-maker regarding terrorism? Historians, with a discipline emphasizing long-term developments, do not easily market themselves to governments interested in a quick fix and more receptive to current events specialists. Clio, an ambivalent muse, pales in comparison to the scientific confidence of her rival disciplines in modeling, statistical gymnastics, or trendy terminology. Exactly what happened, when, and why – historical 'facts' – are always subject to debate and interpretation. Historians worth their salt avoid the phrase 'history shows'.[3] Simple conclusions prove elusive either from assertion of each event's historical uniqueness or reducing texts to metaphysical puzzles. Extreme period specialization within the profession limits a broader historical perspective, and outside the profession it is often assumed that nothing important happened before the Industrial Revolution or the Second World War, as if the human animal and his social groups are captives of a modern environment formed *ex nihilo*.

History offers education in the broadest sense: it instructs without dictating a definite course of action, but it provides a perspective from which to make pragmatic decisions. The limits of historical knowledge, Clio's ambiguity, do not reduce history's use for the policy-maker to an inferior role *vis-à-vis* political science, sociology, or psychology. Discovery of universal laws of human behavior (whether as individuals or groups) is an ultimate (if currently often ignored) goal of all these disciplines, and it is debatable whether history's rivals have had more success. Recognizing that the mechanisms of societal development are still too inadequately understood to permit regular and accurate predictions does not imply that history has no meaning or utility for understanding contemporary problems. History need not be teleological to have value nor offer definite laws in order to show discernible patterns.

This essay does not seek historical examples to support specific policy recommendations for ridding the world of terrorism. The moral judgement implicit in such a goal is not the dispassionate historian's prerogative. Rather, late twentieth-century terrorism as an idea will be placed within the larger framework of universal history, in hope of shedding new light on terrorism's conceptual origins and theoretical debts. Deriving policy decisions solely from a problem's immediate context is myopic, as terrorism has deep roots immune to Band-Aids. Wise policy, formulated with a view to past, future, and current conditions, can benefit from history's broader pool of examples and their consequences.

Defining Terrorism

Study of terrorism continues to suffer from the lack of a widely accepted definition of the subject matter. Terrorism is like pornography: everyone has a general impression of what it is without agreeing on a detailed definition. The now hackneyed aphorism: 'one man's terrorist is another's freedom fighter', epitomizes this relativistic and politically charged topic. Is terrorism a plague to be wiped out, a technique of liberation, or a recurrent societal problem? Although neither scholars, governments, nor even departments within the same government find accord on a definition, Rapoport's 'extra-normal violence or deliberate use of atrocities to achieve particular public ends' is succinctly serviceable.[4]

Problems of definition stem in part from using 'terror', until recently not a technical term in psychology, political science, or history, as the criterion for determining the subject matter. Few professors before the late 1960s would have considered offering a course on terrorism. To some extent scholars are really concerned with apples and oranges but insist on speaking of fruit.[5] Hence classifications of terrorism often can be as instructive as definitions. A division into terrorism 'from above' or 'from below' the power structure has some popularity, although classifications can betray a particular scholarly interest: Vought and Fraser [*1986: 75–76*], military officers propose state-directed, state-supported, non-state-supported; Taheri, writing on Iran, discerns five types, of which Islamic terrorism is the fifth.[6] Hanle's seven types is the longest list.[7] All these schemes can be criticized. Taheri's distinction between publicity-seekers and Islamic terrorists implies that members of the PFLP are not Moslems and that Islamic terrorists are uninterested in publicity. Similarly, Hanle's criminal category ignores the new type of narco-terrorism, best illustrated by the Latin American drug lords and also the drug traffic financing some Lebanese groups [cf. *Taheri, 1987: 146*]. Narco-terrorists operate as a *Staat im Staat* and enjoy various international connections. Likewise Hanle's class of mystical terrorism fails to appreciate the religious basis of much Islamic terrorism, often state-sponsored or state-directed.

My own system, no doubt also open to criticism, would limit the subject matter to states or groups desiring to govern or revolutionize states. Acts of 'terror' associated with mental or emotional disorder, profit-seeking, or religious ritual (Hanle's categories of psychotic, criminal, and mystical), even if alleging a political motive, would not qualify as terrorism, unless of sufficient frequency or producing enough victims to shake confidence in a government. Thus three general types of terrorism can be posited: state terrorism, domestic terrorism, and international or transnational terrorism.

State terrorism (Hanle's 'repression')[8] is essentially a government's rule through violence and fear, although its techniques can be extensive and sophisticated even in primitive societies [cf. *Walter, 1969*]. In modern times it first appears in the French Revolution's Reign of Terror (1793–94), the event to which scholars point as the origin of the word 'terrorism' The internal policies of Nazi Germany, Stalinist Russia, Ceausescu's Romania, and perhaps Israel's response to the *Intifada* offer other examples. Domestic terrorism (terrorism from below) denotes the activities of revolutionaries, rebels, and vigilantes within a single state (for example, IRA, Shining Path, white supremacist groups, Red Brigade). International or transnational terrorism signifies terror by one group or government against another, or use of third parties as agents against nationals of another state either within the territorial domains of that state or in a third state's territory. Narco-terrorists, publicity-seekers, mercenary terrorists, Taheri's Islamic terrorists, and all state-sponsored or state-directed terrorism would fit this category.

However terrorism may be defined and its manifestations classified, policy-makers should be permitted to view late twentieth-century terrorism from a broader historical perspective. How new is terrorism as an idea or a strategy and how unique are its current forms? Scholars generally mark the current wave of terrorism as beginning in the 1960s, when transnational terrorism emerged as an international concern.[9] At the same time scholarly interest in terrorism, which had languished since 1933 (see Hardman, in Laqueur [1978: 223–30]), revived mostly among social scientists but with largely an ahistorical perspective, paying lip service only to the French Revolution and nineteenth-century anarchists. Modern technology (that is, cheaper, more powerful, more accessible means of destruction and exploitation of the mass media) seemed to characterize a 'new', unparalleled phenomenon. US policy-makers, for example, always ready for a quick fix, took in part a psychological approach: a personality profile of terrorists was needed to handle 'crazies', and the psychological perspective (not limited to work by psychologists or psychiatrists) is notable in American bibliography on terrorism. Needless to say, a history of terrorism from the universal perspective of world history has not been written. Such a work would be premature as long as debate over a common definition persists and the multiple historical roots of modern terrorism remain obscure. But important groundwork for a history of terrorism has appeared, from which some historical 'lessons' can be derived.

Three historical approaches to terrorism can be cited. For state terrorism Walter [1969] examined the role of terror in primitive African societies, especially Shaka's development of military and state terror among the Zulu in the early nineteenth century. His intention to complement this work by a general study of terroristic despotism in advanced states was not realized. Rapoport in a series of articles [1982, 1984, 1990] has developed the genre of religious terrorism in the Judaic, Islamic, and Hindu traditions. The studies of Walter and Rapoport refute the notion of dependence of terrorism upon modern technology. Furthermore, Rapoport has demonstrated that transnational terrorism long predated the twentieth century and that terror in a religious tradition can influence modern practitioners. Menachem Begin as leader of the Zionist Irgun consciously avoided the errors of the Zealots and *sicarii* of the first Jewish revolt against Rome (66–70).[10] Likewise in Islam the Ismaili Assassins (11th–13th centuries) and ideas of *jihad*, which can include extermination of apostates (e.g. Anwar Sadat's assassination in 1981), offer examples and doctrine for a living tradition.[11] Hence in this view [*Rapoport, 1984: 674–5*] the transition from religious to modern terrorism, beginning with the Russian group Narodnaya Volya in the late nineteenth century, marks a change from divine to secular justification, although religious aspects continue to have effect.

Besides these Semitic origins of modern terrorism, to which Hebrew behavior and ideas of holy war in the Old Testament should be added, Graeco-Roman antiquity offers a third historical approach in its justifications for tyrannicide. This Classical tradition has perhaps the most traceable lineage: medieval commentators, political and religious propagandists of the sixteenth and seventeenth centuries, French revolutionaries, and nineteenth-century anarchists.[12]

Nevertheless, this is not the whole story of terrorism's debt to antiquity. The Greeks invented Western military theory, and modern terrorism, particularly since the 1960s, can be viewed as a form of warfare. Thus some attempt is merited to place the phenomenon of terrorism within the conceptual framework of developments in military theory. Traditionally military theory has treated conventional warfare: the organization and training of armies as well as tactics and strategy for winning wars. The concept of military theory, however, expanding *pari passu* with the growth of the role of military power and military institutions in the post-Second World War era, has lost a precise definition.[13] Inclusion of 'small wars' within military theory from the eighteenth century on led ultimately to the development of written guerrilla theory, which represents an aspect of this expansion.

I would like to suggest that from the viewpoint of traditional military theory – the hypothetical principles behind military acts in the conduct of war – terrorism forms a subset of the ideas included within the ancient concept of stratagem, and in modern practice it has become a conceptual offshoot of guerrilla warfare. The Western military doctrine of stratagem was first formulated in Graeco-Roman military thought and has not ceased to exert its influence in the present age. As a fourth historical approach to the origins of modern terrorism, stratagem interacts with other perspectives. Like the state terrorism described by Walter, it initially appears in primitive societies; but stratagem also has a role in Islamic military thought, and modern practitioners (both Islamic and non-Islamic) still overtly express its principles in word and deed. I shall first discuss terrorism as a form of war and the theory reflected in terrorism, before introducing the concept of stratagem and examining how terrorism conforms with this Classical doctrine.

Recognition of terrorism as a form of war has significant implications for public policy. Terrorism can be demystified, when method is found in the madness of 'crazies' and terrorism stands revealed as a rational (if certainly radical) strategy of psychological warfare and coercion. Furthermore, study of another root of terrorism will once again confirm that terrorism in its late twentieth century form, while unique in some ways, represents merely new wine in an old bottle. The cyclical nature of terrorism can also be seen. Terrorism is not a passing phase of contemporary international politics which has now largely run its course [cf. *Laqueur, 1986: 86–100*], but a strategy bound to occur and recur when favorable conditions exist.

Terrorism as a Form of War

Why should terrorism be considered a form of war, and if so, do all three types of terrorism (that is, state, domestic, trans- or international) indicate acts of war?[14] War, in the Clausewitzian view, may be the continuation of policy by other means, but it also is an act of force to compel one party to do the will of another. War, as opposed to feud or violence between individuals or small groups, further requires the existence of political communities with at least a recognized de facto status and with some kind of formal military organizations sanctioned to use violence for the achievement of a group goal.[15] Legalistic views need not be considered, since in the contemporary euphemisms of international law all war except in self-defense is illegal, and what might be called wars are today, technically speaking, mere 'armed conflicts' [cf. *Schindler, 1979: 3–20*]. As freedom fighters, terrorists can claim to be representatives of a state pursuing a political goal.

Common arguments against identification of terrorism as a form of war are strained: for example, that in terrorism political circumstances outweigh strategy; and that in war an audience is defended, but in terrorism parties compete for an audience. Successful strategy cannot be contradictory to political circumstances, but rather derives its essence from them. Similarly, a party at war must compete well or it may lose the support of its audience, for all war can be reduced to a conflict of wills, which especially in the late twentieth-century becomes a competition for the desire of populations in conflict to continue the struggle or to quit. The real question is not whether international and domestic terrorism are a form of war, but whether enough substance stands behind the alleged political end for the violence to avoid the charge of criminality. Indeed, many agree that trans- or international terrorism is a form of war.[16] The domestic terrorism of revolution or rebellion can also qualify [cf. *Hanle, 1989: 132–63*], especially since civil wars today fall within the scope of military theory and often occur with the active support of outside third parties, thus giving an international aspect to an internal conflict [*Lider, 1982: 2*; cf. *Rapoport, 1988: 32–58*].

State terrorism would appear to pose the greatest difficulty for interpreting terrorism as a form of war [cf. *Hanle, 1989: 165–71*], since conceptually a government cannot, except in civil war, wage war against its own citizens. This problem once again signals the quandry of defining terrorism and the problematic status of the assumption that the use of terror, regardless of the agent, circumstances, or the rationale, determines a common phenomenon. Although it can be argued that the proverbial 'man on the street' in the 1970s and 1980s would not include state terrorism in a definition of terrorism [cf. *Quester, 1982: 328–9*], this hypothetical response, no doubt conditioned by media exposure of domestic and international terrorism in this period, is not an argument for exclusion of state terrorism from the subject matter of terrorism. Likewise, an operational definition of domestic and international terrorism witnessed since the 1960s (that is, murder/assassination/massacre, piracy/ hijacking, kidnaping/hostage-taking, sabotage/destruction of public facilities) does not help, since a repressive regime may use all of these tactics or their equivalents (for example, executions, arrests of political prisoners, intimidation through destruction of a dissident's property) openly or surreptitiously through its secret police or a similar arm. The fallacy of this operational approach is clear from the comparison (so popular with pacifists) of soldiers and common criminals – both soldiers and criminals kill, steal, and destroy. Given continued debate on the definition of terrorism, abstract discussions cannot be conclusive, but history can be instructive.

One of the strongest arguments for inclusion of state terrorism within the modern concept of terrorism is the original use of the word to describe the activities of the Committee of Public Safety in 1793–94, although I venture to guess that a close examination of the contemporary sources would show that the word 'terrorism' in this sense first generally appeared after the Ninth of Thermidor. Robespierre and his contemporaries spoke only of 'terror'. As the phenomenon of terrorism in various forms long antedates the word's origin, the French Revolution's 'terrorism' loses at least some of its authority as a milestone in this phenomenon's history, and 'terrorism' becomes like other 'isms' invented in the nineteenth century (for example, imperialism, militarism) a conventional but, strictly speaking, an anachronistic term for events in earlier periods. Indeed from the viewpoint of world history, repressive regimes have been common and only the unhistorical application of late twentieth-century Western values to earlier periods permits characterizing violence and fear for control of domestic resistance or inhibition of social deviation as 'extra-normal'.

Walter's classic study of state terrorism in African societies illustrates the point. The terror of secret societies in some tribes at the chieftain level of political development to enforce conformity to tradition [*1969: 80–108*] is a *customary* practice, not an 'extra-normal' one. Furthermore, Shaka's institution of state terror among the Zulu occurred rather late (1816–28) in the history of terrorism and, although continued by some of his successors, it remained isolated, unless one wants to posit a tradition of African state terrorism influencing the likes of Idi Amin and others.

From the perspective of world history, overestimation of Robespierre's Terror also leads to the argument that terror as a tactic of rebellion represents a second dimension to state terror – the one developed from the other. This view rests on the proximity of Robespierre's Reign of Terror to the ideas of Gracchus Babeuf (d. 1797), whose colleague Filippo Michele Buonarotti (1761–1837) popularized revolutionary secret societies and propagated Babeuf's views in the bible of nineteenth-century revolutionaries, *Conspiration pour l'égalite dite de Babeuf* (1828). The terroristic aspect of Babeuf's thought (all's fair against tyrants) owes much, however, to Graeco-Roman views of tyrannicide, and Babeuf was a devotee of the French Revolution's cult of antiquity.[17] Even theoretically, the precedence of state terror as a general rule is false: Shaka's state terrorism for domestic control developed *after* his use of terror as a military policy for conquest [*Walter, 1969: 123–43*].

Certainly terroristic despotism and political repression merit scholarly examination. As terrorism, however, remains at present a study of fruit, it is not necessary to assert that apples and oranges are the same in every respect.[18] State terrorism can only metaphorically be understood as a form of war and will therefore be excluded from further discussion. The variety of terrorism does not impede a thesis that domestic and international terrorism can be a form of war.

Terrorism as Primitive Warfare

But what kind of war is terrorism? Do all uses of terror and inducement of fear in attempting to break enemy morale constitute terrorism? As a psychological technique, terrorism may imply violence or force without necessarily employing them: the threat per se may often be sufficient to achieve the goal of creating fear and uncertainty. Indeed the potential 'power to hurt,' whether demonstrated or merely perceived, can be more compelling to an opponent than any damage actually done.[19]

As a military technique, terror has probably never been absent from warfare, although (as I argue) if the term 'terrorism' is to have any rigor in its definition all uses of terror do not constitute 'terrorism'. When an opponent can be disarmed psychologically, whether merely unnerved or alarmed, his defeat in battle is facilitated, although not guaranteed, and sometimes a strategic goal can be achieved without battle.[20] In warfare of primitive (or pre-state) peoples the often horrifying appearance of the warriors exploits this psychological technique. Romans of the Late Empire dreaded even the sight of the Huns. Polybius indicates that the Romans of the Middle Republic also knew this stratagem, for in his day the *hastati*, the first rank of the legion, wore tall plumes on their helmets to make each man look twice his height and thus to terrify opponents. Similarly, terror could be applied by certain tactical formations or types of units. Onasander (*fl.* 49–59) recommends keeping armor and weapons clean and shiny to increase their fearful psychological effect on the enemy, and the Roman general at Pydna (168 B.C.), Aemilius Paulus, said that the Macedonian phalanx in action had the most dreadful appearance he had seen. The corps of scythed chariots employed in late Achaemenid Persian armies and imitated by Hellenistic rulers, such as Antiochus III and Mithridates VI Eupator, despite their dismal record of tactical failure at Cunaxa (401 B.C.), Gaugamela (331 B.C.), Magnesia (189 B.C.), and Chaeronea (86 B.C.), must have been largely a psychological weapon. Vegetius, the Late Roman military theorist, calls such chariots a joke; the same could be said for elephants.[21]

Terror also appears as a policy of conquerors toward the subjugated. The Assyrians (8th–7th c. B.C.) ruthlessly massacred, flayed, beheaded, and impaled great numbers of rebellious subjects – an aspect of their imperial policy seen in both inscriptions and their notable bas-reliefs. Terror became a way to ensure loyalty, to intimidate potential foes, and was even considered a means for kings to increase their personal fame. Roman custom in the third century B.C. according to Polybius called for massacring all living beings within a captured city – animal as well as human – to inspire terror.[22] Roman intentions in such acts scarcely differ from those of the Assyrians.

All these examples involve some kind of terror and from one viewpoint could be said to constitute terrorism (cf. Hanle's military terrorism: n. 8 *supra*). Likewise all these examples, except that of the primitive warriors, belong to regular conventional warfare, understood as the legally recognized armed forces of sovereign states (or would-be states, that is, revolutionaries) openly pursuing their respective strategic goals according to the internationally approved rules of the game – *ius ad bellum* and *ius in bello*. Conventional warfare requires, above all, open battle and observance of rules, although many of these remain unwritten. The exception of primitive warriors is notable, since the terrorism of the 1970s and 1980s has been particularly characterized by its unconventionality, that is, legally unrecognized agents of political groups, who are also (apart from state-directed terrorism) legally unrecognized or only marginally so, committing and/or threatening acts of violence sporadically and surreptitiously without regard for traditional rules and limits on their actions. Thus terror as a strategic/tactical tool has ancient roots, and terrorism like primitive warfare is unconventional in its most literal sense: the parties in conflict lack a shared set of rules.

Of course primitive warfare is a diverse phenomenon. Intra-cultural (or in-group) warfare among pre-state peoples can be so rule-bound as to be ritualistic. Only inter-cultural (or out-group) conflicts, those without a shared set of rules, would correspond to modern terrorism. Thus the shock of modern terrorism resembles the outrage of seventeenth- or eighteenth-century European regulars in North America when ambushed by Indians who ignored the European rules of the game (for example Braddock's Defeat in 1755).[23]

Indeed one anthropologist, H.H. Turney-High, would interpret contemporary trends toward guerrilla warfare and terrorism as a return to primitive warfare in every way except motivation, to which I would also add technology. This view rests in part upon his concept of the 'military horizon', that is, advancement of a society to a stage in which *inter alia* its armed forces employ the column and line tactics of conventional warfare, have a definite command structure, and can supply forces for a campaign as opposed to a single battle.

Terrorists as primitive warriors have generally not yet reached the 'military horizon'. In their roles as revolutionaries or agents of national liberation, they are truly in a pre-state stage. They have definite leaders and plan for a campaign rather than a single battle, although the life span of many terrorist groups signals their dissolution before any goal is achieved (see Crenshaw, this volume). Above all, terrorists avoid pitched battle and confrontation with regular armed forces, relying on the tactics of primitive warfare – surprise, ambush, deception, and hit-and-run maneuvers (see n.58 *infra* for bibliography). As Service writes [*1971: 104*]:

> Continued threat, sniping, and terrorization which will discourage and harass the enemy is the typical form of action in primitive warfare. In fact, terrorization, or psychological warfare, seems to be at its highest development in tribal society. Head-hunting, cannibalism, torture of prisoners, rape, massacre, and other forms of atrocious nerve-warfare are probably more effective means to the end at the tribal level than is true combat.

Indeed the Zulu under Shaka avoided direct military confrontation when possible and preferred terror and deception – conquest by stratagem [*Walter, 1969: 143*].

The Shining Path movement in Peru, combining Andean mysticism,

Maoism, and a personality cult of its founder Abimael Gusman, offers a good example of effective, contemporary primitive warfare, especially in its rejection (in its early days) of the modern media for publicity and in its diverse arsenal ranging from dynamite to slingshots (a good survey in McCormick [*1988: 109–26*]). Avoiding the media limelight and technological backwardness are unusual for many current terrorists.

Although Turney-High's military horizon has its critics, the identification of terrorism and guerrilla activity as primitive warfare illustrates the paradox of military developments in the twentieth century.[24] High technology and the nuclear stalemate have fostered retreat from the total mobilization of societies for war, as seen in the Second World War, to manipulation of high technology in military situations of lower intensity, of less structural as well as less legal formality, and of less temporally definable periods. Nuclear weapons have dammed the stream of large-scale warfare for nearly a half-century, but guerrilla warfare and terrorism represent the inevitable leaks in the dyke.

Nor should terrorism as a modern form of primitive warfare seem so anomalous to the 'progress' and sophistication of late twentieth-century life. Contemporary modernism on the one hand has nurtured a rejection of the cultural past and promoted a cult of the primitive [cf. *Amon, 1982: 62–76*], while also producing in some quarters reaction for a return to the basics and religious fundamentalism. Besides political, social, and psychological studies, perhaps scholars could do more to set contemporary terrorism into its cultural context, as Tololyan [*1988: 217–33*] has done for Armenian terrorist groups, who perceive their acts to have an affinity with the great mid-fifth-century Armenian revolt against the Sassanid Persians.

If terrorism and guerrilla warfare both constitute modern forms of primitive warfare, terrorism's relationship to guerrilla warfare should be clarified. A developmental scheme projecting the emergence of terrorism from guerrilla warfare, which in turn is viewed as an offshoot of conventional warfare (that is, conventional warfare leading to guerrilla warfare leading to terrorism) would not only be simplistic but also historically inaccurate. Conventional warfare developed from primitive warfare, with which modern notions of guerrilla warfare share many traits, and guerrilla warfare in various forms has frequently appeared throughout history concurrently with conventional warfare. In the murky era of prehistory, acts of violence by individuals or small groups for a political (as opposed to a personal) motive, acts considered terrorism today, could conceivably be the *Urquelle* in the developmental transition to conventional warfare. Indeed the frequency of terror in pre-state warfare has already been mentioned. Accordingly, terrorism may be the original seed from which conventional warfare eventually developed rather than an aberrant mutation of traditional warfare.

Origins and development are not the problem, since terrorism, guerrilla warfare, and conventional warfare have at times been concurrent, but rather an issue of tactical prevalence. The current wave of terrorism has followed a period of guerrilla warfare characterizing the national liberation movements of the Third World in the post-Second World War era. Guerrillas of the liberation movements often used terrorism. In Hanle's analysis of revolutionary warfare, terrorism occurs in the preparatory and initial violence phase (the pre-guerrilla phase) and in the consolidation phase after victory to reprogram the populace – another example of state terrorism following terrorism in war. But these distinctions are too neat. For the revolutionary guerrilla, terrorism is a constant option, being discriminate or indiscriminate depending on circumstances and political goals at a particular time.[25]

Despite conceptual, historical, and tactical relationships between guerrilla warfare and terrorism, some scholars wish to distinguish terrorists from guerrillas and even to discern urban from rural guerrillas, while denying that terrorists are urban guerrillas.[26] But some guerrillas use terrorism and some terrorists are more ruthless than others.[27] Che Guevara is often cited to argue that guerrillas and terrorists should be distinguished. This is misleading: Guevara opposed indiscriminate violence but approved of assassination and sabotage [*1961: 15–16, 85, 93–4*]. Attempts to draw up rigid classifications distort the very fluid options available. Marighella's urban guerrilla strategy, formulated in the 1960s before terrorism became a buzzword, certainly approximates terrorist strategy: the countryside will fall if authority in the urban centers collapses through havoc wrecked by freedom fighters and manipulation of the media. The goal is to transform a political into a military situation.[28]

In discussing the strategy behind the Arab revolt he led in the First World War, T.E. Lawrence notes that ' "murder" war' (that is, terrorism) was an option against the Turks, if other methods failed. Similarly, Liddell Hart, in his skeptical evaluation of the wisdom of allied support for partisan movements in the Second World War, contends that such movements bred post-war civil wars (that is, revolutionary insurgency) and terrorism.[29] For these two major military thinkers of the twentieth century, guerrilla warfare and terrorism clearly represent related but distinct points on the continuum of military violence.

Any denial of connections between terrorism and guerrilla warfare should consider how terrorists see themselves. No terrorist group has publicly referred to itself as 'terrorist' since the Zionist Stern Gang of the late 1940s [*Vought and Fraser, 1986:2; Cordes, 1988: 150, 160,*

168 n.2]. The IRA, various factions of the PLO, numerous urban guerrilla groups in Latin America, and young anarchists (for example, Weatherman, Baader–Meinhoff Gang) have adopted military organization and terminology and proclaim themselves guerrillas in a 'people's war'. The 'war', especially for young anarchist groups, may be the terrorists' own fantasy, but the concept of war aids rationalization of actions by depersonalizing the 'enemy'.[30]

A terrorist-guerrilla connection also finds support in the first European treatise to outline a strategy of national liberation through guerrilla warfare: Carlo Bianco advocated terrorist tactics against enemies of the revolution in his *Della guerre nazionale d'insurrezione per bande* (1830) [*Laqueur, 1977c: 24–5*]. The connection, continued into the post-Second World War era, led one commentator in 1966 to characterize modern insurgency as almost entirely terroristic [*Schelling, 1966: 27*]. Certainly the term 'terrorist' has become pejorative, whereas 'guerrilla' retains a more neutral (or even at times a positive) sense. The Sandinista government of Nicaragua in 1987 illustrates the point by calling the Contras 'terrorists for hire' by Washington.[31]

Another problem in denying the relationship between terrorism and guerrilla warfare is to conceive the latter too narrowly and solely within the framework of twentieth-century guerrilla theory as developed in the writings of T.E. Lawrence, Mao Zedong, and Che Guevara. Hence, notions that guerrilla groups are of one size, terrorist groups another; guerrillas have popular support, freedom of movement, and secure bases, whereas terrorists do not, etc.[32] But the twentieth century did not invent guerrilla warfare in either practice or written theory. Reliance on surprise, ambush, hit-and-run tactics, trickery, and avoidance of open pitched battle are the hallmarks of primitive warfare, which some primitives continued to use in conflicts against more advanced societies, and which weaker forces have often exploited against numerically or technologically superior foes. The Byzantines of the tenth century produced the first treatise exclusively devoted to guerrilla and low intensity border warfare.[33]

Furthermore, many guerrillas and most terrorists share a dubious legal status: is their violence legally sanctioned? Are these perpetrators of violence soldiers or criminals? These complex questions can not be discussed here, but the problem of legal status (not exclusively modern) is relevant to the connection of guerrilla warfare and terrorism with primitive warfare. In the Graeco-Roman world a soldier was a legally defined enemy (*iustus hostis*) as opposed to pirates and outlaws, whose violence was criminal and who lay without claim to any legal status or rights.[34] The ancients classified all unconventional warfare, whether the acts of primitive barbarians or nationalistic resistance movements, as banditry.[35] But if the criterion for legally sanctioned violence is existence of a state for which one acts, then it should be noted that the concept of the state is a metaphysical idea which a group acknowledges and to which it pledges allegiance even in the absence of sovereign territory or institutions. Hence the right of racial or national groups to form new states from older empires or kingdoms. Terrorism is a means to make the metaphysical state physically felt in the international system [*Hanle, 1989: 89*]. As pre-state warriors, most terrorists and some guerrillas straddle the fence between criminality and politically sanctioned violence, although the Geneva Protocols of 1977, if universally adopted, would facilitate recognition of guerrillas (and in some cases terrorists) as *iusti hostes*.[36]

Terrorism and Military Theory

So far I have tried to point out the ancient roots of terrorism and to suggest that from the viewpoint of military theory, domestic and international terrorism can constitute a modern form of primitive warfare and stand in a fluid relationship with guerrilla warfare. It is now time to examine terrorism in more detail, to establish the theoretical principles upon which it is based, and how these relate to general military theory.

Although it can be maintained that a general theory of terrorism is impossible because of its diverse forms and lack of a generally accepted definition [*Hahlweg, 1977: 133; Laqueur, 1978: 183*], these difficulties have not deterred the proliferation of books on the subject, including a reader by Laqueur on terrorism's conceptual development. Likewise, as is often the case in the matter of written theory and actual practice, the problem arises of the extent to which practitioners read books or, if they do, allow theory to influence practice.[37] In the parallel situation of twentieth-century guerrilla theory, for example, some assert that T.E. Lawrence's theoretical writing and influence are overrated; that Mao lacked both originality and any coherent theoretical doctrine, although he did know Lawrence's *Seven Pillars of Wisdom*; and that neither Castro nor Che Guevara read Mao until after the Cuban Revolution.[38] Connections between theory and practice are rarely simple.

Apart from the conceptual origins of modern terrorism found in ancient and medieval political and religious thought and, as I shall argue below, also ancient military thought, certain modern 'classics' of terrorism have appeared. The essays of Karl Heinzen (1809–80), published in the late 1840s, suggest calling him the first theorist of terrorism, although a case for founding modern terrorism can also be made for the Russian anarchist Sergey Nechaev and his *Revolutionary Catechism* (1869) [*Laqueur, 1977c: 26–7; Amon, 1982: 70*]. Of more recent vintage is the *Minimanual of the Urban Guerrilla* by the Brazilian terrorist Carlos Marighella (d.

1969), popular with young anarchists. Finally, perhaps less well-known but proof that government-directed terrorism can be formulated in written theory, is the so-called 'Document on Terror', a supposed Communist monograph of ca 1948, originally in Polish but passed to the West in German translation.[39]

Despite the existence of such 'classics', the terrorists of the past two decades have published scarcely anything theoretical, nothing at least that would distinguish terrorist theory from guerrilla theory (and Marighella's book would not support this distinction). The ideological pronouncements of some groups, such as the Palestinians, or the pamphlets of the Euro-terrorists, have little to do with the practical theory.[40] The lack of published manuals detailing 'how to do it' and of justifications for terrorism should not be taken to imply that modern terrorists act without having theoretical principles to support them or that they are somehow divorced from any traditions in guerrilla and terrorist thought. Heinzen still cited Classical examples in the tradition advocating tyrannicide. The influential revolutionary theorist Louis Auguste Blanqui (1805–71) also appealed to ancient history, as did the theorist of urban guerrilla warfare Abraham Guillen (1912?–) in his *Estrategia de la guerrilla urbane* (ca 1971).[41] For the Islamic tradition a notable exception to the lack of theoretical literature is the pamphlet, *The Neglected Duty (Al-Faridah al-Gha'ibah)* by Abd Al-Salem Faraj, leader of the Egyptian Al-Jihad (also called the Islamic Group of Egypt), responsible for the assassination of Anwar Sadat in 1981. Faraj justifies the deed by appeal to the concept of *jihad*, the command to exterminate apostates, and, above all for this essay's purposes, a Muslim tradition of stratagem, to which I return below.[42]

No doubt an underground technical literature exists, for example, on bomb construction and training manuals for weapons (cf. W. Powell, *The Anarchist Cookbook* [1971]). Such works have a precedent in the anarchist Johann Most's *Revolutionäre Kriegswissenschaft* (1885). At Niavaran, Teheran's northern suburb, where the Volunteers for Martyrdom established a training camp in 1980, cadets received instruction in Islamic law and history, the works of Ayatollah Khomeini, and technical military textbooks of the Shah's army. Significantly, however, the cadets could also peruse in Persian translation the ancient Chinese classic of stratagem and Mao's alleged vade mecum – Sun Tzu.[43] The absence of a distinct body of written theory on terrorism may result from a belief that the guerrilla literature is sufficient. On the other hand, theory can also be deduced from practice, which may derive its theoretical basis ultimately from the written word, but which may stem more directly from oral tradition or consistency with the acts of earlier generations.

Terrorism, a psychological technique relying on the effects of surprise and shock to unnerve or to coerce, aims at an opponent's eventual demoralization and surrender on the issue in dispute.[44] After all, the objective in war is not necessarily physical defeat of an enemy or conquest of territory, but rather breaking his will. Just as in guerrilla warfare, the pinpricks of terrorism permit a numerically or technologically weaker party to annoy and embarrass a superior foe without the face-to-face confrontation in which the superior party can exert its strength.[45] But like strategic nuclear weapons, terrorism bypasses conventional military forces, thus avoiding any local contest of strength, and can hit the civilian population directly. Terrorism combines a counter-value attack (that is, inflicting pain on the enemy without impeding his military capability) with guerrilla warfare, in which no definite lines are defended [*Quester, 1982: 329*]. Furthermore, unlike conventional warfare, the conflict is temporally ill-defined: terrorist strikes can be extended over time without loss (or perhaps with an increase) of efficiency in producing fear. Contemporary terrorism illustrates Quincy Wright's notion of war's 'nuisance value'.[46]

The goals of terrorism can be both short- and long-term [cf. *Vought and Fraser, 1986: 73*] Besides the obvious purpose of creating terror, a terrorist act advertises a cause, can gain sympathy for that cause in some quarters, and can either ridicule and embarrass the terrorist's foe or provoke that foe to rash retaliation resulting in further sympathy for the terrorist's cause. Terrorism attacks an opponent's cohesion, but it can also produce serious material destruction of utilities, industries and communications, as well as economic damage, when commerce dissipates and investment deserts areas prone to terrorist activity [*Rapoport, 1982: 15; Mallin, 1978: 397*].

Above all, however, terrorism is psychological warfare, aimed at society as a whole rather than at a particular state's armed forces, and tied to a strategy of exhaustion. Except in instances of assassination, the terrorist views his victims as a means to an end. The real target is public opinion, and the success of a terrorist act can often be gauged by the amount of publicity received.[47] By brutal acts against civilians the terrorist seeks to create the impression that no one anywhere at any time is safe from attack. He hopes that the fear sown will destabilize society, alienate people from the support of their governments, and thus break his opposition's will through demoralization [cf. *Schelling, 1966: 180*].

Recognizing 'public opinion' as terrorism's prime target does not imply, however, that the effectiveness of all terrorism is dependent on the mass media. Terrorism, as I argue, existed as a strategy before mass media appeared, and contemporary terrorism successfully occurs in some societies where mass media have little impact, for example, Vietcong assassination squads and the early years of the Shining Path movement in

Peru. Public opinion and publicity can be manipulated without mass media. On the other hand, some terrorists do play intentionally for television cameras. It would be difficult to argue that the massacre at the Munich Olympics was not produced for a world stage. Once again, the phenomenon of terrorism defies gross generalizations.

If terrorism is to have any chance of success, certain favorable conditions must be present. As already noted, the nuclear stalemate of the superpowers in the post-Second World War era has encouraged small wars and low intensity conflicts. Terrorism, often tinged with ideological fanaticism, is tailor-made for nationalistic and religious strife, and few armed conflicts in today's world occur without some kind of participation from outside third parties. Successful terrorism is usually not the warfare of indigent or technologically unsophisticated groups, but is fueled and supplied by various interests.[48] Furthermore, since many terrorists hope their acts will become media events and be cost effective, that is, that millions not on the scene will be terrorized vicariously, terrorism functions best either in open democratic societies with a free press or in ineffective authoritarian states.[49] Similarly, terrorists can exploit the reluctance of democratic regimes to impose restrictions on individual freedom as a response to terrorism, and also take advantage of a government either intimidated by possible terrorist threats against its own nationals, or having an ambivalent attitude to the terrorists because of that government's moral or political embarrassment about its own conduct.[50] Of course, the more unstable a government, the more vulnerable it is to terrorism.

As a final note on the theory of terrorism, two aspects of terrorism's emphasis on psychological shock deserve attention: first, terrorism's apparent disregard of all rules of war, and second, the preference of terrorists for civilian targets. As a form of unconventional warfare, terrorism would be more remarkable if rules were observed. In fact, terrorism is a strategy of desperation and extremism, which often operates within a mind-set of absolutes: compromise is equated with surrender and negotiations often become a ploy for milking even more publicity from the media and for further embarrassment to the target government [*Livingston, 1978: 22; Rivers, 1986: 216*]). Moreover, since terrorist groups tend to lack any official political recognition, they operate outside traditional international law from the beginning, and heeding only the expediency of their own cause as their morality, they are free to create their own rules and to make a mockery of recognized norms.[51]

Perhaps the most obvious and most shocking terrorist method of flouting the rules is an apparent preference for civilian targets, including women and children. Certainly civilian targets make for maximum horror. Many have interpreted this trend to mean that the victims are seen merely as symbols of the class, government, or policy opposed by the terrorist, and as part of the 'system' the victims deserve punishment in the terrorist's eyes. Hence the terrorist's *Weltanschauung* of absolutes depersonalizes his act.[52] This interpretation appears valid, so far as it goes, but from the viewpoint of military theory another view is possible.

Mallin raises the question of terrorism's uniqueness in comparing terrorism to aerial bombing. Destruction of an enemy's cities is an accepted practice of modern warfare, and terrorism's results resemble an air raid: it is conducted in the enemy's rear, aims at installations, officials, and morale; and the deaths of civilians, although an unacknowledged goal, are often deliberately sought.[53] But the view can be carried further. With the democratization of modern war in the French Revolution the army became the nation in arms: every soldier was a citizen and every citizen a soldier.[54] As the theory and practice of total war continued to develop in the nineteenth and especially the twentieth centuries, civilian morale and civilians *per se* became regular military targets, whose protected status could be circumvented if attacked collectively and/ or incidentally. Traditional distinctions between civilians and military personnel asserted in traditional rules of *ius in bello* were blurred. One can ask if the distinction of military from civilian is not an anachronism in the nuclear age. From this viewpoint contemporary terrorism in preferring civilian targets merely exploits the heritage of modern total war, and Mallin's point is valid: the difference between a terrorist car bomb and a bomb dropped by plane is only a matter of means. Furthermore, any depersonalization of killing by terrorists reflects the battlefield of modern conventional warfare: the age of the bayonet charge and hand-to-hand combat is largely past.[55]

Terrorism as Stratagem

If terrorism, as I have argued, is a form of war, closely related to guerrilla activity and characterized by emphasis on psychological factors and abandonment of normal rules of warfare, then it should be possible to place terrorism within the framework of military theory. Stratagem, commonly interpreted as military trickery, deception, and surprise, but actually a much broader idea in Graeco-Roman use, can be shown from a military viewpoint to be a conceptual ancestor of modern terrorism. This view coincides with what Crenshaw calls the 'instrumental approach' to terrorism, whereby terrorism is associated with surprise attack, a topic generating in the last decade a considerable literature from the viewpoint of both nuclear strategy and the relatively new field of military intelligence studies.[56] Both surprise attack and the aspects of deception in intelligence, however, are categories of stratagem.

Force and trickery offer alternative means of military action. The strong tend to flex their muscles openly and directly, while the reaction of the weak to a stronger opponent may be to seek escape, to rebel, to submit abjectly, or to cheat.[57] The idea of cheating implies a set of rules for conduct, which the strong usually see in their own terms as the expectation of confronting force with force. Stratagem, however, derives its essence from the unexpected in bending, breaking, or ignoring the rules completely.

I define stratagem as either a strategic or a tactical act of trickery, deceit, or cunning in war, whereby one attempts to gain psychological or material advantage over an opponent, to neutralize some part of an opponent's superiority, to minimize one's own expenditure of resources, or to restore the morale or physical state of one's own forces. Stratagem may take such common forms as ambush, surprise attack, feigned retreat, and reversing a pattern of behavior which the enemy has been conditioned to expect, but stratagem may also manifest itself as disinformation, betrayal, treason, assassination, the use of poison, sophistic interpretation of treaties or other agreements, new weapons or equipment (technological surprise), and various other tricks, deceptions, and psychological ploys too diverse for more specific classifications.

Stratagem pervades all aspects of war [cf. *Gentili, 1933: I, 28=II, 142*], and the connection of trickery with war surely occurred early in the development of military practice. In fact primitive warfare is largely characterized by stratagems, such as ambush, surprise attack, feigned retreat, and often treachery.[58] When the Greek and Chinese civilizations in the fourth century B.C. became the first to theorize in written form about war and the conduct of operations, stratagem formed a major motif of this literature [*Wheeler, 1981: 74–9*]. In the West Frontinus (d. 103) and in China Sun Tzu became its most notable exponents. Thus independent but conceptually related Western and Oriental traditions on military trickery arose simultaneously and only with the development of twentieth-century guerrilla doctrine did the two streams of thought finally merge.

In the West open battle and direct use of force received preference over trickery, although the tradition of stratagem did not die out. Rather, the history of the Western military tradition displays a tension between rival norms: the Achilles ethos, advocating chivalry, pitched battle and open, direct means, and the Odysseus ethos, favoring trickery, deceit, indirect means, and avoidance of pitched battle but not necessarily denial of the use of force. Ages of stratagem have occasionally emerged. Indeed the second half of the twentieth century could be characterized as an age of stratagem, in which theories of deterrence exploit the idea of bluff, intelligence agencies have become masters of deceit, and guerrilla warfare and terrorism consistently employ surprise, psychological tactics, and avoidance of battle.

Terrorism, seen as a form of primitive warfare and likewise exploiting surprise, ambush, avoidance of direct military confrontation, and abandoning conventional rules of conduct, would seem *a priori* connected to stratagem and its Odysseus ethos. The attachment of terrorism to Classical doctrine on stratagem, however, need not depend on *a priori* assumptions concerning concepts only apparently related, for whether terrorism is interpreted as an offshoot of guerrilla warfare or an outgrowth of theories of tyrannicide, citation of Classical examples and Classical doctrine throughout both traditions is demonstrable.

From the perspective of tyrannicide the story has, to some extent, recently been told.[59] A few examples will suffice. From the late eleventh to the thirteenth century the Ismaili sect called the Assassins waged perhaps the most effective terrorist campaign in history – first in Iran and Iraq, later in Syria. Operating from remote, inaccessible mountain-top fortresses, the Assassins succeeded in dominating the plains below by a policy of conversion, alliance, and hostilities constantly supported by assassination of key rulers, generals, and ministers, which prevented attacks on their bases and kept their Seljuk Turk and Sunnite opponents in perpetual disarray. Assassin terror was so effective that even a mysteriously placed message transfixed by a dagger could precipitate panic and a change of enemy plans.[60] This relatively bloodless method of waging war through terror represents the Odysseus ethos carried to a high degree.

Unfortunately, the study of medieval Moslem military thought is still in its infancy and direct citation of Graeco-Roman sources is not yet in evidence for the Assassins, most of whose writings have long since been destroyed by the Sunnite opposition. But it is known that Arabs delighted in stratagems, made collections of stratagems in the tradition of Frontinus and Polyaenus, translated some Greek and Byzantine military treatises into Arabic, and absorbed some Graeco-Roman military thought through treatises of the Sassanid Persians.[61]

Sunnites, however, also share in the Islamic tradition of stratagem. Faraj in *The Neglected Duty* (para. 106, cf. para. 113) justified Sadat's assassination by appeal to Mohammed's tactics for the *jihad*: believers with few resources should rely on intelligence and deceit – a succinct expression of the Odysseus ethos. Indeed Ibn Khaldun (1332–1406) quotes Muhammad that 'War is trickery' and cites an Arab proverb that 'Many a trick is worth more than a tribe'. These citations derive from a chapter of his *Muqaddimah*, in which he argues that 'hidden factors' (stratagem interestingly coupled with the 'celestial cause', that is, Allah's intercession) are superior in war to external factors (for example, numbers, weapons, battle formations).[62]

In current Islamic fundamentalism the Assassins, especially Hassan Sabbah their founder, are hailed as heroes for their terrorism against the European Crusaders. Lectures on Islamic history to the cadets of the Volunteers for Martyrdom at Iranian training camps, such as that at Niavaran, could hardly ignore the Assassins, although the Assassins' sectarian strife with the Sunnites is today usually glossed over. In Sunnite Iraq, however, Khomeini is equated with Hassan, seen as a Zoroastrian magus dreaming of reviving the ancient Persian Empire and restoring fire worship.[63]

Principles of the Odysseus ethos also appear in the Communist 'Document on Terror' (ca 1948). The anonymous author cautions against conditioning target populations to terror, recommends 'camouflage maneuvers' (that is, make terrorist acts appear the work of someone else), and even recounts a Russian stratagem from the Second World War on how to stop desertion, which recalls similar Carthaginian stratagems in the Punic Wars.[64] An example of a 'camouflage maneuver' occurred in 1957, when the wife of a French administrator was murdered by a bomb disguised as a box of cigars for her husband. The act was blamed on a West German Neo-Nazi group, the *Kampfverband für ein Unabhängiges Deutschland*, but in reality the perpetrators were the Czechoslovak intelligence service. In its early days camouflage maneuvers often characterized PLO activities, but more recently the situation is reversed and the PLO suffers the blame for the acts of others.[65]

The tradition of stratagem is even clearer and more direct in the theoretical development of guerrilla warfare. When small war (*petite guerre, klein Krieg*) began to be recognized as a distinct type of war in the mid-eighteenth century, the genre of military theory on this topic originated, which (further developed in the nineteenth century) led to modern guerrilla theory. Stratagem and the Odysseus ethos, a part of the Classical military legacy hitherto associated with the large-scale operations of conventional warfare, acquired new prominence in the literature on small war.[66] Furthermore, one of the founders of modern guerrilla theory, T.E. Lawrence, trained in Classics and archaeology, based his views to some extent on ancient ideas and drew inspiration from Maurice de Saxe (1695–1750).[67] De Saxe, a major military figure of the early eighteenth century, reinforces Lawrence's Classical emphasis, since de Saxe based his treatise largely on Classical doctrine and epitomized for his age the Odysseus ethos.[68] Even Che Guevara initiates his treatise with expression of the Odysseus ethos and advocates various stratagems, while Luttwak, in his recent analysis of the logic of strategy, classifies guerrilla warfare as 'relational maneuver' – in some respects his equivalent of what I call the Odysseus ethos.[69]

Terrorism as Warfare – Implications for Public Policy

Terrorism, however shocking and morally objectionable to the general public, has become a form of warfare in the twentieth century. Despite new facets, such as exploitation of the modern media of democratic societies and the use of sophisticated technology, contemporary terrorism combines the trends toward depersonalization of combat and the blurred distinction between civilians and soldiers in the twentieth-century practice of total war with the psychological techniques of stratagem, perhaps warfare's oldest method of operation. Terrorism represents an extreme form of the Odysseus ethos – Odysseus gone mad.

Viewing terrorism as a form of war can demystify this phenomenon for both the general public and policy-makers who must contend with this Odysseus *furens*. Terrorism may strike civilians unexpectedly, but it should not be equated with unavoidable and inevitable acts of God excusing the negligence of commanders (even of peace-keeping forces) in a war zone (for example the 1983 bombing of the Marine barracks in Lebanon). Centuries ago, Greeks and Romans rejected 'I didn't think' as an acceptable defense for being surprised [*Wheeler, 1988b: 164–5*]. Nevertheless, identification of terrorism with war does not mean that every terrorist act can be rationally explained. War like history can have its own logic, and the reasoning of terrorists need not correspond to that of intelligence agencies or political office holders. Here the 'organizational process' approach to terrorism has much to offer [cf. *Crenshaw, 1988: 28–9*].

As an aspect of stratagem, terrorism approximates the same point on the continuum of military violence as primitive warfare and guerrilla warfare. The apparent uniqueness of contemporary terrorism and its conceptual distinctions from guerrilla operations soon dissolve when terrorism is set within a broader historical context. Indeed after its initial splash in the 1960s and 1970s, terrorism has displayed few new *tactical* wrinkles in the 1980s, although narco-terrorism has emerged as a new category of the phenomenon. Terrorists have not obtained access to nuclear devices or targeted the infrastructures of industrialized countries. Achievements of terrorism have been minimal or negative in changing major policies of governments or producing new regimes.[70] The Jewish revolt of 66–70 remains the only case of a mass uprising sparked by terrorism [*Rapoport, 1984: 669, 672–3*]. Its nuisance value, however, remains occasionally atrocious (for example the bombing of Pan Am

Flight 103 in 1988). Indeed Falk [*1988: 17–18*] would even argue that the American government in the 1980s exploited public fear of terrorism to justify its intervention in the Third World and to boost its leadership role in the face of declining American economic preeminence.

Three observations derived from this essay's historical perspective of terrorism may be of interest to policy-makers. First, terrorism as a form of psychological warfare strikes at the will and the morale of its target and uses a strategy of exhaustion. Like the defensive aspect of war, terrorism can preserve its perpetrators and their cause, but it cannot achieve any positive goal unless its target party yields to negotiation or acknowledges defeat. Contemporary Western-style democracies have, despite public statements of 'no negotiation' with terrorists, not displayed an unshaken resolve, particularly regarding hostages. The premium placed on individual human life and public pressures to act, exacerbated by media attention to hostages, have elevated the centuries-old practice of hostage-taking to a useful means of embarrassing superpowers and promoting political paralysis (for example the Carter administration; [cf. *Taheri, 1987: 196–7*]). Retaliatory air strikes, as advocated (15 May 1990) by the presidential commission on the Pan Am Flight 103 disaster, would satisfy the public's demand to act, but could also aid terrorists by creating a backlash of world opinion, especially if the wrong 'terrorists' were bombed. Terrorist success in secluding hostages also eliminates the viability of commando rescue missions, which could easily fail and result in a greater loss of life besides signaling still another superpower policy disaster regarding terrorism. Hostages only have value if someone presses for their release. In an age of terrorism the public may have to accept small sacrifices of hostages, however politically unpopular, to eliminate the desirability of this tactic.

Second, the prominence of terrorism as a form of war should alter the perspective of policy-makers and suggest modifications in military education. Except for nuclear strategy, military thought since 1945 has been marked by a void of new ideas and a plethora of new technology. The tail sometimes seems to wag the dog. Officers are still primarily trained to fight large-scale conventional conflicts, although guerrilla warfare and terrorism represent the most common form of war in the last four decades.[71] With the end of the cold war officially proclaimed and a conflict of the two post-1945 superpowers increasingly unlikely, the trend toward low intensity conflicts will probably continue. Study of Clausewitz remains important, as does a knowledge of conventional conflict, but some reform is needed.

Finally, identification of terrorism as a form of war does not necessarily, as Wardlaw suggests [*1988: 247*], lead exclusively to a preference for military analyses and military solutions over political ones. Hanle [*1989:*

86–8, 208] characterizes the current prevalence of guerrilla warfare and terrorism as a new era of 'social war', in which winners will be the parties best mobilizing and sustaining sociopolitical resources within a populace, while disrupting and destroying those of opponents. As the United States learned in Vietnam, superior logistics and firepower will not win this kind of war. Xenophon (d. *ca* 354 B.C.), an early exponent of stratagem, said it best: 'Battles are won by men's souls' (*Cyropaedia* 3.3.19).

It has almost become a truism to suggest that a more social approach to terrorism might be profitable in the long run, and this proposal might appeal to those believing that terrorism is a problem with a solution. But billions could be spent worldwide to improve the lot of millions of potential terrorists without an appreciable return on the investment. Political and religious motives for terrorism will not necessarily be eliminated by social programs.

Terrorism has a long history stretching from pre-state societies to the present, but scholars have really only begun to uncover and analyze it. Grandiose 'lessons' from history about terrorism are still somewhat premature. We can say that generally a strategy limited to terrorism alone is ineffective in producing major changes of regimes of policy and that terrorism has success mainly as advertising. Lack of effectiveness and success, however, seem not to affect longevity: the wave of modern terrorism begun *ca* 1879 (cf. Rapoport in n.9 *supra*) has already entered its second century. The Assassins lasted nearly 200 years; the Thugs of India (killing as religious ritual) even longer; and the IRA, over a half-century old, shows no signs of dissolving. The phenomenon appears cyclical, taking advantage of political watersheds, exploiting technology but not dependent on it, and drawing inspiration from religious, cultural, and historical traditions. Clausewitz's metaphor of war as a chameleon [*1976: 89*] is also apt for terrorism – ever changing its color to fit new circumstances.

Although it is not the historian's role to play futurist, chances are we have not seen the last of terrorism. Apart from the continuation of current terrorist causes, new potential seeds of terrorism lie in resentment at shifts in political and economic power, frustrations within states learning the democratic process and the realities of a market economy, and rising nationalistic, racial, and religious sentiments. On the positive side, the end of Soviet domination in Eastern Europe has eliminated some former sanctuaries for terrorists, in East Germany for instance. But the union of Common Market countries in 1992 will lead to decreased border controls that may open new opportunities for terrorism.[72] Like guerrilla warfare, terrorism is a strategy and an idea which cannot be once defeated and forgotten. The will of the weak always finds an ally in the wily Odysseus.[73]

NOTES

1. See Falk [*1988: 17*], who asserts that fewer than 25 Americans per year in the 1980s died from terrorism and that being struck by lightning is four times more likely than death from a terrorist. See Clark [*1988: 41*]. Falk's statistics do not include the 1983 bombing of the Marine barracks in Beirut or the downing of Pan Am Flight 103 in 1988.
2. For overviews of the scholarly literature on terrorism see Bell [*1978: 36–43*], cf. Laqueur [*1977c: 132–49*]; Romano [*1984 (non vidi)*]; Schmid and Jongman [*1988*].
3. Clark [*1988: 44*] uses this phrase twice on one page.
4. Rapoport [*1988: 56* n.14 with bibliography]; cf. Rapoport and Alexander [*1982: passim*]; Jenkins [*1980*]; Nef [*1978: 7*]; for governments see Dugard [*1982: 77–98*]. The US State Department, Department of Defense, and the Army all have different definitions [*Vought and Fraser, 1986: 73–4*]. A representative of the US Department of Defense at the seminar cited the need for an historical study of the definition of terrorism.
5. I question whether every bombing in political protest merits the term 'terrorism', although bombs are a terrorist tactic. Anti-abortion and animal rights activists hardly compare with the IRA. Scale and frequency should be considered in distinguishing use of terrorist tactics from terrorism. By analogy with an Aristotelian problem, does terrorism occur if no one is terrorized?
6. Taheri [*1987: 4–6*]: national (for example IRA, Basque ETA), urban guerrillas (for example Italian Red Brigade, West German Red Army Faction, Belgian CCC), old-style guerrillas (for example Sandinistas), publicity-seeking (for example Popular Front for the Liberation of Palestine, African National Congress), Islamic terrorists (for example Iranian trained or supported groups in Lebanon).
7. Hanle [*1989: xiii*]: psychotic, criminal, mystical, revolutionary, repression, military, state-sponsored.
8. In Hanle's system [*1989: 165–6*] state terrorism includes repression against internal opponents and military terrorism and state-sponsored terrorism against external parties. Terror as a common wartime strategy or tactic by a state's military forces against the enemy would hardly satisfy Rapoport's definition that terrorism is 'extra-normal'.
9. Chaliand [*1985: 141*]; Crenshaw [*1988: 15*]; Rapoport [*1988: 34*], who discerns two earlier waves: 1879–First World War (mainly assassinations in Europe) and First World War–1960s (national liberation movements in colonial territories).
10. Rapoport [*1982: 31–3*]: Begin refused to attack other Jews, did not provoke the local Arabs, centralized his command, and struck only the British. Hanle [*1989: 115*] erroneously dates the *sicarii* to the Jewish revolt of 132–35.
11. Rapoport [*1984: 664–8; 1990: 103–30*]; on the Assassins also see Lewis [*1967*]; Franzius [*1969*]; Tahari [*1987: 27–35*].
12. Laqueur [*1977c and 1978*]; Dowdling [*1978: 224, 226*]; Rapoport [*1971*]; Ford [*1985*]; Ivianski [*1988: 129–49*].
13. See Lider [*1982*]: an examination of the problem from both Western and Marxist–Leninist perspectives with a solution for restoring rigor to the term.
14. As this essay is the revision of a 1987 conference paper, I must acknowledge that Hanle [*1989*] has independently and in much greater detail formulated ideas very similar to mine on identification of terrorism with war, although his views are much more Clausewitzian and emphasize belief in 'immutable principles of war', for the validity of which he frequently appeals to the authority of the US Army's Field Manual 100–5, Field Service Regulations – Operations. Historians and military theorists, however, have never agreed on the existence of such principles, their number, their identity, and their definition, although such 'principles' continue to be standard in modern military education and training. See Wheeler [*1988a: 8, 25* n.10 with bibliography].
15. Clausewitz [*1976: 75–89*], cf. Otterbein [*1970: 3–4*]; Turney-High [*1981: 25–45*]. Hanle [*1989: 1–55*, esp. 52] argues three criteria for war: lethal force for a political end, use of force on the moral plane (that is, an entity's cohesion is targeted), and the principle of engagement (that is, force is used according to seven principles of combat).

16. For example, Laqueur [1977c: 116]; Livingston [1978: 19]; Mallin [1978: 391]; Nef [1978: 16]; Cooper [1978: 287–96]; Rumpf [1985: 388–9]; Fields [1986: 10]; Rivers [1986: 21, 101, 152]; Wardlaw [1988: 258 n.43]; Hanle [1989: 181–93]. See Burgess [1986: 8–15]. A flawed argument asserts that terrorism differs from the strategy of war because territorial gain is not involved [Mickolus, 1978: 45, cf. Wolf, 1978: 297–306], but territorial gain need not be the cause of war and many terrorists are, at least ultimately, concerned with the possession of territory, for example Northern Ireland, Palestine.

17. Rapoport [1982: xiv]; Laqueur [1977c: 23]; for Babeuf see Rose [1978]; for Buonarotti, Ivianski [1988: 129 with 145 n.2 for bibliography]; on the cult of antiquity see Parker [1937]; Clauss [1979: 81–94].

18. For further criticism of the term 'terrorism' and rejection of 'terrorism' as a scholarly discipline see Zulaika elsewhere in this volume.

19. Schelling [1966: v–vi, 10, 172], cf. Luttwak [1976: esp. 195–200] on the distinction between power (something perceived) and force (something empirically employed).

20. See Liddell Hart's strategy of indirect approach based upon psychological as much as physical dislocation of the enemy [Liddell Hart 1967: 5–6].

21. Primitive warriors: for example Karsten [1967: 320–21]; Ammianus Marcellinus [31.3.2–3]; Polybus [6.23.12–13]; Plutarch, Aemilius Paulus [19.1–2, cf. 18.3–4]; Vegetius [3.24].

22. Assyrians: Ferrill [1985: 68–70], cf. Röllig [1986: 116–28]; Romans: Polybus [10.15.4–5].

23. Although some might object to the validity of this comparison (for example trees are not the equivalent of a terrorist concealing himself in the civilian population), the persistence and vitality of gentlemenly rules of fair play among early modern European commanders should not be underestimated. For the distinction between soldiers and civilians as an anachronism in the nuclear age see below.

24. Turney-High [1981: 24–45], cf. Laqueur [1977a: vii]; criticism: for example Otterbein [1973: 945]. Clutterbuck's analysis of primitive warfare [1977: 22–4] is cursory and extremely superficial.

25. Hanle [1989: 132–63, esp. 134–5]; cf. Chaliand [1985: 15, 67–79].

26. Rapoport [1971: 44]; Laqueur [1977a: ix, 1977c: 5, 100, 217–18]; Mallin [1978: 371–72]; Rumpf [1985: 391, 394].

27. See Laqueur [1977a: 400; Rumpf 1985: 391]. Luttwak's analysis of revolutionary warfare as a grand strategy [1987: 132n] would designate guerrilla warfare as the military component and subversion, consisting of propaganda and terrorism, as the political component. Since grand strategy in his view [1987: 179] is the sphere in which military and political elements continuously interact, his distinction of guerrilla warfare from terrorism can hardly mean a rigid separation of the two, or that terrorism cannot be a guerrilla tactic. Rather, Luttwak's coupling of terrorism and propaganda would seem to emphasize terrorism's psychological effects.

28. Williams [1989: 1–20]; Clutterbuck [1977: 92]. Marighella's handbook has recently been reprinted: Carlos Marighella, The Terrorist Classic: Manual of the Urban Guerrilla, tr. Gene Hanrahan (Chapel Hill, NC: Documentary Publications, 1985).

29. Lawrence [1939: 111]; Liddell Hart [1950: 53–7]; cf. Bond [1977: 8–9]. In seminar discussions Post asserted that many members of the Italian Red Brigade are the offspring of former partisans in the Second World War.

30. Laqueur [1977c: 188, 1978: 122–79, cf. 226–7]; Ford [1985: 264]; Cordes [1988: 154–5, 157].

31. Richard Threlkeld, ABC Evening News, 4 Nov. 1987.

32. Certainly guerrilla movements that can field armies are larger than many terrorist cells, although such movements may have grown from originally minute groups, and many terrorist organizations would like to be guerrillas, if they could.

33. Available in English and French translations: Dennis [1985]; Dagron and Mihǎescu [1986].

34. See Cicero, De officiis [3.107–8], Philippicae [4.14]; Ulpian, Digesta Justiniani [49.15.24].

35. For example Livy [1.15.1; 2.48.5–6; 3.2.12–13; 7.28.3; 8.34.10; 21.15.2]; MacMullen

[1966: 223–4, 225]; Milan *[1979: 171–97]*; cf. MacDonald *[1984: 77–84]*.

36. *Contra*, Wilkinson, *[1982: 317–22]*, but I find his views too legalistic.
37. See Amon *[1982: 68–9]* on terrorists' ignorance of history and even of literature on the revolutionary tradition.
38. Laqueur *[1977a: 154–6, 169–71, 244–45, 260, 302, 334]*; *English* [1987: 10]; *Kuhfus* [1985: 57–91].
39. Reprinted in English translation in Rapoport and Alexander *[1982: 186–216]*.
40. Laqueur *[1978: 121]*; Cordes *[1988: 150–71]*; cf. Rapoport *[1988: 32–58]* on terrorists' memoirs.
41. Laqueur *[1977c: 55–6, 121; 1977b: 157, 118, 235]*; on Blanqui also see Ivianski *[1988: 130–33]*.
42. For bibliography and discussion of the pamphlet see Rapoport *[1990: 103–30]*. My thanks to Professor Rapoport for sending me an advanced copy of this paper.
43. Hahlweg *[1977: 125]*; Taheri *[1987: 90, 94]*.
44. See J.F.C. Fuller's military definition of treachery as demoralization of the enemy *[Fuller, 1923: 105]*.
45. See the remarks of the Russian terrorist Serge Stepniak-Kravchinski (1883), in Laqueur *[1978: 89]*: 'A victory, immediate, splendid, and decisive, such as that obtained by an insurrection, is utterly impossible by means of terrorism. But another victory is more probable, that of the weak against the strong, that of the "beggars" of Holland against the Spaniards. In a struggle against an invisible, impalpable, omnipresent enemy, the strong is vanquished, not by the arms of his adversary, but by the continuous tension of his own strength, which exhausts him, at last, more than he would be exhausted by defeats.'
46. Schelling *[1966: 25, 33, 172–4]*; Wright *[1965: 319–20]*.
47. Laqueur *[1977c: 109]*; Fields *[1986: 3]*. Hanle *[1989: 112–15]* distinguishes direct (classical, triadic) terrorism from indirect terrorism: in the former the target of terror and the target of influence are the same, whereas in the latter they are distinct (for example revolutionary terror, in which the target of terror is the government, but the target of influence is the population at large).
48. Laqueur *[1977c: 219–23, 1978: 120]*, cf. Cooper *[1978: 289]*. On terrorist networking see Rivers *[1986: 88–104]*.
49. Laqueur *[1978: 120]*; Rivers *[1986: 21,142]*.
50. Wolf *[1978: 303]*; Rapoport *[1982: 16]*. Cf. Luttwak *[1987: 132–3]*.
51. Wilkinson *[1982: 327]*; Rapoport *[1982: xiv]*; Terry *[1986: 61]*. Cf. Gros *[1978: 450]*.
52. Laqueur *[1978: 224]*; Rapoport *[1982: xiii]*; Rivers *[1986: 16–17]*; Terry *[1986: 62]*; Fields *[1986: 3]*; Ford *[1985: 240]*.
53. Mallin *[1978: 393, 397]*. The analogy of terrorism and an air raid also appears in Nef *[1978: 8]*.
54. See Auguste Blanqui, *Instructions pour une prise des armes* (1869), in Laqueur *[1977b: 157]*. On the date of this work see Ivianski *[1988: 133]*.
55. On depersonalization of modern battle see Keegan *[1976: 203–336]*.
56. See Crenshaw *[1988: 13–19]*. For terrorism as a stratagem I would not accept all the premises of her Table 1 [27].
57. See Bowyer *[1982: 3–4]*; Luttwak *[1987: 16]*. Throughout this section I draw freely from my current research on the history of stratagem as a concept in military thought and international law. I offer a brief summary of the topic in 'Ruses and Stratagems', in Trevor N. Dupuy (ed.), *International Military and Defense Encyclopedia* (Pergamon-Brassey's) forthcoming.
58. See Otterbein *[1970: 27–44]*; Turney-High *[1971: 109–37]*; Davie *[1929: 176–81]*.
59. Ford *[1985]*. Cf. Rapoport *[1971]*; Laqueur *[1978: 26, 34, 55, 63–4, 80, 89]*.
60. Franzius *[1969: 40–42, 55–6]*; Lewis *[1967: 96, 99, 129]*; cf. Rapoport *[1984: 664–8]*.
61. For example Khawam *[1976]*; Kolias *[1984: 129–35]*; Christides *[1984: 137–48]*; Tantum *[1979: 187–201]*.
62. Rapoport *[1990: 113–14]*; Ibn Khaldun *[1958: II, 73–88, esp. 86]*; cf. the Arab proverb quoted by Callwell *[1906: 232]*: 'War is stratagem applied by force.'
63. Taheri *[1987: 34]*. At the seminar Sprinzak posited that the Assassins provide a model

for Khaddafi's terrorist activities.

64. Rapoport and Alexander [*1982: 190, 197–99, 202*]. Cf. Frontinus [*Strategemata 3.16.2, 4*]. Russian stratagem: favorable German treatment of deserters encouraged Russian desertion, so the Russians adopted a policy of mistreatment of captured Germans. Reports of this policy led to German reprisals and Russian desertion rates declined.
65. Bittman [*1972: 1–3*]; Rapoport [*1988: 53*].
66. See, for example, Laqueur [*1977b: 17, 19, 21, 61, 94, 111–12, 235*].
67. Lawrence [*1939: 109, 115, 116, 117–18, 132*].
68. De Saxe [*1971: v, 70, 74, 122, 129, 132, 136, 141, 149, 150, 159, 163–5, 187–8*].
69. Guevara [*1961: 6–7, 10, 13*]; Luttwak [*1987: 132–3*].
70. See Chaliand [*1985: 141, 162–3*]; cf. Crenshaw [*1988: 15*] on innovations in terrorism.
71. Chaliand [*1985: 11, 19*]; Martin van Creveld, speech at the annual meeting of the American Military Institute, Virginia Military Institute, 15 April 1989. Van Creveld's recent book on officer training [*1990*] unfortunately contains few of the speech's criticisms of curriculum.
72. See Richard Clutterbuck, *Terrorism and Guerrilla Warfare: Forecasts and Remedies* (London: Routledge, 1990) and *Terrorism, Drugs and Crime in Europe after 1992* (London: Routledge, 1990).
73. My sincere thanks to Theodore Ropp, Clark McCauley, Martha Crenshaw, and David Rapoport for beneficial suggestions and criticisms.

Terror, Totem, and Taboo:
Reporting on a Report

Joseba Zulaika

Should we analytically constitute or dissolve the category of terrorism? The Basque case is adduced to illustrate the dynamics of constructing and deconstructing a reified notion of terrorism. Two approaches are confronted: the legal-technical work of a committee of terrorism experts and the ethnographic work of an anthropologist. The experts' position that social science should be subservient to police and intelligence counter-insurgency is questioned. The intellectual history of cultural anthropology is invoked for advancing a critique of current theories of terrorism; in particular, the resurgence of psychological fallacies and unicausal arguments in explanations of terrorism is reexamined. It is argued that ritual situations are typically not governed by intrinsic or instrumental means-ends connections and that the search for positive causes may not be the best strategy for studying contexts of behavior, such as terrorism, in which the element of chance plays a key role. Anthropologists have learned a disturbing lesson from the history of their discipline: after having elaborated dozens of theories on cultural institutions such as animism, totemism, taboo, and witchcraft, the conclusion was reached that their best theoretical advance consisted in analytically dissolving the category in question. The paper concludes that this literature should caution students of terrorism about making similar categorical mistakes and that the adoption of crusading attitudes under the mask of expertise has more to do with religion than with scientific objectivity.

In the summer of 1985 a news item appearing in a Basque newspaper grabbed my attention: an international panel of five terrorism experts had been commissioned by the regional Basque government to find out the causes and consequences of Basque terrorism and propose appropriate measures to contain it. I had spent seven years doing ethnographic research on Basque political violence and the news prompted me to reflect on what kinds of 'expertise' I could claim for myself in the matter. There was no question in my mind that policy-makers have a right and a need to ask for expert advice, yet in this case, with which I was so familiar, the prospect of a committee of scholars offering expert diagnoses and solutions directly contradicted my own experience. For years I had struggled with the intellectual and ethical problems posed by my country's violence, and the more I reflected on the issues the more I became convinced that they were rooted in cultural perceptions and political impasse. Suddenly a panel of experts could bring to bear real 'scientific' knowledge on the issues and, by treating them as if they were technical ones, resolve once and for all the intellectual or policy challenges posed by Basque violence. I felt their expediency made a mockery of my own anthropological work.

Since my argument will be mostly methodological, I have resorted to the work of Max Weber, a towering figure in the methodology of the social sciences. I also have recourse to the history of anthropological theory and have been struck by the similarities between our present theories of terrorism and those produced decades ago by pioneering anthropologists in the fields of magic, religion, and totemism. So I will be proposing that we learn from them how to avoid basic categorical errors.

The Findings of the Report

The committee of experts was composed of an Italian psychiatrist, a French criminologist, a German jurist, an English historian, and headed by Sir Clive Rose (1986), a British ambassador to NATO. Their specialties being in other areas, none knew much about Basque history or culture, nor could they speak the native language, yet they were to understand the Basque problems and propose solutions. When the report was made public, my worst fears concerning their methodology and value impositions were confirmed. It was not simply that the experts and I subscribed to competing approaches to the same phenomenon, but rather that they provided the logistical scheme for a grand anti-terrorist campaign in which anthropologists were exhorted to contribute along with police and intelligence agents in the eradication of terrorism. The gist of the enterprise can be gathered from the following quotation: 'More information is needed about the aims, membership, personalities and methods of ETA. This information should be sought in parallel with the implementation of the counter-measures recommended later in this report, which should not await the outcome of the research studies indicated below' (9.1.21). Social science is needed because 'such research will enable action to combat terrorism, particularly in the social, cultural, educational and legal fields, to be progressively refined and focused, thus becoming increasingly more effective as knowledge about the phenomenon of terrorism in the Basque country is improved' (9.1.14).

The experts are concerned with the cultural values that support Basque terrorism. They recommend an ethnographic study that would try to 'enter' the value system of the people in the culture (9.1.16.2). We are told that such a study's goal is 'implementing a politics of reinsertion and pacification', which is a key strategic element in the Spanish Ministry of the Interior's fight against terrorism. Their understanding of 'value' is reflected in the following paragraph: 'Recruitment into ETA seems slow and gradual (this would imply a subcultural explanation, with slow, progressive infusion of norms and values, through family influences ... and peer pressure (the subculture of the groups)' (9.1.11). Thus the experts fall little short of accusing family members and peer groups of being responsible for their relatives' and friends' induction; the experts seem to be calling for the reevalutation and eradication of the cultural being of the native Basque as a means of halting terrorism.

Approximately two-thirds of the entire report is devoted to describing other European terrorist groups. One might question whether the specifics of Italy, Germany, or the South Tyrol are crucial for understanding what is happening among Basques, but for the experts the fundamental thing about Basque violence is that it *is* terrorism; that is to say, it belongs to a particular category of behavior. Once such a categorization is established, describing other cases of terrorism is much the same as describing the Basque problem. The remaining one-third of the report is made up of a short introduction plus the concluding chapters recommending action. In these essays the experts propose an anti-terrorism strategy that includes social science, legal and juridical dispositions, socio-economic measures, police provisions and intelligence recommendations, security measures and a 'Plan for Consciousness-Raising'. The consciousness-raising is premised on clearly stated ideological and moral imperatives that include an active use of media exposure of the plan, detailed indoctrination against radical nationalist values at all educational levels from primary school to the university, and advice to political parties regarding the role they should play combatting terrorism.

All of this seems well thought out for the Ministry of the Interior, but the question from a social scientific viewpoint is how these experts know what 'ought to be' in the Basque case. How do they know, for instance, what is best for Basque children to be taught at school? The assumption is, of course, that we all know that terrorism is bad and that anything that contributes to preventing it should be considered positive. This is, however, a position closer to religion than to social science. Weber's [1949] categorical distinction between factual and normative propositions cannot be reconciled with the experts' imposition of value-judgment at all social and normative levels. If science means anything, it should be its readiness to question any presupposition, a readiness inconsistent with the zeal of anti-terrorist crusaders.

These concerns became pressing for me when foreign scholars with only the remotest knowledge of Basque society, history and culture, but with claims to scientific expertise in the field of terrorism, burst into my own area of concern with great media fanfare while raising the hopes of policymakers that a definite solution to the problem of Basque violence was at hand. As far as I could learn, they were never seen in public, did not give an interview or a talk in the Basque country, made no presentation of their results during or after the research, nor consulted any Basque scholar. The figure of the expert became for me almost as problematical as the figure of the terrorist itself. Finally, when the report came out, it provoked a public controversy as to its uselessness and subservience to the political interests of those who commissioned it in the first place. Far from providing a solution, it became part of the problem.

Why Terrorism?

Causal thinking is the main intellectual strategy concerning issues of war and political terrorism, namely, the search for the 'causes' that will unveil the source of the problem. Thus we have a rapidly growing body of literature devoted to suggesting 'hypotheses relating to the causation of civil violence and terrorism' [*Wilkinson, 1979: 46*]. A stock definition of terrorism becomes 'violence for effect' [*Jenkins, 1975: 1*]. Cause and effect are linked in a rational-instrumental chain that echoes the military action-reaction mentality. Likewise the panel of experts is quite specific about the major goal of terrorism research: 'The explanation of "why terrorism" has so far eluded scholars and politologists, and the research studies suggested should aim to find the answer to this question' (9.1.18). This search for 'why terrorism' may appear to be the best strategy for getting at the heart of the matter yet, unfortunately, it may also be the safest way to ignore the advances over the last 50 years of the social and cultural sciences.

An investigation which uncritically relies on the idea of 'cause' tends to ignore categorical differences in various kinds of causation. Bateson stresses the distinction between 'causal explanation' and 'cybernetic explanation' on the grounds that the former 'is usually positive' and the latter 'is always negative' (1972: 399). Cybernetically, what matter are the alternative possibilities which could have occurred but which did *not* occur due to restraints. By concentrating on the positive causes of the violence we are partly reproducing the military type of thinking in which the encounter between the contending parties is a one-way, functional, nonprobabilistic, causal relationship. Devoid of feedback and different orders of prediction, in this type of thinking all creativity is reduced to the purposive means-ends syndrome. The shift from the physical event to the idea of the physical event, from function to meaning, has yet to take place in such thinking.

Ritual situations are typically not governed by intrinsic or instrumental means-ends connections. Nor are those in which the element of chance plays a key role. Such ritual contexts are most relevant for the anthropologist who distinguishes categorically among the following three types of behavior: (1) rational behavior aiming at specific ends in a strictly mechanical way; (2) communicative behavior, in which there is no mechanical link between means and ends but only culturally defined connection; (3) magical behavior, which is efficient in terms of cultural conventions of the actors but not in a rational-technical sense [*Leach, 1975*]. Types 2 and 3 are basically ritual behavior, and in my work on Basque violence I argue extensively that such behavior is an essential component of it. Positive causal explanations limit the perception and analysis of violent processes as if they were type 1 behavior alone, when from a culturally integrative perspective types 2 and 3 make up most human performances.

The terrorism experts demand that the social scientist determine nothing less than 'why terrorism'. This genetic and aetiological approach to social institutions was fashionable in anthropology at the turn of the century when the most pressing intellectual problems were thought to be the discovery of the 'origins' of religion, law, family, and so on. The obsession with the origins, sources or reasons of an institution, however, long since disappeared from the social science agenda. Thus, Evans-Pritchard could write in 1951: 'We would, I think unanimously, hold today that an institution is not to be understood, far less explained, in terms of origins, whether these origins are conceived of as beginning, causes, or merely, in a logical sense, its simplest forms' [*1951: 38*]. This is required knowledge in any undergraduate anthropology course, for 'how they (the institutions) originated and developed is in any case a problem which, however relevant to the problem of how they function in society, is a different problem and one that has to be separately investigated by a different technique' [*1951: 39–40*]. If an anthropologist were to start asking, say, 'why witchcraft?' or 'why ritual?' or 'why religious belief?' we would instantly know that his sophistication does not transcend Frazer [*1922*]. Or if a linguist were to propose to his colleagues that the key issue for research is 'why language?' he would be derided. Yet this is what the international panel of terrorism experts is demanding of us, simply to find out 'why terrorism?'.

Terrorism and the Concept of the State

It might appear the experts take a neutral stance when they state that 'it has not proved possible to define "terrorism" as an offence in such a way as to distinguish it from a normal criminal offence' (8.36). Here the Spanish State provides the source of legality, since 'under Article 149 of the Constitution, the judiciary is among the matters over which the state holds exclusive jurisdiction' (9.2.1). The unquestioning acceptance of the state as the guarantor of legitimacy is, however, a presupposition to which a social scientist may not subscribe.

Weber's essays specifically underline the problematic nature of the concept of the state; such difficulty, theoretical as well as practical in the Basque case, completely escapes the terrorism experts. A stark indication of the extent to which Basques accept the current constitutional order can be gathered from the fact that none of the Basque parties from center-right to left voted in favor of the Constitution. More than two-thirds of the Basques voted against or actively abstained during the referendum of 1978, not primarily because the Constitution failed to endorse Basque pro-independence goals, which do not enjoy majority support among Basques, but because it was thought that it did not provide sufficient political autonomy for the preservation of Basque historical identity and language. The experts' solution to the political stalemate is to reinforce the State's control mechanism.

The categories of 'law' and 'crime' are no less problematic for an anthropologist. In fact this has been a salient field of research since Malinowski [1926] and Radcliffe-Brown [1937]. Most human societies are ruled by oral procedures and tradition; although written and codified law-making is essential to our state-governed societies, we should remember that in the context of global human history it is rather unusual. One does not need to go to a primitive society to discover the obvious reality that legitimacy and criminality depend not on the facts of the case but on what we believe to be the case, as was clearly shown by the hearings on the Iran–Contra affair. In nearly all the major nation-states, recent history provides striking examples to illustrate that the legitimate actions of the ruler become the criminal acts of the ex-ruler.

In contemporary life terrorist acts are perhaps the most blunt instances of how little we have progressed from regicides and headhunters. To the extent that our knowledge is technical we can discern advancement or recession in types of warfare and their institutional organizations. It is perhaps worth noting that after the Second World War guerrilla 'terror' and nuclear 'terror' are the two forms of warfare which have superseded conventional war and that in both new forms actual combat is largely replaced by the interchange of threat messages and ritual simulation; in Aron's words, 'in the treatise of a twentieth-century Clausewitz, the Communist theory of revolutionary warfare would figure just as prominently as the theory of nuclear weapons' [1959: 67]. As shown by Wheeler's study in this volume, understanding terrorism as a mode of warfare appears to be a most promising area of research.

Related to the problematic status of the terrorist's 'offence' is the apparently simple problem of counting terrorist incidents. Quantifiable variables and statistical samples are all necessary for scientific progress and we need them in the study of terrorism. Any sequence of human behavior presents, however, the conceptual problem of distinguishing the context of action from the acts themselves, as well as the question of whether there are isolable units of behavior. Supposing we have types of behavior classifiable as 'joking' or 'love' or 'aggression', which are *classes* of behavior, if we are asked how many single pieces of events have occurred in a given sequence (how many jokes in half an hour, how many acts of aggression in a day) we will run into difficulties in identifying the single units, and therefore in meeting the elementary requirement of statistics which is uniformity of sample. Some investigators doubt whether there are such isolable units in human behavior (see Bateson [*1975*]). The conceptual problems behind statistical samples become glaring in the literature on terrorism. One is not surprised to find out that 'the figures produced by the best-known data-bases on international terrorism vary considerably. This is due mainly to differences in definition and categorization – as regards what constitutes not only an act of terrorism, but also an "incident" [*Wilkinson, 1986a: 45*]. As a result of such differing understandings of terrorist acts we are told for instance that the CIA's 1979 report claimed there were 3,336 terrorist incidents from 1968 to the date, whereas the 1980 report claimed that there have been 6,714. The reasons for the dramatic increase in just one year were that the data sources previously used were too narrow and that it was decided to include threats and 'hoaxes' as incidents. Depending on the categorization of the phenomenon the acts of terrorism multiply, which is to say that as long as we do not solve the conceptual problems behind what constitutes terrorism as a class of behavior the statistics are not worth much.

The panel of terrorism experts is not bothered by questions of classification or value and instead simply portrays Basque violence as criminal terrorism. We are bound to question who defines the criminal. The real definition of public figures comes in the end from their own communities and the experts themselves recognize that during Franco's years ETA activists were considered 'heroes'. What the experts do not say is that until democracy – during all those years from 1959 to 1979 – ETA was much the same 'terrorist' group for the Spanish government and media. It is normal for a politician to define a situation according to his own needs and to use the semantics of terror as a weapon to legitimize the state's violence and stigmatize that of its opponents. Yet what are we to think of experts who go to a foreign country and, under the guise of scientific expertise, impose a set of definitions that criminalize the political options of large segments of the population?

Terror, Totem and Taboo: Dissolving Categories

'Totemism is like hysteria', wrote Levi-Strauss of that much debated topic in anthropology,

> in that once we are persuaded to doubt that is possible arbitrarily to isolate certain phenomena and to group them together as diagnostic signs of an illness, or of an objective institution, the symptoms themselves vanish or appear refractory to any unifying interpretation ... but the comparison with totemism suggests a relation of another order between scientific theories and culture, one in which the mind of the scholar himself plays as large a part as the mind of the people studies; it is as though he were seeking, consciously or unconsciously, and under the guise of scientific objectivity, to make the latter – whether mental patients or so-called primitives – more *different* than they really are' (1962: 1; his emphasis).

By substituting 'terrorism' for 'totemism', it is hard to imagine a more precise characterization of our terrorism studies.

Anthropologists have concluded that, for categories such as 'totemism', their best theoretical chance is the 'dissolving' of the category in question. Concerning totemism, for instance, its theoretical framer McLennan characterized it as fetishism plus exogamy and matrilineal descent. W.H.R. Rivers defined it in 1913 as a combination of (1) a social element (the connection of an animal or plant with, typically, an exogamous group or clan); (2) a psychological element (a belief in a relation of kinship between members of the group and the animal, plant or thing); (3) a ritual element (taboos on eating the totem). By 1920 Van Gennep reviewed forty-one theories of totemism. Yet as early as 1916 Boas had charged that totemism is an artificial entity existing nowhere but in the mind of the anthropologist; his own suggestion was that a necessary condition of totemism is the formation of a social system. There is no doubt that totemic groups are exogamous, for instance, but is not exogamy *per se* a more basic feature than totemism in marking social groups? Totemism established relationships between human groups and objects of the natural environment, but does that make it a phenomenon *sui generis*? A.P. Elkin, after defining totemism according to the three criteria of form, meaning, and function, tried to preserve the reality of the phenomenon by recognizing a multiplicity of forms; he differentiated between 'individual' totemism, 'sexual' totemism, 'clan' totemism, and 'dream' totemism. But the one thing that does not occur to the analyst is that it is 'the very idea of totemism that is illusory, not just its unity' [*Levi-Strauss, 1962: 45*].

This discussion illustrates the state of affairs in the study of terrorism which, like totemism, defies a unifying interpretation and in which the scholar himself plays a crucial role in making his subjects more different than they really are. In the field of terrorism, too, the category rests on the obvious existence of a social system, with persons and groups which are interdicted, the breach of certain norms being tantamount to the fearsome breach of a taboo, with ideological and psychological premises being essential components,and ritual elements playing a significant role. Yet here, too, after describing elaborate taxonomies and typologies of terrorism [*Schmid, 1983*], one cannot help but question the categorical unity of the phenomenon and the validity of the idea itself of terrorism. The various types of terrorists ('nationalists', 'ideological', 'religious fanatics', 'single issue', 'state-sponsored') are united by one basic feature – terrorizing.

An anthropologist can hardly avoid recalling similar approaches in areas such as witchcraft and sorcery, which elicited these comments:

> The various papers presented in this A.S.A. conference all mention witchcraft and sorcery, and yet these terms seem labels for social phenomena that differ radically from society to society .... Taxonomic preoccupation may sometimes distract us from recognizing ambiguities inherent in social beliefs and acts. When applied on a cross-cultural, comparative level, such labels may conceal problematical interdependencies. We feel we have explained matters away through having imposed some nominal category' [*Beidelman, 1970: 351*].

This is said of anthropologists who have carried out extensive and detailed studies of witchcraft and sorcery in many societies; it applies more poignantly to our field in which we are in possession of hardly any ethnographic knowledge of terrorist groups, while the literature tends to concentrate on 'international terrorism' in the most general manner, as if we were dealing with the real 'thing' itself.

As did Levi-Strauss with totemism, Crick has proposed that 'our understanding will advance when "witchcraft" is analytically dissolved into a larger frame of reference' [*1976: 112*]. Instead of piling up new definitions and theories, what is needed is a new approach to the entire phenomenon which will decrease the employment of the term. It can be argued that witchcraft may have become a separate topic in anthropology simply because of its significance in Europe's history during the sixteenth and seventeenth centuries, although it had very little to do with practices in primitive cultures. If the notion of witchcraft in Europe was parasitic on categories such as natural philosophy and a theological system, the relevant categories among, say, the Azande are quite different, and no easy translation is possible between the two worlds.

These sorts of intellectual subtleties do not seem to concern students of terrorism, who find no problem in applying the very same concept to most diverse groups and acts of violence. Typological qualifications ready at hand will soon order any differences. We should learn a lesson from the anthropologists who devoted themselves to producing dozens of theories on animism, totemism, witchcraft, and so on, only to realize that the category in question should be dropped as semantic nonsense. This does not mean, of course, that totems, dreams, witches, evil eyes and the like are not real, or that once they are analytically dissolved they disappear from the face of the earth, but that such unsound categorical constructs become a hindrance to objective knowledge. We are thus confronted with the dilemma of whether we shall advance in understanding terrorism by adding new definitions and typologies and by trying to grasp the essence of the phenomenon in its most general context of international and cross-cultural comparison, or whether our theoretical task is to rethink critically the very category of terrorism and possibly dissolve it within a wider politico-military space into the types of behavior and persons that are constitutive of the phenomenon.

As an instance of conceptual reification we could point out just one such typological category, 'ethnic terrorism', since this is the one chosen by the panel of experts to explain Basque violence. The analysis of the present situation starts with these words: 'the basis of the Basque problem is ethnicity which, in the case of the Basque country, means the feeling of shared identity and unity which comes from being Basque' (9.1.1). It appears that misguided sentiment is at the origin of the whole problem. Other factors contribute as well, but ethnicity is singled out as the root of the matter and, in what is the greatest analytical effort of the report, the experts lay out an inventory of 15 cultural traits to identify 'ethnos'. They do not blush to list side by side historical origins, family surnames, marriage, religion and philosophy, dress fashions, cuisine, voluntary associations, psychological attributes, and so on, as constitutive of a single category. An egregious monument to conceptual reification was erected in the near past by explaining cultural events as products of racial characteristics. Such thinking is anathema nowadays, yet it is hard to imagine a closer substitution for it than asserting that 'ethnos' (defined as 'race and nationality') is 'the basis' (root, source, cause) of 'the Basque problem' (or terrorism). Once we are set in search of 'why terrorism', explanations of the type 'ethnos causes terrorism' are almost unavoidable. It requires an effort to take it seriously, but in fact a major advance in our field seems to be that terrorism is motivated by the two alternative sources of either ethnicity or ideology. Thus we are told that in ETA 'ethnocentrism may have taken the place of ideological struggles which have marked the birth and evolution of terrorism in other western countries' (9.1.12). Basques support terrorism, which is of an ethnic nature, because they are ethnocentric, is the kind of explanation that eclipses the explanation that opium puts people to sleep because it has a 'dormitive principle'.

Formerly anthropologists used to associate totemism with the taboo on incest. As the literature on totemism illustrates the making and dissolution of an unhelpful category, the literature on taboo shows that perception of risk calls for cultural analysis. In his *Totem and Taboo* Freud wrote: 'The meaning of "taboo" as we see it, diverges in two contrary directions. To us it means, on the one hand, "sacred", "consecrated", and on the other, "uncanny", "dangerous", "forbidden", 'unclean" ', [*1950: 19*]. The ambivalent quality of persons being simultaneously consecrated and dangerous can be made to describe the characteristically dual nature of the subjects we study, of whom it is often remarked that, depending on the beholder, they are at once 'freedom fighters' and 'terrorists'. It is in the very nature of proscribed persons that they should provoke such contrary reactions.

The connection between terrorism and taboo rests in that both are fundamentally concerned with dangerous behavior. Steiner [*1967*] concluded that two quite separate social functions of taboo are: (1) the classification and identification of transgressions; (2) the institutional localization of danger, both by the separation of the dangerous and by the protection of society from it. In contemporary society, terrorism functions largely as a device for identifying and localizing military danger. If with pollution we enter the realm of fear and terror, we could add that with terrorism we are at the center of political taboo, its true value residing more on ritual and magical system which defines dirt as disorderly and out of place. Terrorism, likewise, appears as an anomaly within a national or international order. Uncleanliness must not be included if a pattern is to be maintained; like dirt, terrorism is a residual category.

The degree to which we are dealing with tabooed people can be gathered from the fact that one can be an 'expert' on terrorism without ever having seen or talked to one terrorist. Those who wrote the report on Basque terrorism admitted that they did not talk to ETA. Such complete lack of contact with the subjects under study is not only usual but even appears inevitable and desirable in the study of terrorism. The source of this anomaly is that we, too, abide by the general view that terrorists are by their very nature 'untouchables', highly dangerous people whose contact should be avoided under any circumstances. Terrorist researchers follow the perception fostered by the media that, whatever else they are,

terrorists are best categorized as 'people wholly unlike us' [*Leach, 1977: 85*].
Having any dealings with them amounts to breaking a taboo.

Not only must one avoid personal contact with terrorists but even seeing
one of them on television is high danger, and so the experts stress at
various points that 'television should not enjoy the same degree of lati-
tude in reporting as is accorded to the press'. For 'people can see as well as
hear the person being interviewed' (8.18). God forbid seeing a terrorist on
television! Beware of hearing a terrorist's voice! It is indeed strange that
the experts are driven into championing specific instructions for tabooing
pivotal members of Basque society, when in fact any Basque is likely to have
known and lionized them, and for hundreds of families the existence of a
member in prison or exile is an intimate and ongoing tragedy. The strategy
consists in first ignoring the fact that for hundreds of youths ETA membership has amounted to a baptism by fire akin to an initiation ritual, and then,
surrounding them with an aura of estrangement and aberration, to literally
taboo them. This is a clear example of the interdependence between
terrorism and terrorism experts: The militant must be first be stigmatized,
the figure of the tabooed terrorist must first be created, so that the anti-
terrorist crusade can make sense.

To illustrate the dynamics by which tabooing people and adopting
crusading attitudes feed into each other, Leach [*1977*] resorts to history and
mentions the case of Pope Gregory IX who harangued Christianity to a
crusade by depicting the Mongols as dog-headed people who ate the bodies
of the dead leaving the bones to the vultures. He also recalls that when
Columbus first encountered the Caribbeans he found them to be human
beings and not monsters, but soon rumors were spread that dog-headed
cannibals (the term 'cannibal' derives from Columbus's name for Carib)
inhabited the as yet unvisited islands, which then provided a moral justification of the extermination of the locals in order to found European plantations
worked by African slaves. Leach goes on to compare the political oppor-
tunism against terrorism with the 'cannibalism by imaginary monsters'
in which 'every imaginable form of terroristic atrocity is not only attributed
to the other side but becomes permissible for oneself. Indeed, counter-
terrorism becomes, in a bizarre sense, a religiously sanctioned duty' [*1977:
36*]. The panel of experts in possession of such a burning anti-terrorist zeal
might have done well to consider for a moment to what extent they were
simply possessed by a religious illusion (it happened after all that the dog-
headed cannibals against which Pope Gregory IX preached his crusade had a
far more sophisticated civilization than anything that existed in Europe at
the time). This 'spirit of religious self-righteousness', that would strike us as
an aberration in other social disciplines, may appear to students of terrorism
not only legitimate but also morally required once we have succeeded in
defining and experiencing it within the taboo framework.

Conclusion

The panel of terrorism experts was commissioned by politicians who later claimed that the report's finding supported their own view concerning Basque violence. For one Basque nationalist leader the report had at least the advantage of showing that ETA was not part of the international network directed by the KGB [cf. *Sterling, 1981*]. Other leaders declared that the report lacked credibility; one called it ironically 'the childbirth of the mountains'; another contended that the Basque government had been ridiculous in sponsoring such an expert report. (The costs of the report amounted to half a million dollars.) The man in the street was simply amused that the much publicized panel of international savants, after nine months of painstaking research and deliberations, had reached the astonishing conclusion that the violence is the result of Basque nationalism; they had never imagined that science and common sense were so well attuned.

While the experts were investigating Basque terrorists, some Basques were investigating who the experts were. The group Gatzaga Taldea (1985) produced its own report trying to show, as announced in front-page news by a pro-ETA newspaper, that 'Four of the five experts [were] under the influence of the CIA'. The unconvincing allegations consisted mostly of connections between the experts and research centers and publications partly funded by the CIA. Still the disquieting result was that for the general public the allegations were sufficient news to reinforce the perception of what Conor Cruise O'Brian had called the 'counter-revolutionary subordination' of scholarship. The information gathered on the ETA by the experts and the counter-information assembled by pro-ETA journals and media was processed in similar fashion: in both cases it was partly secret and inaccessible to the public; it was presumed to be technical; it was gathered indirectly (never were the actors, terrorists, or experts personally interviewed); it relied principally on written sources or programmatic statement; and the intellectual work itself was subservient to extraneous political interests. Thus to the taboo of terrorism was opposed the taboo of the CIA.

The armchair anthropologists of the turn of the century were full of self-serving rationality and moral superiority when they criticized the super-stitions, logical errors and ritual killings of savages. Wittgenstein wrote of such interpretations of savage killings: 'Frazer is much more savage than most of his savages, for these savages will not be so far from any understanding of spiritual matters as an Englishman of the twentieth century. His explanations of the primitive observances are much cruder than the sense of the observances themselves' [*1971: 34*]. We should take those armchair anthropologists as our intellectual ancestors and learn from them how to avoid categorical mistakes when dealing with savage practices.

Needless to say, these errors in the elementary comprehension of cultural and political phenomena have grave consequences when policy is decided with such misunderstanding. I believe our first advice to policy-makers should be this conclusion by Leach: 'The point of my sermon is simply this. However incomprehensible the acts of the terrorists may seem to be, our judges, our policemen, and our politicians must never be allowed to forget that terrorism is an activity by fellow human beings and *not* of dog-headed cannibals' [*1977: 36*; his emphasis]. Another closely related suggestion should be for policymakers to beware of experts who do not want to see the untouchable terrorists even on their television sets; they are part of the problem in the same manner that the inquisitors' perceptions and definitions were as much part of the problem of the inquisition as the victims' beliefs and rites. It has been said of the Church that, by creating and sustaining the witchcraft institution, it was part of it; likewise it can be said of modern states that, by turning terrorist groups into collective representations and perpetuating them by punitive means, they have become their accomplices.

'I simply cannot give you answers. There aren't answers', was Brian Jenkins' reply when in 1974 the House Subcommittee of the Near East and South Asia held hearings on international terrorism. Yet the experts hired to investigate Basque terrorism were far from such honesty. Their assertion that there is a solution to the problem of Basque violence by following their recommendations reminds one of Weber's remark on the eighteenth century's rationalistic optimism, that it 'obstructed the dis-covery of the problematic character' [*1949: 85*] of social reality. The experts' report does an excellent job in obscuring the real problems.

Since the brunt of my essay is on how not to advise policy-makers, I am likely to be asked what positive steps do I propose to end the conflict. I believe that sound scholarship should be my main contribution and this demanded from me a sustained ethnographic research during several years [*Zulaika, 1988*]; by describing and analyzing the cultural context in which Basque violence is situated, I have paid special attention to the ritualized models of performance drawn from the traditional culture for the ongoing violence. I am far from presenting to the Basques overall solutions to the violence, which would only betray on my part ignorance of political realities. Yet at the conclusion of my ethnographic study I did present my results for public discussion to the community of villagers where I did my fieldwork, which is also my native village. The various perspectives on the ongoing violence were confronted and we were forced to interpret within our own community the differing premises underlying irreconcilable political positions. This might appear as a minor solution, but at least one that respects the subjectivity of the actors without the fieldworker falsely presuming to have ready-made solutions to existential dilemmas, and one in which it is the native community as such that is faced with the task of criticizing and recreating new cultural forms. We were challenged to compare opposing models of heroism and to reflect on divergent kinds of politics.

Beyond the ethnographic boundaries of my own community, while teaching at the Basque University I did also attempt to bring together intellectuals of various political persuasions to provoke a national debate on the present stalemate and force the political parties into a negotiation. The initiative almost materialized, but in the end ideological commitments prevailed over intellectual flexibility. Rather than approaching the issues on grounds of technical expertise, my preliminary argument was that Basque intellectuals, artists, and clergy had sufficient moral authority to request from politicians in Madrid and the Basque country a negotiated solution to the deadlock. I also proposed to the 200 ETA prisoners in Herrera de la Mancha that under the guise of an anthropology course we systematically discuss the findings of my research; the prisoners were willing but the director of penal institutions in Madrid did not grant permission.

Before we engage ourselves in tasks commissioned by politicians we should think twice about whether it is intellectually acceptable that our work should be at the service of whatever government's immediate policy interests. The dangers of such subservience are that it risks betraying the standards of scientific objectivity. Our best service to the general public and to policy-makers is not to promote the self-serving cult of the expert but to promote sound scholarship. Weber reminds us that the task of social science is interpretive in nature. Cultural anthropology could not exist without such a premise and its tradition compels us to question the very category of 'terrorism'. Following the steps of thinkers such as Vico, Nietzche, Marx, Freud, Durkheim, and Weber, contemporary thought is engaged in hermeneutical, semiotic, or deconstructivist interpretations of cultural texts. Terrorism is one such prominent text in our times, and to think of it oblivious of anything we have learned from such thinkers is to engage in intellectual obsolescence. The kind of 'expertise' we are criticizing is far from engaging in such interpretive effort but prefers to lend itself to the assertion of the existing power. If we are going to operate in the context of crisis management we can hardly think critically of the adequacy of our basic premises concerning terrorism. In such circumstances the worst that could happen is that policy-makers should pay attention to us.

NOTES

The author is indebted to the Harry Frank Guggenheim Foundation for financial support, and to William Douglass for intellectual stimulation and editorial help. He also benefited from Clark McCauley's suggestions concerning the organization of this contribution. Full citation of the panel report is:

Rose, C., Ferracuti, F., Horchem, H., Janke, P., & Leaute, J. (1986). *Report of the International Commission on Violence in the Basque Country*. Vitoria, Espagna: Eusko Jaurlaritza.

The Process of Delegitimation: Towards a Linkage Theory of Political Terrorism

Ehud Sprinzak

The purpose of this paper is to close the gap between terrorism and other non-terroristic conflicts which exist in the normal world, and to identify the *behavioral links* between various forms of terrorism and less radical disputes. The paper argues that all rebel terrorist organizations have a long pre-terroristic history, and are products of a prolonged process of delegitimation with the powers that be. It shows that this rather lengthy trajectory of radicalization can be divided into smaller development stages, and is open to an unconventional theoretical manipulation. Three consecutive ideological and behavioral stages are identified: *Crisis of Confidence; Conflict of Legitimacy*; and *Crisis of Legitimacy*. The paper also offers a new classification of terrorist organizations, according to the type of the delegitimation processes they undergo: 'Transformational Delegitimation'; 'extensional Delegitimation'; and 'Split Delegitimation', and demonstrates and analytic and empirical usefulness of the new approach.

The purpose of this study is to show that terrorism does not exist in isolation and that as a form of human behavior it is integrally linked to the normal world. Rebel terrorism, this paper argues, is a direct behavioral extension of non-terroristic opposition politics. It is the most dramatic part of a longer political *process of delegitimation* undergone by an opposition movement *vis-à-vis* the regime. Only a small splinter fraction of the opposition movement reaches terrorism, which is the highest peak of the process, and it usually does not stay terroristic too long. The full story of terrorism is therefore not simply the climax of the radicalization process, in which terrorist practice is resorted to by a small group, but the process of delegitimation in its entirety. Not only is the understanding of this process necessary for a better scholarly account of terrorism, but it may help policy-making a great deal. New research in this direction may open new ways of policy intervention against terrorism long before it emerges.

Terrorism and the Process of Delegitimation

Any analytical examination of terrorism must start with the recognition that terrorism appears in a variety of forms. Students of the subject

50

recognize today that the terrorism of nationalist-separatist groups, which fight for self-determination and independence, differs significantly from the terrorism which is conducted against autocratic regimes or against democratic governments. And they know, just as well, that religious terrorism introduces yet another dimension to the comparative map of terrorism from below. Variations of culture, historical experiences, religious traditions, governments opposed and involvement of outside forces – all make for plurality and multiplicity of terrorist action.

Despite the variations, there are shared characteristics which make the vast majority of the terrorist groups open to generalization. The available information on terrorism indicates that most of the known organizations have been splinter groups of larger radical movements. None of the known terrorist groups started its career by the application of terrorism. Most modern terrorists had reached their terrorism *gradually. They had been radicalized into it.* It is extremely difficult to understand the decision of the nineteenth century Narodnaya Volya to go terrorist (1878), without an understanding of the radicalization of the Russian youth and intellectuals in the previous two decades [*Billington, 1958: Chs. 5, 6, 7; Venturi, 1960*]. It is just as impossible to account for the Baader–Meinhoff Gang of the 1970s without a return to the SDS of the early nineteen sixties or, perhaps, to the German pacifists of the 1950s [*Becker, 1977*]. Sometimes, the history of the radicalization is longer and goes back to older roots of anti-regime struggles and rebelliousness as in case of the Irish Republican Army [*Becket, 1971*]. But whatever the radical past is, it is lesser in intensity and brutality than terrorism and moves to terrorism by gradual evolution. Unprovoked people do not become brutal killers in the service of politics until they have experienced weaker methods of opposition and engaged in less intense forms of political action [*Bandura, 1973*].

The common denominator of the vast majority of the terror organizations, regardless of their immense differences, is thus their radical life history, a formative past of intense social and political opposition to some regime. These terror-producing histories, which bring together mutual struggles, shared experiences, extremist ideologies, idiosyncratic symbols and common methods of operation, make terrorism a distinct psycho-political phenomenon. Each terrorist group may have an identity of its own and a special group psychology, but they all have a common *structural genealogy* which sets them apart from groups which do not reach terrorism. What brings together such immensely different terror organizations as the Russian Social Revolutionaries, the Israeli Lehi (Stern Gang), the Armenian ASALA, the American Weatherman, the German RAF, the Palestinian PFLP, the Lebanese Hesballa, the Italian Ordine Nuovo and scores of others, is not only their terrorism but also their developmental skeleton, their patterns of radicalization *vis-à-vis* their respective regimes or enemies. It is this *evolutionary trajectory* of the would-be terrorists, which makes it possible to identify the *linkage* between terrorism and the normal world and to discuss it in terms and concepts broader than the language of terrorism itself.

What then is terrorism? In the final analysis it is a political phenomenon par excellence, a struggle of a very radical group to either assert power or protest against a perceived abuse of power. And it is a struggle that presupposes a total rejection of the regime's legitimacy. *Terrorism implies a crisis of legitimacy.* What terrorists do – and other radicals do not – is to bring their rejection of the regime's legitimacy to the point of challenging it with unconventional violence. However, since terrorism never emerges overnight, this crisis of legitimacy unfolds through a prolonged *process of delegitimation* of the established society and the regime. The beginning of this process, and usually its end, are non-terroristic.

While the process of delegitimation is the universal linkage between terrorism and the normal political process, it appears useful to distinguish among three types of delegitimation.

Transformational Delegitimation – A process of radicalization which involves the rise of a *new* social or political movement (with no past record of activity) that opposes the regime and goes all the way from a peaceful opposition into terrorism. Transformational delegitimation usually takes place inside democratic regimes and starts with a deep disappointment with the functioning of democracy. It involves profound psychopolitical transformation of former democrats into terrorists. It is characterized by the rise of a new terrorist morality which rejects both the political and the socio-cultural norms of the established society.

Extensional Delegitimation – A process of radicalization which starts when an *existing* opposition movement, or an old dormant sentiment of opposition, is radicalized quickly against the ruling authority and reaches terrorism without many psychopolitical inhibitions. Extensional delegitimation usually takes place in the context of a nationalist struggle for independence or separation. It may also appear in the context of a struggle against an autocratic and violent regime. It involves a radicalization of one or more segments of an existing nationalist or left-wing movement. The terrorism which is produced by this abridged process of delegitimation is often one strategy of combat among many non-terroristic ones.

Split Delegitimation – A process of delegitimation in which the radical collectivity is involved in conflict with *two opposing entities*: a community (or class) of people who are considered illegitimate, and a regime, whose legitimacy is primarily not challenged, but which protects the 'illegitimate' community. Split delegitimation usually produces a situation in which the main bulk of terrorism is directed against the delegitimized community, but violent confrontation with the regime also occurs. Split delegitimation is likely to take place in a society plagued by ethnic, national or religious divisions. It often provokes counter-terrorism and a massive emergence of terrorism all over the board.

Transformational Delegitimation

Transformational delegitimation is the most extreme form of the radicalization process that produces terrorism. It involves a full and complete transformation of the lovers of the regime into its staunchest enemies. It epitomizes the entire phenomenon of terrorism from below. Transformational delegitimation usually takes place in the context of democracy. It involves democrats, mostly young and idealistic, who find out about the seamy side of the regime and are shocked by what they see. In time, some of them radicalize and reach terrorism. But terrorism, in this case, does not come easily. It is often a result of a profound and painful psychopolitical process in which all the former political, cultural and moral codes of the individuals involved are inverted. The reason this particular process is so exhaustive and tortuous is that the individuals concerned are, among the known terrorists, the least prepared for the experience. Initially, they are idealistic democrats who grow and function within a democratic framework and state of mind. A move to terrorism from such a background requires a complete separation from reality, a fantasizing of another reality that does not exist, and against which it is legitimate to apply terrorism. We know today that normal young people can undergo this transformation but there is no doubt that it taxes the psychology and mind very heavily. Terrorism, in this case of delegitimation, is not reached before each of the psycho-political stages of the process (see below) is fully consummated.

A careful dissection of the process of transformational delegitimation reveals three distinct evolutionary stages: *crisis of confidence, conflict of legitimacy, and crisis of legitimacy* [*Sprinzak 1987b*]. Each of these stages pertains to an ideological movement composed of activists and followers who interact with the regime as well as among themselves and who obtain in the process a collective psycho-political identity. The group identity, which changes rapidly as radicalization proceeds, contains a combination of political behavioral components, ideological and symbolic tenets, and psychological traits. As radicalization deepens, the collective group identity takes over much of the individual identity of the members and at the terrorist stage it reaches its peak. The individual terrorists may not lose their former identity but their actual behavior may best be understood in terms of 'groupthink' and the group personality [*Crenshaw, 1986: 395–400; Kaplan, 1978: 248; Post, 1986: 16*].

Crisis of Confidence

This is the psycho-political stage reached by a movement or a challenge group whose confidence in the existing political government is greatly eroded. Crisis of confidence implies a conflict with specific rulers or policies. It does not presume a structural delegitimation because the foundations of the established political system are not questioned or challenged. In many instances, crisis of confidence involves an angry critique of the established authorities or rulers from the very ideological assumptions upon which the regime itself is founded. The black students who later established the SNCC (Student Non-Violent Coordination Committee) came to their first demonstrations and sit-ins, in 1960, well dressed and shaven. In one hand they carried the Bible and in the other, a copy of the American Constitution [*Newfield, 1970: 30–3*]. The Port Huron Statement of the SDS (1962) did not call for a revolution in America. It recommended instead a democratic system of 'Two genuine parties, centered around issues and essential values ... with sufficient party disagreement to dramatize major issues, yet sufficient party overlap to guarantee a stable transition from administration to administration' (The Port Huron Statement [*1964: 46–7*]).

The existing rulers against whom the protest movement is first established are seen as wrong not because of fundamental faults in the system itself but as a result of their rulers' own misleading behavior or misguided policies. A crisis of confidence, therefore, does not indicate an all-out ideological break with the powers that be. It represents a profound disenchantment with what is usually projected as 'the establishment' in that it goes far beyond ordinary political opposition.

From an empirical-operational perspective, the crisis of confidence is marked by the rise of a distinct ideological challenge group, or movement, or counterculture which refuses to play according to the established rules of the game. The group articulates its critique of the establishment in loaded ideological terms, descends from mainstream politics and opts for protests, demonstrations, symbolic resistance and other forms of direct action. While not illegal, its behavior, group mentality and language are likely to be countercultural. Early confrontations with the authorities and the police, including small scale and unplanned events of violence, are highly likely. The American SDS and the SNCC, so too the German SDS, Commune 1 and Commune 2 [*Becker, 1977*], the French 'groupuscules' [*Schnapp and Vidall–Naquet, 1969: 314–15*], the Japanese Zengakuren [*Krauss, 1974: 4–5*], and many similar new left groups that emerged in the democratic world between 1962 and 1966 were not extra-legal collectivities. But they introduced a new ideological and symbolic style of radical opposition into their respective countries.

Conflict of Legitimacy

This is the radicalized continuation of the crisis of confidence. It is the behavioral stage that evolves when a challenge group, previously engaged in anti-governmental critique, is ready to question the very legitimacy of the whole system. Conflict of legitimacy emerges when the challenge group discovers that the erroneous rulers are able to 'mislead the people' not because they shrewdly manipulate the otherwise benign system but because the system itself is manipulative and repressive. The way to do away with the oppressive rulers is to transform the system altogether. Conflict of legitimacy implies the emergence of an *alternative ideological and cultural system*, one that delegitimizes the prevailing regime and its code of social norms in the name of some better ones.

Empirically, the conflict of legitimacy is usually started off by a great disappointment of the challenge group with its previous stage of radicalization. The former 'moderate' radicals are enraged and frustrated either by the government's hostile (sometimes excessively violent) response to their passionate critique or by their own failure to score successes. They now develop the need to channel their outrage into a more extreme form of protest. A proper course to follow seems to be the development of an *ideology of delegitimation* which communicates a complete break with the prevailing political order. The new frame of reference or symbolic system advanced is, in most cases, an existing and unoriginal ideology. Very few radicals are capable, during their intense process of delegitimation, to initiate a new system of critical thought that fits the new situation analytically and empirically. It is a great deal easier *to consume* existing prestigious ideology of delegitimation (like Marxism, Maoism or Third World Trotskyism) and to believe that it is relevant. Most of the student new left groups in the West, which were later to produce small terrorist undergrounds, had undergone their conflict of legitimacy between 1966 and 1968. Young people, who grew up with the conviction that Karl Marx was the founding father of all modern evil, now became Marxists. They would come out of the university co-ops with bags full of Marxist books and incessantly debate whether the young Marx meant violent revolution or whether Herbert Marcuse, their new guru, was loyal to the legacy of Vladimir Lenin and Rosa Luxemburg. Caught between trendy schools like Trotskyism, Maoism or Castroism, they would sometimes not hesitate to invent their own 'campus made' Marxism [*Sprinzak, 1977*].

A very popular version of Marxism among the American student movement was the 'new working class' theory. At the core of the new approach was the idea that modern society had created a new proletariat composed of middle class and professional workers. This 'new working class' was presented as a class not because of its relation to the means of production (as classical Marxism requires) but because of conditions of 'unfreedom' in society, conditions affecting 'deprived minorities, high salaried middle class professionals, and students living in factory-like multiversities' [*Teodori, 1969: 515*]. The theory had, of course, no relation to classical Marxism or to the reality of America of the second half of the twentieth century, but it was essential to the psyche of the student-revolutionaries. It was a most helpful instrument for expressing one's total delegitimation of the 'American corporate capitalism' and of making sure, at the same time, that in spite of one's personal affluence, one was still a legitimate partner of the exploited.

The evolution of the conflict of legitimacy is not marked by ideological, symbolic and psychological changes only. It is equally manifested by intense political action that ranges between angry protest (demonstrations, confrontations, and vandalism) and the application of small scale intentional violence against the regime. The challenge group or movement, which is the concrete collective carrier of the conflict of legitimacy, lives now in a stage of intense radicalization. It solidifies itself and closes ranks. The individuals involved are totally consumed by the movement and emotionally change a great deal. Their language and rhetoric – which are the expression of their inner collective identity – are revolutionary and their jargon is full of slanders and desecrations directed at a totally discredited social order.

Crisis of Legitimacy

This is the behavioral and symbolic culmination of the two preceding psycho-political stages. Its essence lies in the extension of the previous delegitimation of the system to *every individual* person associated with it. Individuals who are identified with the 'rotten' and 'soon to be destroyed' social and political order are depersonalized and dehumanized. They are derogated into the ranks of the worst enemies or subhuman species. Dehumanization makes it possible for the radicals to disengage morally and to commit atrocities without a second thought [*Bandura (in press): 17–18*]. It bifurcates the world into the sons of light and the sons of darkness and makes fully legitimate the 'fantasy war' of the former vs. the latter [*Ferracuti, 1982: 136–7*]. It makes the few radicals who have made it to the third stage of the process of delegitimation, usually a second generation of radicals, accomplished revolutionaries. They convince themselves that they are soldiers in a just war and that their terrorism is bound to create revolutionary conditions in which thousands of people would later join.

La Gauche Proletarienne, the first radical organization to go underground in the aftermath of the 1968 student 'revolution' in Paris, portrayed itself as La Nouvelle Resistance (the New Resistance). It proclaimed that France was in a situation similar to the one in which she found herself in 1943, a situation of illegitimate occupation. Instead of the Germans and their collaborators of the Vichy regime, the occupying forces were now the French patrons (the owners of the shops and the factories – the true rulers of France) and the functionaries and activists of the French communist party, who deserted the revolutionary battle-field in order to live well with the bourgeoisie. As in the case of the Nazi occupation it was now necessary to take arms against the brutal conquerors and the battle had to take place in the street [Sprinzak, 1976: 294].

The first external indication of the evolution of the crisis of legitimacy is linguistic and symbolic. Expressions of political delegitimation are no longer limited to political terms or social concepts but are extended to a language of objects, animals or 'human' animals. The regime and its accomplices are now portrayed as 'things' or 'dogs' or 'pigs' or 'Nazis' or 'terrorists'. The portrayal is not accidental and scant but repeated and systematic. It is now part of a new lexicon. The 'pigs' or the 'Nazis' or the 'terrorist lackeys' can be killed or eliminated because by definition they no longer belong to the human species or to the legitimate community of the 'people'. Each individual who is or belongs to the powers that be is a potential target for assassination or indiscriminate murder. 'We say' wrote Ulrike Meinhoff, 'the person in uniform is a pig, that he is not a human being and thus we have to settle the matter with him. It is wrong to talk to these people at all, and shooting is taken for granted' [Demaris, 1977: 228].

The crisis of legitimacy – which brings together all the earlier clusters of the process of radicalization – presupposes an acute stage of psychological transformation. The group that undergoes this profound mental change often displays antinomian behavior [Rapoport, 1985: 12–13]. Its members free themselves from the yoke of conventional morality and demonstrably engage in sexual perversity and promiscuity, drug orgies and criminality of many forms. The boundaries between political and personal illegality are totally removed and certain forms of deviant behavior are hailed as right, even sacred. New revolutionary morality emerges, an antinomian weltanschauung is crowned. Young couples, members of the Weatherman, the American terrorist organization that emerged in 1969 out of the SDS, were required to 'smash monogamy'. The 'Weather Bureau' ordered that all women revolutionaries sleep with all men revolutionaries and vice versa. Women were also to make love to each other. 'Weather' mothers, suspected of devoting too much time to their babies (born in the course of the 'revolution'), were ordered to give the babies to other, less committed, members of the organization so they could devote all their energies to the cause [*Sprinzak, 1987b: 7–8*]. 'Dig it', said Bernardin Dohrn, the Weatherman leading lady, after hearing about the brutal murder of the pregnant movie actress Sharon Tate by Charles Manson and his 'family', 'first they killed those pigs, then they ate dinner in the same room with them, then they even shoved a fork in the victim's stomach! Wild! [*Jacobs, 1970: 347*].

The operational manifestation of the crisis of legitimacy is systematic terrorism. It amounts to the formation of a small terror underground, which is engaged in unconventional attacks on the regime and its affiliates, and is capable of committing a wide range of atrocities. As a social unit, the terrorist underground is totally isolated from the outside world. It constructs a reality of its own and a whole new set of behavioral and moral standards that are very authoritatively enforced. The members of the group are so involved and entangled with each other, that every individual act has a collective meaning of utmost importance. The psychodynamics of the whole unit, including its acts of terrorism against the outside society, assume a logic of their own and may often be unrelated to any external factors [*Knutson, 1980: 211–15; Post, 1984: 250–58; Wright, 1982: 12–13*]. Very few of the terrorist-leaders who reach the crisis of legitimacy and are fully consumed by it are capable of reversing their radicalization to the point of going back to normal life. Their immense personal metamorphosis which, in many cases, leads them to nihilism, despair and extreme fear of the group's sanction, often drives them to unconscious self destruction and suicide.

The process of transformational delegitimation is the purest and most exhaustive form of rebel terrorism because it evolves under the most unlikely conditions and against all odds. It is easier, morally and emotionally, to become a terrorist in the context of a repressive and violent regime. A great deal more of a crisis of confidence, conflict of legitimacy and crisis of legitimacy is required from an American student under Lyndon Johnson than from a Chilean student under Pinochet. Had Max Weber studied modern terrorism, he would have probably referred to transformational delegitimation as the *ideal type* of the entire phenomenon of terrorism. He would have rightly noticed that this case provides the most accentuated and pristine gist of the large variety because *it conveys the essence of terrorism, the complete transformation of sane human beings into brutal and indiscriminate killers*. The study of terrorism, we should recollect, is not the study of a unique plague with no beginning or end. It is *a study of human transformation*, of a psycho-political passage in time from normal to extranormal behavior. Nowhere is this transition demonstrated so clearly as in the case of transformational delegitimation.

Extensional Delegitimation

Most terror organizations do not go through the complete trajectory of transformational delegitimation. Their members do not rebel against a regime they once identified with and do not have to undergo a profound psychopolitical transformation in order to become brutal killers. Their terrorism is an *extension* of a deeply rooted sense of bitterness and historical opposition, a terrorism launched in the name of national liberation or a simple quest for freedom. The terrorism of movements for national or civic liberation has, in modern history, included anti-colonial campaigns, struggles against traditional foreign rulers, fights for separation or autonomy on the basis of ethnic or national authoritarian governments. Comparative observation of many of these movements suggests that, like transformational terrorist organizations, only a small number of their members reach terrorism. What distinguishes trans-formational and extensional terrorism is that the latter's *actual* road to terrorism only goes through conflict of legitimacy and crisis of legitimacy and that a lot more politics, and less of psychology, is involved.

National and Ethnic Terrorism

Most nations or ethnic minorities, living under what they consider 'foreign domination' can be said to constantly experience a *latent crisis of confidence*. Long before the feeling of an unjust repression or discrimination becomes political, it is cultural. This dormant sentiment is highly detect-able in the nation's folklore, historical legends, literature and daily con-versation. However, as long as this sense remains cultural and intellectual and is not institutionalized politically, it does not have an operational significance. Crisis of confidence, in the sense discussed earlier, comes into being when a modern movement for national liberation is established and is making concrete political demands for greater independence. Irish quest for some self-determination, let us recall, existed long before the modern drive for Home Rule [*Strauss, 1951: Ch. 8*] and rudimentary Indian nationalism preceded the Indian National Congress by many years [*Bhagwan, 1954: Ch. 8*]. Most nationalist movements, moreover, do not start with radical and totalistic demands. Rather, they ask for greater cultural freedom, larger political representation and a broader partici-pation in determining their collective future. While these demands are meant to reduce the government's authority a great deal, they are unlikely to create a major confrontation. The main agenda of the nascent nationalist movement implies peaceful negotiations and accommodation. It exists long before the beginning of the actual terror-producing radicalization.

Conflict of legitimacy in the struggle for national liberation is usually reached when either the main thrust of the nationalist movement or a seceding fraction of it becomes impatient with the ruler's slow response to the previous demands. The movement, or its seceding component, is radicalized a great deal and the issue at stake becomes 'liberation now'. The demand for either a comprehensive liberation or a total independence not only implies a vision of an alternative political regime but also an immediate and unconditional rejection of the prevailing authority. The heretofore legitimate sovereign becomes an illegitimate 'foreign occupant'. It consequently has to be replaced, immediately, by the independent legitimate government of the nation. The conflict of legitimacy is usually expressed by such symbols as 'occupation', 'resistance' and 'revolution'. It is manifested politically by a significant mass mobilization of the indigenous population and by the combination of tough political negotiations on the elite level and mass demonstrations in the streets. It may often involve moderate amounts of violence – a product of an unintended collision with the regime – but sometimes the violence escalates into massive physical resistance and insurrection. David Ben Gurion (Israel), Mahatma Gandhi (India) and Ferhat Abbas (Algeria) to name a few leaders of moderate modern national liberation movements, did not recommend violence and terrorism. But their activities and struggles for independence produced a great deal of unintended violence which became instrumental in the emergence of terrorist organizations that did not uphold their moderation.

Crisis of legitimacy and terrorism emerge in those cases in which the conflict of legitimacy does not lead to full independence or to an agreed upon autonomy. Modern history teaches us that nationalist struggles that reached terrorism had often involved one or more of the following conditions:

(1) A denial of the claims of the nationalist movement for self determination and its suppression by the authorities.
(2) The presence of two indigenous ethnic communities which struggle for independence from the foreign ruler but sharply disagree about the post-independence structure of authority.
(3) The emergence of a significant ideological fragmentation within the movement for national liberation.

The first condition reminds us that terrorism is a strategy of last resort.

Great amounts of disappointment and frustration are required in order to make a terrorist. The struggle for national liberation usually involves sincere and idealistic individuals who are aware of the moral and political implications of terrorism. Most leaders of nationalist movements would prefer politics to violence and street demonstrations to guerrilla war and terrorism. Their turn to underground activities and terrorism does not take place unless triggered by repeated rejection of peaceful demands and repression of riots and demonstrations. Impatient, despairing and frustrated, they convince themselves that the foreign rule is helplessly brutal, made up of 'animals', and that in the struggle against such an enemy every act is permissible. The moral argument employed by the terrorists, in order to justify their atrocities, is that they were desecrated and brutalized first. Survival dictates reciprocation. Dehumanization breeds dehumanization.

The second condition for the emergence of large-scale terrorism indicates that many nationalist rebels wage a terror campaign against the foreign ruler only after they are socialized into the 'politics of atrocities' by a local communal struggle. This is what happened between the Jews and the Arabs in Palestine, between the Turks and the Greeks in Cyprus and to some extent between the Muslims and the French Colons in Algeria. The issue at stake is either a long memory of historical intercommunal atrocities or a controversy about the post-independence form of the state, its borders and structure of authority. Each of the communities involved has its own version of independence in mind, which appears highly threatening to the other side. Intercommunal terrorism is highly probable in such situations because intense ethnic conflicts almost always lead to atrocities. Low level brawls, fist fights and street clashes evolve to pogroms and counter-pogroms. Special underground militias or 'gangs' or 'phalanges' are then organized. Their manifest purpose is one of self defense, but self defense is a very expandable category. And since most of the operations are illicit in the first place (considered illegal by the foreign ruler) conventional warfare and full military code can rarely be applied.

Compared to opening a terror campaign against a foreign ruler, it is far easier to extend a campaign of intercommunal terrorism into a struggle against the ruler. *Rebels who are accustomed to terrorism do easily switch targets.* Once they convince themselves that the 'occupant' 'collaborates' with the other side – which is usually the case with a regime that is trying to maintain law and order – they are highly likely to strike at the top. The Irgun, in Palestine, developed in 1938 a clandestine terror campaign against the British because they were perceived as pro-Arab for having moved to prosecute Jewish 'freedom fighters' [*Niv, 1975: 251–76*]. General Grivas was authorized, in 1954, by the Greek clergy to wage an anti-British guerrilla-terror campaign because the British 'favored' the Turks and opposed Enosis – the unification of Cyprus with Greece [*Crenshaw, 1978: Part 4*]. And the French authorities became a prime target of the FLN in Algeria after it was found out that all of France was united behind the French Colons in their aspiration to keep Algeria French [*Horne, 1977: Ch. 3*]. The alleged or real association of the authority with the other side always facilitates the application of terrorism.

The third condition for the rise of nationalist or separatist terrorism is the development of ideological fragmentation within the main movement for national liberation. It is true that the ideological bone of contention is usually the very question of the application of revolutionary violence, but in many cases the issue is broader. Nationalist rebels had been divided in the past over such questions as the form of the future regime (Marxist–Leninist vs. Liberal–Democratic), the shape of the future borders and the relationship with the other ethnic community (expulsion vs. co-operation). When ambitious personalities are involved, as well as conflicting economic interests and foreign interlopers, conflict tends to get out of control. The intensity of the external struggle against the foreign ruler heightens the tensions within and the former separatist consensus is eroded. Hostile groups are purged, or executed, and internal terrorism pops up. There are occasions in which the most extreme faction takes over and, as in the case of the FLN in Algeria, monopolizes the use of terrorism against its external and internal enemies [*Hutchinson, 1978*]. But in most other circumstances it is the minority which goes for less-selective violence (the Stern Gang, the IRA Provisionals, Abu Nidal). In order to prove its greater dedication to the cause it will outbrutalize the rest of the movement.

Anti-Authoritarian Terrorism

The terrorism of anti-authoritarian movements which struggle against oppressive, albeit native, regimes is also extensional delegitimation and structurally similar to nationalist terrorism. It usually comes after a long time of perceived repression and does not require a new crisis of confidence and deep psychological transformation. Conflict of legitimacy and an advanced radicalization are likely to be triggered by the application of ruthless methods against the critics of the regime. Most movements of this category have, in the second half of the century, emerged in Latin America and have adopted some kind of Marxist ideology. They have consequently appeared dangerous to the respective authoritarian leaders long before the actual beginning of the revolution. The repression that followed the perception was a self-fulfilling prophesy. It triggered crises of legitimacy and terrorism all over the sub-continent. None of the modern terrorist groups in Latin America, however, was devoid of a passion for national liberation. This unique nationalism has been expressed through a profound resentment of American imperialism. Its proponents argued that without the American economic intervention and the backing of the CIA, no local tyrant could have survived the hatred of the people. For the vast majority of the Latin American revolutionaries, 'Revolution' has come to imply not just an overthrow of the old regime but also a total elimination of the American presence in their countries.

The main difference between nationalist terrorism and its anti-authoritarian variant is that the latter rarely gets the support of the masses. It is, of necessity, less sophisticated and strategic. While a broadly based nationalist movement can apply terrorism along with other strategies of combat, because it has the support of the masses, the terrorism of a small anti-authoritarian group is usually its only remaining method of struggle. A score of Latin American guerrilla and terrorism theorists, from Che Guevara to Carlos Marighella and Abraham Guillen, have failed to identify the formula that could turn small groups of anti-imperialist revolutionaries into big and effective fighting movements [*Laqueur, 1987: 245–54*]. The exceptional cases of Cuba and Nicaragua do not reveal such a rule.

The process of extensional delegitimation, unlike the process of transformational delegitimation, develops under *favorable* conditions. It is the nature of mankind to wish to be free and to aspire for national self determination. And it is, just as well, the nature of ruling powers to cling to their 'property' and to be most unwilling to give it up. The conflict involved, unlike many conflicts that evolve within democracy, is real and substantial. The likelihood that the authority will resort to harsh repression and apply excessive violence, including state terrorism or violence that looks like state terrorism, is high. Radicalization under those circumstances is not unnatural and the chances that some radicals will opt for terrorism without many inhibitions are good. This is the reason that nationalist and anti-authoritarian terrorism do not involve transformational delegitimation: *the potential rebel does not have to exhaust all methods of conflict and go through great personal metamorphosis in order to become a terrorist.* No extraordinary effort is required to become radical in the first place and to switch from a latent crisis of confidence, which is built into most situations of unfreedom, to a manifest crisis of legitimacy and terrorism.

Split Delegitimation

Rebel terrorism usually associates anti-regimist terror with claims for universalistic norms. The atrocities involved are committed against an oppressive government that is charged with a flagrant violation of the fundamental human rights of either its citizens or subject nations. One common form of rebel terrorism, however, is neither directed primarily against governments nor committed in the name of universal values. The terror organizations involved, usually right-wing collectivities, vigilante groups, ethnic or religious splinter sects, do not speak in the name of humanity. They are particularistic by their very nature and respond to the perceptions of insecurity and threats. They fight private wars against hostile ethnic communities, illegitimate religious denominations, classes of undesired people or 'inferior races'. The enemies they feel threaten them are, variably, the Jews, the Arabs, the Catholics, the Blacks, the Communists and other classes of people 'who want to get more than they deserve'.

The most significant political difference between the 'universalistic' terror organizations and the 'particularistic' ones is their relation to the prevailing authority. While left-wing and nationalist collectivities are involved in a direct conflict with the ruling government and their terror campaign is directed against its agents, the conflict of many right-wing, religious or vigilant groups with the regime is secondary. The government is rarely considered an opponent and in many cases is expected to cooperate or remain uninvolved. Conflict with the authorities and an occasional anti-regimist violence emerge only after the terrorists do not obtain official help or favorable silence. The reason the Nazi SA and SS are hardly mentioned in the terrorism literature is not because they did not practice violence and terrorism, but because they rarely applied it against the regime. Hitler was extremely hostile to the Weimar Republic but for tactical and strategic reasons he reserved the atrocities of his thugs for his direct rivals, the socialists, the communists and some Jews [*Laqueur, 1987: 66–7*]. The Ku Klux Klan, in America, is in principle extremely hostile to the 'big government' in Washington and to the 'Eastern Establishment' it thinks it represents. But its violence and terrorism are reserved for the blacks or for their supporters within the community [*Trelease, 1971: 419–22; Lipset, 1970: 123–31*].

The fact that particularistic terror organizations usually avoid confrontation with the authorities and direct their operations at non-ruling groups suggests a different pattern of delegitimation from the two portrayed before. It indicates the possibility of *two cotemporaneous processes of delegitimation*: an intense delegitimation *vis-à-vis* the hated non-governmental collectivity and a diluted delegitimation towards the regime. Thus, while the crisis of confidence, conflict of legitimacy and crisis of legitimacy are all present, or historically implied, their sequential order and direction are not the same. The issue at stake is one of split delegitimation, i.e., *a case where an uneven radicalization of a group of extremists develops against two separate entities.*

The typical feature of the radicalization process of a particularistic terror organization *vis-à-vis* the collectivity it primarily despises is that *it does not begin with a crisis of confidence but rather with a conflict of legitimacy*. The majority of these organizations start their historical career with a conviction that the object of their intense opposition is illegitimate. It does not belong to the same humanity they see themselves part of, and should either be kept in an inferior legal status or expelled. Such a belief, which is usually a product of a long held tradition or cultural heritage, does not imply an immediate violent action. As long as the particularistic movement does not monopolize the political power in the community or senses no immediate existential threat by the 'outsiders', it will not resort to violence. Instead it will wait for its future political success and do its best in the meantime, to strengthen and perpetuate the existing social and cultural mechanisms of discrimination. Violence and, eventually, terrorism, only emerge when the group involved feels insecure or perceives an immediate threat. The Jews may suddenly appear too rich, the Blacks too influential, the Arabs too treacherous and the Communists too close to a Marxist revolution. Something has to be done in order to have them restricted. The effort is likely to start by campaigns of intimidation and (under specific conditions) escalate to terrorism. A historical and comparative examination of occasional terrorist eruptions of the Arabs in Mandatory Palestine [*Arnon-Ohanna, 1981: Part 4*], the Ku Klux Klan in America [*Lipset, 1970: 276–82*], the Fascists and Neo-Fascists in Italy, France and Germany [*Wilkinson, 1981*] and the followers of Rabbi Kahane in Israel [*Sprinzak, 1985*], as well as many of the others, show the same pattern of radicalization: a constant but non-violent sense of delegitimation, a growing anxiety, prolonged campaigns of low level vigilante violence, and finally outbursts of terrorism.

While the main violence of the particularistic terrorists is expected to involve non-ruling populations, some of the heat is likely to reach the political authorities. When vigilante movements, ethnic and religious organizations, or neo-Fascists feel threatened by other groups, they usually convince themselves that the government in charge is not doing enough to protect the 'legitimate' community. The rulers, or the most unfriendly elements among them, are then portrayed as 'soft' or 'internationalist' or 'leftist'. Such projection implies a sense of betrayal and *a crisis of confidence with the regime*. The government may not be declared illegitimate, and become of necessity an object of intended violence, yet the group's respect for its authority is likely to decline dramatically and with it the remainder of its obedience to the law. This is, for example, what happened several times to small groups within Gush Emunim (the Bloc of the Faithful), the Israeli radical movement of the settlers of the West Bank. Gush Emunim, a religious and messianic movement, has never maintained a theological opposition to the lay government of Israel [*Sprinzak, 1987a*]. The majority of its rabbis have, in fact, assigned Israel a sacred status, recognizing the secular regime as the holy 'Kingdom of Israel' in the making. Emunim's growing animosity has been reserved, in the last decade, for the Arabs of the West Bank, 95 per cent of whom have constantly expressed support for the PLO. But the theological sacredness of the state of Israel did not prevent serious clashes between Gush activists and the military whenever the government was seen as too 'soft' on the Arabs. A violent confrontation between Gush activists and the military was barely prevented in 1982 when Yamit, the capital of the northern Sinai, was handed back to the Egyptians [*Aran, 1985*]. And when 1150 Arab prisoners, many of whom were known terrorists, were in 1985 exchanged for three Israeli soldiers, Gush Emunim settlers roamed the roads of the West Bank protesting against the Arabs but clashing with the army and the police.

Most particularistic terrorists – religious, Fascist, vigilante, and other right-wing extremists – do not feel bad about their violence and atrocities. They do not have to undergo a profound psychopolitical transformation in order to become terrorists. Their desired world is not a reality of some non-violent universal humanity that is transformed temporarily – and for just reasons – into a bloody existence. Rather, it is a reality, and an implied *Weltanschauung*, which is predicated on conflict, permanent discrimination against certain classes of people and their dehumanization. From this perspective, some people just do not belong to the relevant community. They are outsiders and should be treated properly. Terrorism against these 'aliens' or 'subhumans' is just another means of making sure they do not multiply and prevail. This attitude is perhaps the reason why most particularistic terrorists never try to apologize for their brutal acts and why so very few explanatory ideologies of terrorism exist in this cultural milieu [*Laqueur, 1987: 67*]. Acts that are reasonable and natural do not require explanation.

The terrorism that is produced by a process of split delegitimation is usually not the product of a full-time revolutionary underground. Rather, it is a set of occasional operations of extremists who otherwise live normal lives, work, and sustain families. Since most of them do not challenge the structure of authority, their terrorism is just one additional method of coping with the anxieties they face. And it is usually done through small, part time, secret organizations. Terrorist acts are likely to emerge in this case out of two sets of circumstances: a sudden and intense sense of insecurity which produces an emotional action, or a conviction of rational decision makers regarding the existence of the right political opportunity to strike.

Small, isolated, and poorly organized religious or ethnic groups are likely to respond to perceived threats without much thought. A sudden economic anxiety, a decline in the group's sense of control and a profound disappointment with the authority may produce clandestine vigilante atrocities, an attempt of the secret organization to restore the *status quo ante* by a series of terror acts. The Ku Klux Klan, the Aryan Nation, small European extreme right groups and some Israeli members of Kach (thus!), Rabbi Kahane's movement, usually act that way. Their terrorism is an unplanned mechanism of expressing anxiety and letting the steam out until the next eruption [*Merkl, 1986: 248–51; Sprinzak, 1985: 11–14; Wilkinson, 1981: Ch. 6*].

The more sophisticated and better organized secret organizations do not act this way. Their leaders do not let emotions prevail. Aware of their weakness and of the effectiveness of the law enforcement agencies, they strike only when convenient – when either the government is in disarray, or a left-wing terrorism is around to take the heat. This is an old Fascist strategy which appears to be followed nowadays by the Italian neo-Fascists [*Drake, 1986: 77–80; Furlong, 1983: 68–76*]. Prudent leaders of vigilante groups may also use terrorism to attract the attention of the media and get issues they deem important on to the national agenda.

Conclusion: Policy and Research Implications

Rebel terrorism, it is possible to conclude, does not emerge in a vacuum or out of an inexplicable impetus of a few crazies. Rather, it is an extension of the political world we all live in, a special case of opposition politics. It is, furthermore, a political product of a prolonged process of delegitimation undergone by a large number of people *vis-à-vis* the established order or some non-ruling parts of it. However, while many other forms of political action appear routine and perennial, terrorism is not. There is no indication that the few who survive the ordeal of the process of radicalization in its entirety are predestined to do so. It is quite possible that just as most processes of delegitimation are not consummated in terrorism, the day will come when almost all of them are not. The fact that processes of delegitimation that take place under tyrannical situations are unlikely to terminate (because terrorism from above will usually trigger terrorism from below) does not mean that in other, less severe situations, terrorism is inevitable.

The main policy implication of this conclusion is that effective anti-terrorist policy may be initiated long before the actual appearance of terrorism. If terrorism is the highest stage of a long process of delegitimation, then the prudent policy-maker does not have to wait until all the conditions for the emergence of terrorism are present. We may act much earlier to either stop the radicalization that produces terrorism or be

prepared for its upsurge. The indeterminism of the process of delegitimation makes rebel terrorism extremely vulnerable to prudent intervention.
It implies the existence of weak spots in the pre-terroristic stages at which
wise governmental action can either prevent the evolution of terrorism or
reduce its effectiveness a great deal. It is quite conceivable that research in
this direction could yield 'radicalization indicators' and be developed into
a sophisticated 'anti-terrorist early warning system'.

Finally, it should be stressed, the argument presented in this study is not
an end but a beginning. My several illustrated hypotheses, which are
based on many years of observation of terror-producing radicalization
processes, call for a new and different terrorism research. The problem of
most of the present research on terrorism is not that it is policy oriented but
that its policy orientation is extremely narrow. Instead of trying to explain
terrorism it tries to explain the terrorists. Comprehensive understanding
of large social processes that produce terrorism is subordinated to the
demands of policy-makers for quick solutions. What my hypotheses call
for is a research that has never been conducted before, a comparative
study of the historical evolution and decline of hundreds of terrorist
organizations of both the past and the present. Such a study is bound to
yield important results in the direction portrayed in this essay. It may not
be a small job or a brief job, but it might, in my judgement, produce the
breakthrough that has not been achieved in the last 20 years by thousands
of projects and many millions of dollars.

How Terrorism Declines

Martha Crenshaw

The decline of oppositional terrorism is a critical question for both scholars and policy-makers. The former have neglected the issue, while the latter have tended to assume that government policies of prevention and deterrence are the key determinants of outcomes. This analysis suggests that government actions must be seen in the context of the internal organizational dynamics and strategy of the opposition groups using terrorism. In some cases, terrorism is self-defeating.

How campaigns of terrorism come to an end is a critical question for public policy, but the problem has not attracted the attention of many scholars.[1] Schmid's [1983] review of the general literature contains no reference to explanations of the decline of terrorism. Theories of conflict usually focus on causes rather than outcomes [Gurr, 1980], and research on terrorism follows this tradition. Furthermore, the persistent and often distracting obsession with definition is a reflection of genuine intellectual difficulties in specifying what is and what is not terrorism. The neglect of outcomes also stems from a set of normative biases that influence writing on contemporary terrorism. Adherents of the view that terrorism is an expression of the nefarious designs of the Soviet Union and its cohorts in a world communist conspiracy (for example, *Cline and Alexander, 1984*] confront equally committed advocates of the opposite persuasion, who blame the United States and its imperialistic ambitions for rising levels of global violence (for example, *Chomsky, 1986*]. Fortunately a growing number of scholars remain aloof from these ideological preoccupations, but academic knowledge has not yet reached the level of general explanatory theories. The few relatively comprehensive studies of terrorism contain implicit suggestions about the government role in the decline of terrorism, but these inferences are abstract and inconsistent.

In this contribution I argue that academic research on terrorism can contribute to the development of sound public policy. Analysis of the relationship between specific government actions and the decline of campaigns of terrorism is a case in point. In order to move toward understanding how terrorism declines, I assess the implications of the mainstream literature on terrorism. Finding them unsatisfactory, I survey the available data on the life cycles of post-war oppositions that have been significant practitioners of terrorism. I then suggest that the decline of terrorism occurs because of three factors: physical defeat of the extremist organization by the government, the group's decision to abandon the terrorist strategy, and organizational disintegration.

Public Policy Needs and Terrorism Research

Policy-makers need to understand the comparative historical evolution of terrorism in its diverse forms as well as the importance of theoretical explanations to formulating sound policy prescriptions. Yet the mid-level government officials who come into direct contact with the products of academic research are often hostile to history and to theory, particularly the latter, which the more outspoken and impatient among them regard as irrelevant 'philosophizing' and 'psychologizing' when they want clear-cut operational recommendations. Such disdain reflects stubborn pre-dispositions on both sides of the gulf between academics and policy makers. The fault does not lie simply with the myopia and action-orientation of the official. Historian John Lewis Gaddis [1987] observes that academics often cannot explain the relevance of what they do. Academics cannot communicate effectively even among themselves because different disciplines speak 'virtually incomprehensible dialects' [1987: 4]. The attempt by political scientists to be scientific promises more than it can deliver, frequently turns to arcane methodological debates, employs excessive jargon, and constructs elaborate data bases that are merely recapitulations of The New York Times. Technique is confused with substance. Historians, on the other hand, resist methodology, avoid comparative studies, work only where extensive documentation exists, allow present controversies to bias the interpretation of the past, and display 'conceptual poverty'. Their work tends to be descriptive and narrow.

Another barrier to policy-relevant academic research is the inadequacy of data, a problem common to the field of security studies, and particularly so in the area of terrorism. Gaddis suggests that national archives and records remain an underutilized resource. Nevertheless, much government information on terrorism is classified. Gurr [1988] argues that security requirements seriously restrict the open research that is the hallmark of scholarship. The Reagan administration also tried to restrict access to sensitive nonclassified materials. In 1986, former national security adviser John Poindexter recommended that the National Security Agency be charged with protecting unclassified data if disclosure would adversely affect national security. Congressional and public pressure forced the administration to rescind the measure in 1987 (The New York Times, 30 Aug. 1987: E5). Nevertheless, the national security implications of terrorism make establishing the reality behind terrorist behavior problematic for the academic researcher, not to speak of the concerned public. In the absence of reliable information from official sources, academics and the public are forced to depend on press reports, the accuracy and objectivity of which are frequently criticized by the government.

Gaddis suggests that policy-makers primarily need the assistance of scholarly disciplines because they lack the time to think of fresh approaches to the problems they recognize. Policy-makers require an integrated perspective, combining sequential historical thinking with systemic views. They need to understand the historical evolution of the problems they confront as well as intellectual procedures for generalizing about them. They need to understand the commonalities of issues that appear isolated and idiosyncratic. And they need to question established assumptions. They need to encounter unorthodox interpretations of familiar events. Shared beliefs and backgrounds among government officials as well as the institutional constraints of bureaucratic environments promote cohesion and loyalty but inhibit critical challenges to orthodoxy.

Decision-makers formulating and implementing policy toward terrorism have other specific needs as well. They need to consider a full range of alternatives and their respective consequences, but officials pressed for time in a crisis cannot develop these options. They need to predict future developments and prepare for likely and unlikely contingencies, including terrorist exploitation of high technology resources. They need to understand how an unfamiliar adversary – whose hallmark is the violation of society's expectations – thinks and acts. They need to compare contemporary terrorism to historical precedents, covering as wide a range of experiences as possible. For Americans, a broad knowledge of other cases is particularly important because terrorism within the United States is infrequent. Officials given decision-making roles with regard to terrorism rarely possess direct experience with terrorism or with the geographical areas in which it has become endemic. Turn-over can be rapid. Between 1972 and 1978, seven individuals held the State Department's top position for coordinating American policy on terrorism. Four held the position in the 1978–88 period, with four years the longest period in office. Farrell [1986] further stresses the decentralized character of policy-making. Nine executive branch agencies participate in the Inter-departmental Group on Terrorism, and thirty are represented in the Advisory Group on Terrorism. Views on terrorism inevitably reflect the parochial perspectives of individual agencies, although the Department of State is supposed to be the lead agency with respect to international terrorism, and the FBI is charged with handling domestic threats.

Moreover, as Farrell points out, the threat of terrorism is not constant.

In periods of crisis, which usually involve the high tension and drama of hostage seizures, terrorism preoccupies the top political levels of the government, but in the long periods between crises it cannot compete with more pressing problems. Few policy-makers outside the intelligence agencies and the State Department's office for combatting terrorism (with its high turnover rates) follow developments consistently. Decentralization and inconsistency make it hard for policy-makers to integrate information or develop general interpretations.

The example at hand – how terrorism declines – shows that the same problems interest scholars and policy-makers. Little can be done to resolve the conflict between the desire of policy-makers for certainty and the tendency for scholars to be cautious, but their goals are complementary. Social scientists want to explain why events occur, and policy-makers want to get things done. The researcher attempts to discover the determinants of terrorism's decline, and the official wishes to bring about that decline at the lowest possible cost to the nation's interests. Useful policy recommendations about ending terrorism can only be based on careful analysis. Good operational advice, when it is possible, must be the result of understanding the problem in comparison with other instances of its kind.

Nevertheless, the work of the scholar and the work of the government official must remain separate and distinct. Independence and objectivity are critical to the growth of knowledge, although in a field of research so heavily subsidized by government as is terrorism, the temptation to adopt the government point of view is strong. Yet the concerns of the policy-maker are not identical to those of the academic. Policy-makers are action-oriented by necessity. Their role obliges them to find solutions for problems as quickly as possible. Academic research can contribute to problem-solving by providing critical and reflective judgment, but the primary aim of scholarly analysis is to further knowledge. The accumulation of knowledge is a long-term proposition, and its pay-offs are not always immediately visible. Secrecy is detrimental to its purposes, although necessary to government. Policy-makers are likely to be frustrated when the answer to the question of how to end terrorism does not come in a neat package of instructions.

Nevertheless, the question of how campaigns of terrorism subside is central to combatting terrorism. No estimate of the effectiveness of different policies – concessions versus no concessions, the use of force versus diplomacy, or unilateral versus multilateral responses – is possible without knowing what might have happened without government intervention. Some processes of terrorism may be independent of government actions.

Contradictory Ideas About Outcomes

No general theories explicitly address the decline of terrorism or analyze the role of government policy in that context, but several competing hypotheses about the outcomes of terrorism can be inferred from conceptions of the origins of terrorism. These interpretations focus either on the conditions that motivate terrorists or on the government response to terrorism.

For example, the growth of terrorism is often linked to the development of modern mass communications media. Terrorism is said to thrive on publicity, so presumably media attention, especially sensationalist television coverage, stimulates it [*Picard, 1987: 39–45*]. The relationship is symbiotic. Terrorists want to communicate a message, and the commercial press wants to attract readers and watchers. This view implies that without publicity terrorism would disappear. Yet the causal link between media coverage and the diffusion of terrorism has rarely been investigated, much less established. It has not been shown that publicity serves to communicate the terrorists' message effectively or to change popular attitudes. Furthermore, democratic governments usually reject press censorship as a policy option. The remedy, even if it were effective, is not feasible for liberal democracies.

This perspective finds its opposite in the idea, advanced in great detail by Schmid and De Graaf [*1982*], that lack of access to the news media is actually the source of terrorism. Violence is an effective way of gaining access to publicity and social power in capitalist societies. Lowering the 'threshold of communication' and creating a more egalitarian media should therefore remove the need for terrorism. The authors concede, however, the absence of empirical evidence for the benefits of establishing a 'right to communicate'. Their own analysis assumes the effectiveness of violence in getting attention. Peaceful persuasion is unlikely to be as newsworthy. Nor does it seem possible that governments would wish to guarantee the dissemination of information supporting the grievances or causes that motivate terrorism. In addition, countries with noncommercial media establishments (Great Britain and France, for example) as well are still troubled by terrorism.

Another popular interpretation assumes that terrorism would end if governments consistently adopted hard-line policies and coordinated their international implementation. Wilkinson [*1986)*] argues that firmness and determination, avoiding the extremes of both appeasement and illegal repression, are central to ending terrorism. Although he acknowledges the complexity of the causes of terrorism, Wilkinson assumes that concessions to terrorist demands will encourage terrorism. He recommends resistance and denial of opportunities, although resistance for Wilkinson excludes military retaliation.

Although Wilkinson argues that terrorism is not by and large a rational strategy, his prescription is based on the assumption that reducing the rewards for terrorism and increasing its costs affect the calculations of terrorists. However, the RAND Corporation [*Bass, Jenkins, Kellen, and Ronfeldt, 1981: 5*] observed that the evidence that a no-concessions policy is effective is 'meager and unconvincing'. Certainly American adherence to tough standards (even before the unfolding of the Iran–Contra scandal) did not appear to reduce American vulnerability. In 1985 and 1986, after over a decade of hardline policy, roughly a quarter of international terrorist incidents were directed against American targets [*US Department of State, 1986 and 1988*]. Nor has Israel's defiant response to Palestinian militancy ended terrorism, but it is impossible to know what levels violence might have reached had Israel and the United States pursued different policies.

On the domestic level, Guelke [*1986*] criticizes Wilkinson's dismissal of rational explanations for IRA terrorism. He implies that the key to the decline of terrorism lies in changing perceptions of its legitimacy by the groups who use it. Terrorism is likely to end when terrorism no longer seems justifiable in terms of the ends it serves, or efficacious in moving the organization toward them. Hardline policies, if consistently followed, would not end terrorism but lead to civil war. Governments have become the victims of their own stereotype of terrorism as responsive only to force. Guelke [*1986: 119*] concludes that 'Northern Ireland's prospects for peace, such as they are, are less likely to depend on the techniques employed by government to deal with terrorism than on the evolution of perceptions of those engaged in political violence'.

To other authors, terrorism can only be ended if the underlying social and economic conditions that motivate it are radically changed. Rubenstein [*1987*] implies that terrorism would decline if young intellectuals in society had the opportunity to participate in mass-based movements for change. The absence of viable social movements leads to terrorism as a measure of desperation. Like Guelke, Rubenstein believes that hard-line policies only encourage terrorism. Terrorism will not end when the perceptions of terrorists change but when fundamental structural transformation of society occurs. Genuinely revolutionary alternatives for political expression must exist. Terrorism decreases as the potential for radical collective action increases.

An earlier analysis by Targ [*1979*] is remarkably similar. He sees terrorism as the product of historical conditions, namely settings that are not conducive to mass revolutionary action. Terrorism is characteristic of preindustrial or postindustrial capitalist societies, but not of the industrial state. It is thus a permanent feature of the postindustrial state as we know it.

Chesnais [1981] also argues that terrorism is linked to conditions, although his analysis is more politically focused. He predicts that terrorism will not decline until the structural conditions that permit it – the immaturity of specific Western democracies – change. Terrorism is a remnant of feudalism, to which Mediterranean Europe is highly vulnerable.

A problem with these views is that revolutionary terrorism has declined significantly in both the Federal Republic of Germany and in Italy although fundamental social, political, and economic conditions do not appear to have changed or a new state of democratic maturity to have been reached. Such general concepts of propitious settings for terrorism are extremely difficult to operationalize.

This brief review shows that the theoretical foundation on which policy recommendations could be built is incomplete. It also reveals the need for concreteness and specificity.

Establishing the Facts

The scope of this preliminary survey of cases is restricted to political oppositions that have mounted significant campaigns of terrorism against the state. This preliminary overview questions the conventional wisdom on terrorism and establishes a basis for comparative research on decline.

The search for useful information on the life cycles of underground organizations is frustrating. Table 1 lists 77 organizations, with their country of origin, and the approximate dates of their existence or activity. Simply compiling such a list presents a number of unavoidable conceptual and practical problems. It is important to recognize that treating information on terrorism as though it were unambiguous can lead to false conclusions. Claims of precision are misleading and even controversial.

A first research question is deciding which organizations to include. In order to ensure comparability among the cases considered, this list includes selected organizations active in the post-Second World War period. It focuses on autonomous organizations, whether left, right, or separatist in orientation, that rely significantly on terrorism as a strategy of opposition to regimes in power. It excludes mass-based independence movements against foreign occupiers in colonial contexts. Terrorism is defined as unorthodox and unexpected violence designed to coerce and intimidate rather than to destroy an opponent. It is meant to influence the political behavior of adversaries by attacking and threatening targets that possess symbolic rather than material significance. Consequently its victims are often civilians, but terrorism need not necessarily cause

TABLE 1

ORGANIZATIONS WITH TERRORIST STRATEGIES

I. In existence 1–5 years:

Organization	Country	Dates
Revolutionary Popular Vanguard (VPR)	Brazil	1968–71
National Liberating Action (ALN)	Brazil	1968–71
Armed Proletarian Nuclei	Italy	1974–77
Argentine Anti-Communist Alliance (AAA)	Argentina	1973–76
People's Revolutionary Armed Forces (FRAP)	Mexico	1973–77
Cellules Communistes Combattantes	Belgium	1984–85
Jewish Underground	Israel	1980–84
Hoffman Military Sports Group	W. Germany	1979–81
The Order	U.S.	1983–84
United Freedom Front	U.S.	1982–85
Secret Army Organization	France	1961–62

II. In existence 5–10 years

Organization	Country	Dates
People's Revolutionary Army (ERP)	Argentina	1969–77
Montoneros	Argentina	1970–77
Japanese Red Army	Japan	1969–77
Weatherman	U.S.	1969–75
Black Panthers	U.S.	1966–72
EOKA	Cyprus	1955–60
EOKA-B	Cyprus	1971–78
Prima Linea	Italy	1976–82
South Moluccan Independence Movement	Netherlands	1975–80
Quebec Liberation Front (FLQ)	Canada	1963–72
23rd of September Communist League	Mexico	1974–81
First of October Anti–Fascist Resistance Group (GRAPO)	Spain	1975–82
Popular Front for the Liberation of Palestine – International Operations	Mideast	1972–78
2nd of June Movement	W. Germany	1971–80
Armed Forces of National Liberation (FALN)	U.S.	1974–82
Omega-7	U.S.	1974–82
Armenian Secret Army for the Liberation of Armenia (ASALA)	Turkey	1975–84
Action Directe	France	1979–87
Islamic Jihad/Hezbollah Hezbollah	Lebanon	1983–

III. In existence over 10 years:

Organization	Country	Dates
Dal Khalsa (Sikh separatists)	India	1978–
Tupamaros	Uruguay	1968–80
Grey Wolves	Turkey	1968–80
Turkish People's Liberation Army (TPLA)	Turkey	1969–80
Red Hand Commandos	N. Ireland	1972–82

Armed Forces of National Liberation (FALN)	Venezuela	1961–72
Movement of the Revolutionary Left (MIR)	Venezuela	1960–73
Red Flag	Venezuela	1969–79
		1981–82
Communist Party of India – Marxist–Leninist (Naxalites)	India	1969–72
Breton Liberation Front (FLB)	France	1969–78
Armed Revolutionary Nuclei (and former Black Order)	Italy	1973–82
Red Brigades (BR)	Italy	1968–82
Moujahidin-e-Khalq	Iran	1971–
Fedayeen-e-Khalq	Iran	1971–
Jewish Defense League (JDL)	US	1968–
Croatian National Resistance (or Revolutionary Brotherhood)	Yugoslavia	1950–
Justice Commandos of the Armenian Genocide/Armenian Revolutionary Army	Turkey	1975–
Corsican National Liberation Front	France	1976–
Irish National Liberation Army (INLA)	N. Ireland	1974–87
Ulster Defence Association (UDA)	N. Ireland	1974–
Ulster Freedom Fighters	N. Ireland	1973–
Ulster Volunteer Force (UVF)	N. Ireland	1966–
Red Army Faction (RAF)	W. Germany	1968–
Revolutionary Cells (RZ)	W. Germany	1973–
Armed Revolutionary Forces of Colombia (FARC)	Colombia	1966–
April 19 Movement (M-19)	Colombia	1974–89
National Liberation Army (ELN)	Colombia	1964–
Popular Liberation Army (EPL)	Colombia	1967–89
Movement of the Revolutionary Left (MIR)	Chile	1967–
Farabundo Marti National Liberation Front	El Salvador	1972–
Liberation Tigers of Tamil Eelam	Sri Lanka	1977–
Moro National Liberation Front	Philippines	1972–
New People's Army	Philippines	1969–
Provisional Irish Republican Army	N. Ireland	1970–
Basque Homeland and Freedom (ETA)	Spain	1959–
Popular Front for the Liberation of Palestine (PFLP)	Mideast	1967–
Democratic Front for the Liberation of Palestine (DFLP, formerly PDFLP)	Mideast	1969–
Fatah Revolutionary Council/Black June (Abu Nidal group)	Mideast	1978–
Palestine Liberation Front	Mideast	1977–
Popular Front for the Liberation of Palestine – General Command (PFLP–GC)	Mideast	1968–
Fatah	Mideast	1967–88
Guerrilla Army of the Poor (EGP)	Guatemala	1975–
Rebel Armed Forces (FAR)	Guatemala	1962–
White Hand (MANO)	Guatemala	1966–
Shining Path	Peru	1980–
Popular Forces of 25 April (FP–25)	Portugal	1980–

Note: I have generally used English translations of names but provided the acronyms by which some groups are commonly known, for example, ETA, Euzkadi ta Akatasuna. An important source for the data is Janke [*1983*] supplemented by the Jaffee Center for Strategic Studies [*1986 and 1987*]. See also Schmid [*1983*] and the US Department of State [*1986 and 1988*].

casualties. It is essential, however, that incidents of terrorism are elements in systematic campaigns of violence and not isolated events.

The selection is further limited to groups of substance, measured in terms of coherent organizational structure, longevity, and level of activity. Making such determinations is not simple. Some groups responsible for extensive terrorism are unstructured. While they are perceived as collective entities, in reality they are small, uncoordinated groups linked by a common cause. South Moluccan terrorism in the Netherlands in the 1970s, for example, was the product of several small groups of youths, all motivated by the same goal and inspired by the same models. Islamic Jihad or Hezbollah in contemporary Lebanon, the far right in Italy and the FLQ in Canada in the 1970s, and various Croatian groups also fall into this category. Yet their actions are sufficiently important that excluding them would distort the history of terrorism.

Similarly, it is often difficult to track right-wing groups. They tend to be more decentralized and unstructured than groups on the left. Consequently the right may be under-represented in data bases because its operations are deeply clandestine, loosely organized, and often unclaimed. Right extremism is likely to be represented by a succession of minor groups, rather than a single large organization that dominates a conflict over an extended period of time. Yet the cumulative impact of their violence is as consequential as that of a unified left. For example, in Italy, the New Order, banned in 1973, essentially became the Black Order, which in 1977 became the Armed Revolutionary Nuclei (NAR). This example also demonstrates that organizations can disband or abandon terrorism but individual members may remain active by joining rival groups or forming new ones. The strategy of terrorism may then be continued under different auspices.

Specifying the time period in which groups are active is equally problematic. Some groups turn to terrorism years after their founding. In Peru, the Shining Path (Sendero Luminoso) was created in 1970 but opened its campaign of terrorism in 1980. In general, this list uses the date when the strategy of terrorism was apparently adopted. Similarly, if an organization openly abandons the strategy of terrorism, terrorism is considered to have ended at that point. Accuracy in this matter is an elusive goal, considering the secrecy surrounding the decisions of violent undergrounds. Some organizations undoubtedly continue to exist despite apparent passivity. It is hard to predict when terrorism is likely to be reactivated.

These ambiguities prohibit definitive conclusions, but the survey suggests that some conventional assumptions about terrorism should be reassessed. For example, terrorism seems to end in democracies as often as in authoritarian states, although democracies are most likely to be affected. The opportunities provided by democratic societies are not necessarily conducive to the continuation of terrorism although they may facilitate its initiation. Almost half of the organizations listed no longer exist or no longer use terrorism. However, most currently active organizations have persisted for over ten years. Such stable and tenacious groups pose intractable and long-term public policy problems. At least ten groups have been in operation for 20 years. Possibly there is a threshold point, beyond which the extremist organization becomes self-sustaining. The younger the organization, the greater the likelihood of its ending. In fact there are no notably active new organizations (formed in the last five years). The last date of formation of a serious group was 1984 (the Cellules Communistes Combattantes or CCC in Belgium), a group that remained active for about a year. Possibly motivations for terrorism are decreasing or government policies are becoming more effective in combatting it. Yet it is also possible that there is a time-lag between the establishment of a terrorism-prone organization and public perception of the threat it poses.

Links between terrorism and conditions are hard to establish. For example, it is not evident that the persistence of terrorism is linked primarily to divided societies, where separatist or nationalist movements predominate. In general, revolutionary and nationalist goals appear equally well represented among groups that have lasted over ten years. Nor is it clear that the duration of terrorism is connected to the level of development of the host state, since there appears to be little difference in the duration of terrorist campaigns in the developed West and in the Third World. Nor is terrorism always absent in the presence of mass-based movements. The two forms of pressure for social change may not be mutually exclusive.

With regard to government policies, concessions to demands in specific cases are not always associated with the persistence of terrorism. Brazil, Uruguay, and Argentina, as well as the Federal Republic of Germany and Italy, have met demands, but in all of these nations terrorism has ended or declined significantly. There is no necessary correlation between the government's coerciveness toward terrorism and yielding to specific demands when hostages are seized.

The 'success' of modern terrorism is often deplored. Yet terrorism is rarely associated with political instability or with radical political change. In three exceptional cases revolutionary terrorism preceded military intervention in politics – Uruguay, Argentina, and Turkey – but if organizational survival is considered to be a goal of terrorism, then the strategy failed. The outcome in each case was provocation of a repressive government response. In Argentina, the struggle against terrorism took the severe form of a brutal war to suppress all opposition, leading to thousands of 'disappearances'. In Iran, terrorism was one form of violent opposition to the reign of the Shah, but after the revolution the secular left was soon alienated from Iran's religious regime and unsuccessfully revived its terrorist strategy. It does not seem reasonable to conclude that terrorism declines because it accomplishes its long-term ideological goals.

This brief overview indicates that there are no easy answers to questions about the decline of terrorism. A satisfactory explanation requires analysis that is sensitive to specific historical contexts.

Explaining Individual Processes of Decline

Ross and Gurr [1989] develop a comparative political analysis of the declining incidence of domestic terrorism in Canada and the United States. Their argument is based on an assessment of terrorist capabilities, which they distinguish as coercive or political. Preemption and deterrence are government measures that destroy the terrorists' coercive capabilities. Political capabilities, on the other hand, diminish through 'burn-out' (declining group commitment) and 'backlash' (reduced popular support). These analytical distinctions are helpful in understanding the process of decline, particularly as they suggest further questions about the interrelationships among external and internal variables. For example, what effect does government coercion have on the underground's cohesion and legitimacy, and which are its key political resources? What conditions lead to loss of commitment among the group members or to popular disaffection? When do terrorist groups perceive 'backlash'? Does the withdrawal of popular support that symbolizes decline precede or follow the government's mobilization for pre-emption or deterrence? Are disunity and 'burn-out' synonymous?

The conceptual formulation I propose focuses on a different set of variables and is designed to apply to a wider range of cases. It emphasizes the strategy of extremist organizations. The decline of terrorism appears to be related to the interplay of three factors: the government response to terrorism (which is not restricted to preemption or deterrence), the strategic choices of the terrorist organization, and its organizational resources. The government role can be decisive, but often in non-obvious ways. Attempts to defeat a terrorist underground by destroying its organizational structure, removing leaders, causing large-scale attrition, or blocking recruitment do not always have the same effect. Reforms that decrease the utility of terrorism or positive inducements that encourage individual defections can be as important as the deployment of coercive resources. Decisive defeats are rare in the absence of other contributing factors, such as organizational disintegration. Yet disunity does not necessarily signal the end of terrorism or reflect declining commitment. Disagreements over strategy are common. Members can defect to rival groups or establish a new, more militant organization. Splits and mergers are a form of propagation of terrorism. Power struggles among generations of leaders (especially if the original leadership is imprisoned) and prior patterns of cleavage among supporters, whether states or ethnic groups, also reduce cohesiveness. Strategic reversals may result from dependence on states whose support is withdrawn or sanctuaries that are lost, the appearance of more attractive or justifiable alternatives, or a collective perception of failure. Possibly cycles of terrorism exist. An escalation in destructiveness may precipitate decline, as extreme terrorist activity provokes government intervention, alienates or frightens sympathizers, and generates internal disagreement.

A few examples illustrate these complex interactions. Relevant cases include domestic terrorism in Western and Third World democracies, including both police and military responses (an important difference between the United States and Canada). International terrorist campaigns are also discussed.

Domestic terrorism has not posed a significant threat in the United States, but in the late 1960s it seemed plausible that offshoots of the civil rights protest movement might be capable of serious violence. In 1969 the FBI decided that the Black Panthers were the most dangerous internal threat in the country. By the next year all senior leaders were in prison, in court, dead, or out of the country. Local police forces also reacted vigorously, in large part because they were the chosen targets. In 1972, Huey Newton, the Panthers' Minister of Defense, announced that the program of 'militant self defense' was over. With the original leadership gone, the remaining cadres, who were mostly young and inexperienced, were unable to hold the organization together. Organizing on a national basis posed problems of coordination and continuity. Internal quarrels (frequently bloody) led to significant defections, such as that of Eldridge Cleaver. In retrospect, the FBI's estimation of the threat seems highly exaggerated and police and FBI enforcement of the law overzealous. The apparent success of these policies should not be allowed to obscure the fact that the decline was also the result of organizational over-extension, inexperienced cadres, loss of leadership through defections as well as arrests, unrestrained factionalism, and poor strategic choices (attacks on police).

In contrast to the United States, left extremist groups in Italy enjoyed a measurable popular support and the state appeared weak in terms of both legitimacy and coercive capabilities. Yet terrorism receded because an innovative government policy apparently coincided with the emergence of discontent within the terrorist underground. The government's offer of leniency for 'repented' terrorists was effective because the Red Brigades were in disarray. Gian Carlo Caselli [*1986: 30*], a judge in Turin, claimed that the Italian 'victory' over terrorism was due to applied sociology, psychology, and political science, not police and judicial repression. 'We lost a lot of time before understanding that military measures – I mean the use of the army (in the Moro affair, notably) – accomplished nothing except to create "repressive illusions" '. Once the Italian government recognized the need to attack terrorism at its source and to coordinate the police response, especially in terms of acquiring intelligence, terrorism was quickly suppressed. He points to two laws as decisive: one requiring people renting or selling apartments to inform the authorities of the names of new tenants or purchasers, and the 'repentants' law, by which accused terrorists were offered freedom or reduced sentences in exchange for informing.[2] He also observed that public opinion switched to the side of the government when it became clear that the terrorists were not romantic figures. Open demonstrations of public hostility to terrorism were important to its delegitimization.

The analysis by Tarrow and della Porta [1986] suggests that Italian terrorism was transitory, a sign of the decline of mass protest. It represented the end of a cycle of the rise and fall of social movements. Terrorism only emerged as the momentum of mass protest drew in new political actors with new issues. Small extremist groups were inspired to join the action but were unable to influence events due to receding popular support (the public was often repelled by their violence) and increasing government coercion. Terrorism declined as the Italian government responded with sanctions that would not have been tolerated against peaceful protest but were justified by terrorism.

Legault [1983] argues that terrorism ended because of a poor strategic choice on the part of the Red Brigades, a decision that was criticized at the time by competing groups in the far left. The decision to kidnap and to murder Aldo Moro forced the Italian population to choose sides and compelled a divided government to mobilize. The result was the re-affirmation of the legitimacy of the Italian state, which terrorism was meant to undermine.

Legault also sees left-wing Italian terrorism as cyclical (as does Sprinzak, in this volume). First in the 'pre-revolutionary' or 'pre-discourse' period, opposition movements begin to question the established order in a context of decentralizing authority, especially in the universities, and growing discontent among students and workers. Second, 'the terrorist discourse' involves the elaboration and refinement of ideological themes that legitimize violence. Extremists come to believe that violence is both morally justified and likely to succeed. The third stage, 'implementation of discourse through action', is marked by steadily escalating terrorism. The range of targets expands as the terrorist group abandons 'armed propaganda' for 'revolutionary civil war', culminating in the 1978 attack on Moro, which was deliberately intended to strike at the heart of the state and to provoke destabilization at the top levels of government. In the fourth stage of 'counter-discourse or repression', state and society react by uniting against terrorism as much as by the destruction of the terrorists' coercive capabilities. By 1979–80, Italy had entered the final stage of 'counter counter-discourse'. The clear public preference for security and order accentuated divisions within the terrorist organizations, who became 'schizophrenic' [Legault, 1983: 676]. Violence had become an end in itself, almost a religion based on myths of arms and death. The terrorists vainly sought new constituencies in the subproletariat and among prisoners, but their violence appeared increasingly meaningless to society. The kidnapping of General Dozier – an attempt to renew links with a broader base in the anti-imperialist left – ended in failure. Terrorism lost support when the ambitiousness and over-confidence of the Red Brigades precipitated a direct confrontation between government and terrorists.

In the French case, government policy followed a sequence of coercion, accommodation, then renewed coercion. Action Directe emerged in the 1980s, a decade later than similar groups in West Germany and Italy. When François Mitterrand was elected President in 1981, he amnestied the members of violent left-wing groups who had not been convicted of common crimes. This partial amnesty provoked two responses: a hunger strike by the remaining prisoners, and terrorist pressure from their comrades outside. After 35 days, the hunger-strikers were released on medical grounds [Madelin, 1986: 106–7]. Some members of Action Directe, particularly the two 'historic leaders', returned to the underground and initiated a strategy of political assassinations, whereas before the group had restricted itself to relatively harmless bombings. Although 80 per cent of the amnestied prisoners did not return to violence, the resurgence of a more murderous Action Directe made the government appear naive and weak. Nevertheless, the much smaller organization, even if more committed and cohesive, was also more vulnerable to police penetration. When key leaders were arrested in 1987, the organization was effectively destroyed. The demonstrated failure of conciliatory alternatives as well as the escalation of terrorism, both from Action Directe and from Middle Eastern groups, served to justify government action.

In the United States, Italy, and France terrorism was inspired by revolutionary ideologies. In Canada, the Front de Libération du Québec mixed national-separatism with self-conscious imitation of Third World national liberation struggles. In 1970 the government responded to the FLQ's seizure of hostages, one British and one Canadian official, with a declaration of martial law and the dispatch of 8,000 federal troops to the province. This extremely coercive response, which was implemented with precision and efficiency, apparently halted separatist terrorism. However, Fournier [*1982*] argues that terrorism subsided not because of the numerous arrests made under martial law (which lasted for three months) but because of internal developments in the FLQ (the decision to form a Marxist–Leninist movement based on mass mobilization, not terrorism) and the growth in power of the legal independence movement, which won elections in Quebec in 1976. Ross and Gurr [*1989*] also stress the development of feasible alternatives to violence. However, the FLQ clearly made a strategic mistake in kidnapping Cross and Laporte and murdering Pierre Laporte. This miscalculation or accident was due in part to the unstructured nature of the FLQ, since two independent cells were actually behind the kidnappings. Their actions were not centrally coordinated.

Military responses to terrorism are more common in the Third World, where terrorism is usually linked to rural insurgency and popular grievances. The example of India shows that an attempt to deprive terrorists of coercive capabilities can backfire. In 1984 India responded to Sikh terrorism with a declaration of martial law in the Punjab, in conjunction with a military attack on the Golden Temple shrine in Amritsar, where Sikh terrorist leader Bhindranwale was headquartered. The central government sent in 2,000 troops to seize the temple, with an additional 70,000 troops to seal off the state. Leaf [*1985: 494*] argues that this inappropriate reaction 'far from ending Bhindranwale's influence and activities ... actually served as evidence of what he was trying to prove'. The terrorists did not represent or speak for even a large minority of the Sikh population, urban or rural, but the government response was self-destructive in misrepresenting the real issues in the Punjab (popular discontent actually focused on economic issues, not political autonomy) and confirming Sikh expectations that the government was not responsive to their demands and that Indira Gandhi was motivated primarily by the desire to establish autocratic rule. Consequently Indira Gandhi was assassinated by two of her Sikh bodyguards. In the rioting after the assassination, more than 1,500 Sikhs were killed. The government response appears only to have widened social divisions, and violence continues.

Uruguay is another case of military reaction to domestic terrorism. The Tupamaros were defeated in 1972, after the declaration of a state of siege and the deployment of the armed forces in a sustained military offensive [*Lopez-Alves, 1985*]. The civilian government had already suspended constitutional rights and imposed media censorship. The military (and its allies in the ruling government coalition) may have overestimated the revolutionary threat, due in part to the Tupamaros' own over-confidence as well as a vested interest in increasing the power and resources of the security forces. The Tupamaro threat created a consensus among the armed forces that made intervention into politics possible. Yet the defeat of the Tupamaros was also related to internal disintegration, caused by disagreement over the appropriate response to the military crack-down. The Tupamaros tried unsuccessfully to move back into rural areas they thought would be harder for the military to control. But the movement could not challenge a mobilized army in urban or rural areas.

It is much more difficult for governments to defeat international terrorist organizations, most of which are centered in the Middle East. Decision-making in the Popular Front for the Liberation of Palestine (PFLP) is instructive with regard to the constraints affecting such groups. Abu Khalil [*1987: 361–78*] argues that the PFLP decision to halt hijackings in 1971 (after having initiated the tactic in 1968) was possible only because of the iron discipline and charismatic authority exercised by George Habash, who decreed that international operations were manifestations of petit bourgeois spirit and adventurism. The PFLP's ideology seemed to be as flexible as the organization was autocratic. Every change that Habash approved was presented as 'tactical' rather than 'strategic'. In the 1970s with increasing bureaucratization, resulting from an increase in financial resources, the organization grew more conservative. In 1981 the leadership dismissed guerrilla warfare as inappropriate and instead stressed 'quasi-conventional' war. The 1982 Israeli invasion of Lebanon discredited this strategy, and apparently a new clique, allied with Syria and Libya rather than Iraq, gained power. In 1984, the 'comrades and cadres of the PFLP' split off from the moderate faction. In February 1987, Habash declared extremism to be detrimental to the Palestinian national interest. 'Strikes at imperialist interests' (attacks on foreign targets) in the Middle East were condemned. The PFLP then appeared to wish to abandon its terrorist image in order to gain official recognition, perhaps following the lead of its patron, Syria, a government embarrassed by Britain's severing of diplomatic relations in 1986 and eager to regain respectability. However, after the Iraqi invasion of Kuwait in 1990, the PFLP seemed prepared to return to terrorism.

The Armenian Secret Army for the Liberation of Armenia (ASALA) and the Justice Commandos of the Armenian Genocide, both active internationally, have suffered a serious decline. Tololyan [*1986*] argues that diminished terrorism was not due to instrumental success or failure. Changing attitudes of populations in the Armenian Diaspora and, secondarily, loss of secure bases outside Turkey were the critical factors. Internal quarrels over strategy and over the relevance of the Palestinian model split the movement from the beginning. The collapse of Lebanon, a result of the 1982 Israeli invasion, and subsequent Shi'ite hostility to Armenians deprived them of a base of operations. The British crackdown on Iranians, a response to Iranian-sponsored terrorism, restricted the activities of ethnic Armenians in Britain. Greek Cyprus may also have ceased to provide support for ASALA. The Orly bombing in 1983 resulted not only in repression from the French police (largely ineffective in apprehending actual ASALA members) but also a mixture of alienation, outrage, and fear among French Armenians. Expressions of popular disaffection reinforced existing splits in the terrorist groups, and in turn, bloody internecine quarrels diminished the movement's legitimacy *vis-à-vis* its Diaspora constituency. Terrorism generated strains and pressures that the movement did not anticipate and from which it could not recover. Tololyan concludes [*1986: 19*]:

> The Armenian terrorist movement deeply miscalculated the kinds and amounts of violence and dissension which the Diaspora consensus could tolerate; it miscalculated equally badly the degree to which its own success depended on at least the silent acquiescence, if not the support, that such consensus enables – in part because the terrorists' initial successes led them to overconfidence concerning their ability to manipulate events and opinion....

Tololyan concludes that the beliefs and perceptions of the political community out of which terrorism springs are more important than the physical defeat of the terrorist organization. His analysis demonstrates that specific acts of terrorism can violate the legitimizing beliefs that support violence.

Conclusions

It is difficult for democratic governments to anticipate and forestall the emergence of underground organizations dedicated to the use of terrorism. Before extremist groups turn to action, the most expert intelligence agencies cannot distinguish reliably between legitimate dissent and disloyalty or between potentially violent and nonviolent oppositions. The first indication of the path a group has chosen to follow is not its rhetoric but the commission of an act of terrorism. Governments then need time to organize a response: collecting and analyzing intelligence information, establishing special units in the security forces, coordinating bureaucratic resources, and securing legal changes to facilitate the apprehension and conviction of terrorists. All of these measures would be rejected by public opinion if terrorism were not obviously threatening. By the time the government is equipped to combat terrorism, the task is no longer prevention but bringing an active terrorist campaign to an end. At this point dealing with the causes of terrorism, even if feasible or desirable in the long term, must take second place to restoring order.

The assumption that the decline of terrorism is due simply to the physical defeat of extremist organizations is too simple a conception of the process. Government policies and actions, whether coercive or conciliatory, are only one among several factors contributing to the evolution of terrorist campaigns. These determinants include the organization's cohesiveness and its decisions. Analyzing terrorists' perceptions not only of government policies but of popular attitudes is essential to understanding the miscalculations that discredit terrorism before its supporters, provoke internal dissension, and justify government repression. In liberal democracies where violent oppositions rely exclusively on terrorism, there may be a pattern in which terrorist actions, brought about by overconfidence and misperceptions of consequences, divide the radical opposition and undermine the legitimacy of all violent extremism. It is possible that misjudgments such as the kidnapping and murder of Aldo Moro, Pierre Laporte, or Dan Mitrione occurred because the Red Brigades, FLQ, or Tupamaros, respectively, were isolated from reality (a condition of underground conspiracies) and arrogant in their expectations of success. Terrorists may not recognize failure, but when terrorism becomes an end in itself, it loses its justifiability in the eyes of the public it was meant to convince. In these cases, terrorism is self-defeating.

NOTES

1. There are two recent exceptions, Ross and Gurr [*1989*] and Crenshaw [*1987*]. I am happy to acknowledge the support of the Harry Frank Guggenheim Foundation for this research.
2. Yet similar British policies in Northern Ireland produce different outcomes. Finn [*1987: 119*] notes that IRA defendants plead guilty in order to secure more lenient sentences, but this apparent cooperation is a sign of loyalty to the IRA, not organizational disintegration. The IRA has apparently instructed its members to try to get off as lightly as possible, in order to insure group survival.

Academic Research and Government Policy on Terrorism

Ariel Merari

Since 1968 international terrorism has grown considerably, despite governments' effort to curb it. Part of this failure is attributable to the inadequate contribution of academic research to government policy making on terrorism. The paper identifies three problem areas that hinder academic influence on government policy making in this field. These are: (1) Terrorism is a difficult subject for research because its diversity makes generalizations questionable and empirical data are hardly accessible for the academic researcher. (2) By and large, terrorism has remained outside the interest of mainstream social science. Academic contributions on terrorism have often been occasional and amateurish, lacking in factual knowledge of the subject matter. Many of them are too theoretical to have an applicability value and some are too speculative to be reliable. (3) For a variety of reasons, including resistance to external influences in general and suspicion of academia in particular, government officials have failed to utilize even sound knowledge and competent professional advice of academics. In some demonstrable cases this neglect has had deleterious effects on the quality of government decisions concerning terrorism. In order to improve the utilization of potential academic contribution to policy decisions on terrorism, governments should selectively support academic research on terrorism that has a high practical promise. Preference should be given to subjects of study where academic has a relative advantage over government in depth and rigor. It is also suggested that academic influence on government decision making would be served best by an exchange of people between academia and government.

In the course of the recent two decades political terrorism has become a part of our civilization. Beyond its obvious impact on international relations and, in some countries, domestic political stability, terrorism has had a significant cultural influence. It maintains a very salient existence not only in mass media reporting, but in literature and in cinematographic creations as well. Undeniably, it is part of our culture now.

Despite growing public concern and ever-increasing investment in counter-terrorism measures and equipment, overall the rate of international terrorist activity has shown an almost uninterrupted increment since 1968. In addition to the rise in the frequency of incidents, there has been an escalation in the lethality of terrorist attacks, as measured by several criteria [*Jenkins, 1983; Public Report of the Vice President's Task Force on Combatting Terrorism, 1986*]. The conclusion that, generally speaking, society has failed to cope effectively with this form of political violence is, therefore, unavoidable.

This paper deals with a specific aspect of this failure, namely, the inadequate contribution of academic research on terrorism to governmental policy making. In treating this topic, it focuses on the following constituents of the problem: difficulties stemming from the nature of terrorism; problems relating to the state of academic research on terrorism; and the interface between government and academia. The final section of the study ventures some conclusions and suggestions.

Terrorism as a Subject for Academic Research

It is often mentioned that terrorism is an old form of irregular warfare. However, in its present scope and intensity, terrorism is a young phenomenon. Compared to areas such as common criminality and conventional warfare, systematic data on terrorism are very scanty. In addition to the brevity of our relatively intensive exposure to this form of violence, several factors render terrorism an unusually difficult subject for academic research. On the conceptual side, the geographical, ideological, cultural, contextual and operational diversity of the problem cast doubt on the very justification for identifying terrorism as a fairly homogeneous phenomenon. Even if we exclude the application of terrorism by repressive regimes against their own citizens, we are still left with a great variety of terroristic phenomena from below that seem to have very little in common. At best, there are 'terrorisms', a broad spectrum of violent attempts to attain political, social or religious objectives by subnational groups that may or may not enjoy state support. Repeated occurrences of the same phenomenon are the basis of scientific research. In the case of terrorism, however, there is hardly a pattern which allows generalizations. Clearly, the heterogeneity of the terroristic phenomena makes descriptive, explanatory and predictive generalizations, which are the ultimate products of scientific research, inherently questionable.

On the practical side, terrorism is a very elusive subject for research. My data base at the Jaffee Center for Strategic Studies contains information on more than 800 terrorist groups scattered all over the world. The great majority of these groups are small, with membership ranging from ten to a few hundred. Collecting systematic standardized, reliable information for the purpose of comparisons is next to impossible. Moreover, the customary tools of psychological and sociological research are almost always inapplicable for studying terrorist groups and their individual members. For obvious reasons, terrorists are inaccessible to scientific research as long as they maintain their clandestine activity. In situ studies of group structure and processes, for example, are inconceivable modes of research on terrorism. Psychological studies of captured or repented terrorists suffer from inherent artifacts, since it is doubtful that the conditions of these studies represent the 'normal' terrorist's habitat and that the individual subjects are a representative sample of the active, uncaptured terrorist population. Intelligence agencies have some information on individual terrorists and intra-group interactions which could, conceivably help to reach some psychological conclusions. Nevertheless, these agencies are reluctant to share their information with outsiders and, in the rare exceptions, they cooperate on a private basis, precluding the possibility of publication that might benefit the academic community at large.

Having said this, I should add that my own experience suggests, after all, that the loss of information due to secrecy is not so great, since the kind of information collected by intelligence outfits is a far cry from the accepted minimum for scientific research or for reliable clinical assessment. In addition to the fact that the relevant details are sporadic and fortuitous, they are almost always derived from secondary sources whose reliability is questionable. These shortcomings are attributable in part to the nature of intelligence material and the ways by which it is obtained, and in part to the interests of intelligence agencies, which are almost always focused on immediate operational needs rather than on basic, long-term processes. Thus, an intelligence organization would always give higher priority to obtaining information about the name, passport number and whereabouts of a person suspected of planning an assassination, than to collecting data on the socio-economic characteristics of the organization to which that person belongs. Had there been in intelligence agencies a larger number of people with social science interests, more information relevant to social sciences questions would probably have been obtained, but the clandestine nature of terrorist organizations and the ways and means by which intelligence can be obtained will extremely rarely enable data collection which meets commonly accepted academic standards.

The physical manifestations of terrorism as well as public responses to it are, in principle, much more accessible to research than the psychology and sociology of terrorists. In practice, however, even this research is not easy. Consider, for instance, the difficulties involved in studying the effects of Albanian terrorist activity in Yugoslavia, Afghan terrorism in Pakistan, or UNITA in Angola. Quite often it is impossible to know with certainty what happened, let alone to assess public responses with any scientifically acceptable tools. It is not a matter of chance that most of the existing scientific literature on terrorism deals with manifestations of this phenomenon in Western democracies. The conditions prevailing in a large part of the world, including lack of the necessary domestic scientific infrastructure, lack of intimate acquaintance with the country under consideration among foreign researchers, and limitations imposed by the local government on collecting and disseminating information, are insurmountable for the scientific community.

Shortcoming of Academic Research on Terrorism

The Problem of the Contributors

Until recently, the academic community paid very little attention to the phenomena of terrorism. For academic psychology, in particular, terrorism was nonexistent throughout the 1970s, a period when scores of terrorist groups were established all over the world and terrorist attacks became one of the most frequent topics of media headlines. The *Psychological Abstracts*, the most authoritative compendium of academic publications in psychology, listed no reference to terrorism or to related terms, such as 'hostages' or 'hijacking', until the end of 1981. By this criterion, academic psychology recognized terrorism as a subject worthy of consideration only in 1982. In that year the *Psychological Abstracts* listed ten publications under this topic [*Merari and Friedland, 1985*]. Actually, some psychological and psychiatric articles and books on terrorism appeared before 1982 [for example, *Morf, 1970; Hubbard, 1971; Hacker, 1976; Kaplan, 1978*] but the articles were not published in the journals covered by the *Psychological Abstracts* and the books, apparently, did not deserve a mention in the opinion of the *Psychological Abstracts* editors. Clearly this subject remained outside the interest and attention of mainstream psychology. Although political scientists have devoted considerably greater attention to terrorism than psychologists and sociologists, on the whole the scientific community has so far allocated a very small part of its research effort to this subject – a strange attitude towards a phenomenon that is clearly one of the most common forms of violent domestic and international political conflict in our time.

This neglect has possibly resulted from the compounded influence of several factors, including the already-mentioned characteristics of the phenomenon. In addition, from the angle of the individual scientist's motivation to engage in systematic research on the subject, terrorism falls between the chairs. It has no private commercial appeal like clinical psychology, for instance, and no academic glory of the kind offered by basic theoretical work, which in psychology relies mostly on controlled laboratory experimentation. This may explain the fact that, in contrast to other fields of academic expertise, only a small proportion of the published works on terrorism have been written by devoted students of the subject, that is, by persons who spend most of their research energy on terrorism, however broadly defined. Rather, it seems that the majority of the academic contributions in this area have been done by people whose main research interests lie elsewhere, who felt that they had something to say on this juicy and timely subject.

The result has been, sometimes, an unexpected fresh look at the issue, which carried a promise of generating a new line of research, but more often it has been a superficial treatment of a singular aspect of the problem, ignorant of the complex and heterogeneous nature of terrorism, at times suffering from factual errors. Usually, a contribution of this kind is well-grounded in the empirical and theoretical findings of the writer's particular area of expertise, but lacking in knowledge on terrorism.

Problems of the Contributions

In the absence of systematic and first-hand information, the prevailing academic notion of the psychological and sociological characteristics of terrorists and terrorist groups is often largely speculative. Kaplan [*1978*] for instance, claims without reservation:

> A need to pursue absolute ends, whether or not the need is rooted in anxiety, is characteristic of the terrorist. Personal need can deter-mine social goals, as Lasswell long ago pointed out. Acts of terror on behalf of the just rights of the Palestinians' may be committed by terrorists who are not Palestinians, not even Arabs who might be thought to identify with the Palestinians, but by Japanese, Germans, or Bolivians. The important thing is not *who* they are but *what* they are. An international network of terror is less an organizational reality than the pervasiveness of psychopathology.

Kaplan does not bring any empirical evidence to support his sweeping statement.

Even empirical studies rest heavily on secondary, partial sources that suffer from severe limitations. A case in point is the study by Russell and Miller [*1977*]. This study merits special mention because it is one of the most comprehensive efforts of its kind, it has been widely quoted, has been reprinted several times, and it has led to some of the common misconceptions in the field. This study is an attempt to portray the profile of terrorists, using data on 350 terrorists that belonged to 18 groups of various nationalities. The authors reported that they collected their data from newspapers, some academic works and government publications. The basic problem with the study is a sampling bias. The terrorists who were considered by the authors as a representative sample of their groups were those who had been exposed to the public. Presumably, in most cases they were either leaders of the groups or operational members who had been arrested and their identity uncovered, usually in connection with their involvement in terrorist activity abroad. These two types can hardly be considered a representative sample of the rank and file of a terrorist group. To use an example I am most familiar with, the authors describe Palestinian terrorists as 'in their late twenties' (p. 20),

> ... many Palestinians, including those now affiliated with the PFLP, were educated abroad ... Trained in European and various Middle Eastern universities located in such cities as Frankfurt, Stuttgart, Berlin, London, Cairo, Beirut, and Paris, these individuals were intimately familiar with urban life, normally spoke a foreign language and were able to integrate into and live within any metropolitan area without difficulty. The success of Palestinian terrorist operations in Europe over the past four to five years attests readily to this fact (p. 25).

'Finally, even in the case of the Palestinians, many of whom were educated abroad, universities were frequent recruiting bases' (p. 30).

Russell and Miller do not provide precise statistics to support the statements quoted above. Their main source on Palestinian terrorists seemed to be a personal communication from Dr Paul Jureidini (p. 32). Yet, anybody who has had a close contact with Palestinian terrorists would find it hard to recognize them by Russell and Miller's description. Indeed, a representative sample of the thousands of proven members of the various PLO groups who were captured in Lebanon in 1982 differed significantly from the above description. For example, only 11 per cent of the terrorists had some college education, whereas 15 per cent had no formal education whatsoever and 29 per cent had only partial elementary education. About 51 per cent were city or town dwellers, 15 per cent were villagers and 34 per cent lived in refugee camps. By and large, they came from lower class families: 61 per cent of their fathers were unskilled laborers, 30 per cent were semi-skilled laborers, four per cent were skilled laborers and only three per cent were professionals. Most of them were recruited in their living places, namely, refugee camps in Lebanon and the Palestinian neighborhoods of Beirut. One might think that these demographic features characterize only the PLO organized militias in Lebanon, and that the small terrorist cells that have operated in Israel might be more similar to Russell and Miller's description. However, this is not the case. The typical Palestinian terrorist in Israel and the territories resembles those captured in Lebanon in all of the demographic features mentioned above. Similarly, the characteristics of Palestinian terrorists who had been sent to Israel for the purpose of carrying out high-risk missions (hostage-taking and/or mass-killing) and were captured in the course of their mission, are also quite different from those described by

Russell and Miller. Thus, the average level of education in a sample of twelve of these terrorists was six grades (only one was a high school graduate), their mean age was 22, and all of them were recruited in Middle Eastern countries, usually in Lebanon.

The disparity between Russell and Miller's report and the above mentioned findings apparently stems from the fact that Russell and Miller's sample included what they called 'known terrorists', probably referring to Palestinian terrorists who had been captured in Europe, whereas the great majority of the PLO membership was based in Lebanon (before the 1982 war) and the bulk of the PLO terrorist activity has always taken place in Israel and the Administered Territories. In terms of operational activity, international terrorism constituted only a small part of the total number of terrorist attacks carried out by the Palestinian organizations [*Merari and Elad, 1986*].

The damage done by studies of this kind is not limited to factual errors about the characteristics of specific terrorist groups, but may lead to basic conceptual mistakes. Thus, Russell and Miller conclude that 'one can draw a composite picture into which fit the great majority of those terrorists from the eighteen urban guerrilla groups examined here'. The implication is not only suggestive for security personnel at airports, but also for academics trying to understand the nature of terrorism and the making of a terrorist. The study essentially claims that all terrorists are basically alike and, by extension, terrorism is by and large a homogeneous phenomenon. Another sweeping conclusion in the same vein is: 'Thus, in the final analysis, the philosophical underpinnings of most modern terrorist groups may be found in a loose synthesis of the views developed by Mao, Trotsky, Marcuse, Fanon, and particularly those of Marighella' (p. 31). This statement seems trivially correct concerning left wing terrorist groups, but quite unfounded with regard to right wing, fundamentalist-religious, nationalist and separatist terrorist groups.

The preceding criticism notwithstanding, the Russell and Miller study is, at least, a laudable attempt to collect and analyze empirical data on terrorism. I refer to it in detail because it is one of the better papers in this regard. As Gurr [*1988: 2*] observes, 'With a few clusters of exceptions there is, in fact, a disturbing lack of good empirically-grounded research on terrorism'. This may well be an understatement. Although I have not conducted a comprehensive survey of the psychological and sociological publications on terrorism, it seems to me that only a small proportion of them are based on primary sources. Works on terrorist personality are rarely based on interviews with terrorists conducted by the authors and those that address the question of terrorist motivation are seldom based on content analysis of terrorist manifestos and communiques. Independent data collection by authors is rare even in studies which deal with topics that call for information of a relatively accessible kind, such as public opinion polls, interviews with victims of terrorist incidents or chronologies of terrorist events.

It seems, then, that many – perhaps most – academic writers on terrorism rely not only on empirical data collected by other researchers, but on other writers' conclusions, impressions and suggestions. The body of common academic wisdom on terrorism thus becomes increasingly more remote from the accepted norms of research in the social sciences, occasionally remote from reality, and sometimes resembles hearsay rather than twentieth century science. I am not trying to belittle the role of speculation, but to emphasize the importance of empirical research and the need to differentiate between speculation and research. There is certainly a place in science for speculation, instant insights, and even wild hypotheses. However, when these constitute the bulk of our knowledge about a phenomenon and supersede facts, as is the case with research on terrorism, the state of science becomes a state of art.

Government and Academia

Academic Frustrations

More than a decade ago I invested much time in an attempt to promote a project which, in my opinion, had considerable importance for national security. Following a series of meetings with Israeli government officials, I presented the idea to Professor Yehezkel Dror, a distinguished political scientist who then served as an advisor to the minister of defense. I sought Professor Dror's opinion about the proposal and its likelihood of being accepted by the Minister of Defense. Professor Dror commented that in his experience, government bureaucracies were usually rather reluctant to accept external academic influences. He went on to explain that this attitude stemmed from several motives, including unwillingness to accept advice from anybody, since acceptance of advice may amount to admission by the office holders that their past performance left something to be desired; a general reluctance to share influence and power with any new additions to the system; fear of intellectual superiority of academics; reluctance to make outsiders privy to sensitive information, a sentiment which is particularly strong in the case of academics, who are generally considered as open-mouthed as they are open-minded; resentment of the 'theoretical' (meaning: impractical) nature of the academic approach to problems; and decision makers' disrespect for academic knowledge in the social and political sciences (every politician is a practical political scientist and everybody is a practical psychologist). In short, Dror was not overly optimistic about the likelihood that an academic contribution would be welcome in that case as well as in others. In the wake of that discouraging monologue, I asked what would he advise me to do. His reply was 'arm yourself with stoical enthusiasm'.

Much has been written on the shortcomings of governments' decision making processes in general and resistance to external influences in particular [for example, *Herman, 1972; Janis and Mann, 1977*]. In the context of this contribution it is not my intention to deal with this topic systematically, but to mention briefly some of my personal experiences in this regard, which may illustrate specific barriers in the way of academic contribution to government policy decisions concerning terrorism.

Calling the attention of government officials to the existence of a potential problem and to the need to think in advance about possible solutions is usually not enough to make them act upon it. Even a straight-in-the-face demonstration does not guarantee that a problem will be taken seriously, as long as it has not become a direct, concrete threat. In July 1979 I organized, at Tel Aviv University, an international conference on terrorism. The peak of the conference was a three-day game, which had been designed to examine the possible developments and repercussions of a highly complex hostage incident, which takes place in a hostile country, where a military rescue of the hostages is impossible, and to search for possible strategies to cope with the situation [*Merari, 1979*]. The imaginary scenario involved the hijacking of a TWA airliner, whose passengers included several dignitaries, by Palestinian terrorists to Tehran. The so-called military option was deliberately ruled out, and the choice of Iran as the country which hosted the hijackers was not random. The idea was that, following the precedents of Entebbe and Mogadishu, a military rescue operation would be considerably more difficult to carry out in a hostile country, and the Iranian regime, with its Islamic revolutionary fervor and fuming anti-American posture, seemed a natural candidate to support a terrorist venture of this kind. The game's participants were a mixture of academic experts and high-ranking officials from several countries. The game exposed the fact that there was no ready solution to the problem at hand. In the introduction to the game's summary I noted 'As an imitation of reality and a test of possible coping strategies, the game demonstrated that it is easier to declare and advocate a tough policy than to implement it in actuality under difficult conditions' [*Merari, 1979: iii*]. The Head of the US Crisis Management Team, who was in real life a senior US government official in charge of coping with terrorist crisis situations, commented in the game's summary:

> I was struck by a number of overall lessons. This scenario certainly suggested that it is very hard to devise a strategy in which there are real winners. You are trying to minimize losses by limiting the

number of lives lost, by limiting the political damage which you make from entering negotiations, by limiting the political gains of the other side. However, once a terrorist incident has taken place, you have already lost something: the possibility of a clear-cut victory for one side or the other. I was also struck, as we considered alternatives, by how very little real leverage we enjoyed. We explored a large number of diplomatic strategies; we explored in really great detail the military force option. It was pretty clear to us that these strategies offered only limited chances of success. That was the real world [*Merari, 1979: 136–7*].

Less than four months after the game, the Iranian Revolutionary Guard stormed the US embassy in Tehran. The hostages they took were released 444 days later at a considerable political cost for the United States internationally and for President Carter and his administration domestically. I am not in the position to know whether any of the game's lessons had been acted upon by the US administration prior to the crisis in Iran. The way that the crisis was handled, however, did not suggest that this was done.

To the best of my knowledge, the government of Israel has not done better with regard either to analysis in advance of key policy issues concerning terrorism or utilization of relevant academic knowledge in crisis situations. In April 1978 an Israeli soldier was captured by members of Ahmed Gibril's Popular Front for the Liberation of Palestine – General Command (PFLP-GC). The organization originally demanded the release of fewer than 30 relatively unimportant jailed terrorists in return for the soldier's release. The government tended to accept Gibril's initial demand. A group of psychologists who were consulted by the government proposed an alternative strategy of bargaining, indicating that acceptance of the initial terrorist proposition would lead to escalating demands as well as to prolongation of the bargaining process. Their advice was flatly rejected, due *inter alia*, to direct emotional pressure of the captive prisoner's family on the highest decision making authorities. The soldier was eventually released, about a year later, at a price of 76 of the worst terrorists in Israeli jails, including mass-murderers and hijackers. This was a clear case of erroneous policy, tactically as well as strategically. It was not even another example of populism. A public opinion poll indicated that 82 per cent of the Israeli population opposed the deal [*Merari and Friedland, 1980*].

Did the government of Israel learn the necessary lessons from this episode? Not at all. In May 1985 Israel released 1,150 of the worst jailed Palestinian terrorists in return for three Israel soldiers who were held captive by Ahmed Gibril's PFLP-GC.

The Government's Side

Perhaps out of courtesy to me, Dror's explanation of the cleft between government and academia put the whole blame on the former. It is my opinion, however, that, as in every interaction, both sides contribute for better or for worse. In the specific case under consideration, we should first ask ourselves what we have to offer in order to improve public policy on terrorism. At present, I am afraid it is not much. In some areas we have research tools that can be used to provide inputs that will contribute towards more rational and more effective government decisions. The answers that we already have at hand, however, are partial, tentative, and – in most cases – not sufficiently well-founded.

A considerable part of the academic writing on terrorism is simply irrelevant to government decision making. Even if one takes at face value a conclusion such as 'There is in terrorism a regression to what Freud called the "oceanic feeling" common to mysticism and to the infantile state in which self and other are not yet differentiated' [*Kaplan, 1978: 247*], it is hard to imagine how this knowledge could help the British government's struggle against the IRA, the Spanish against ETA, or the French government's fight against the tiny Action Directe. Should the ministers of interior simply pass the problem over to the ministers of public health?

In his memoirs, Sir Robert Bruce Lockhart, the Director General of the British Political Warfare Executive during World War II, wrote about the contribution of the psychologists who served on his team:

> I have an open mind about psychologists. We employed three, and one, at least did useful [work] for our German section. Psychological analysis has undoubtedly a place in political warfare, but it was not sufficiently tested in the war to justify any firm conclusions. My personal view is that in propaganda an ounce of first-hand experience of a country is worth a ton of theoretical knowledge, and this theory applies not only to our psychologists but to all the propagandists we employed [*Lockhart, 1947: 155*].

On the whole, Lockhart's amusing description seems to apply to the subject of this paper as well.

By and large, the applicability of psychological knowledge to combatting terrorism still has to be proven. There are obvious situations where psychological expertise has a significant potential contribution, for example, in bargaining with hostage takers. Even there, however, the existing literature on bargaining theory is generally inapplicable, because it is presently unequipped to deal with situations where the real issues at stake are intangible, such as prestige, propaganda value, and willingness to die [*Merari and Friedland, 1987*]. Furthermore, even a solid theoretical framework will never exempt the decision maker from the necessity of making an on-the-spot assessment of the actual situation, and generalizations about terrorist personality will never suffice to replace a direct assessment of the adversary.

I am picking on psychology because my academic roots are in this discipline; it is the subject matter I am most familiar with and, perhaps, toward which I feel responsibility more than to other disciplines. In my judgment, however, other areas in the social sciences do not differ much from the status of psychology with regard to the problem under consideration.

Conclusions and Suggestions

Academic Products

Coming to the point of conclusion, I must admit that, from the viewpoint of an academic, I have no real ground to complain in general about governments' disregard for academic wisdom on terrorism and combatting terrorism. The existing corpus of scientific knowledge about the phenomenon does not justify a more serious attitude on the part of decision makers. Before we complain that the client does not appreciate our merchandise, we must be sure that the goods are good, that the client really needs them and that he does not already have a better product that he makes on his own. With some exceptions, these conditions have not been met in the case of academic contribution to government decision making on terrorism.

The 'stoical enthusiasm' advised by Dror may be a good prophylaxis against personal disappointments, but the question remains, what can be done to enhance the contribution of academic research to policy decisions on the problem of terrorism?

A natural first step should be to identify those areas of research that should be encouraged. One might claim, of course, that all research is important in that it expands and enriches human knowledge. I have no argument with this contention, except that the subject of this study is the applicability of scientific knowledge to specific needs, rendering direct relevance a highly important criterion for evaluation. Naturally, the individual scientist ordinarily chooses his research topics by other considerations: personal inclinations, political and philosophical beliefs, experience with specific methodologies, familiarity with the subject matter, etc. It is for the government and non-governmental foundations that wish to promote the practical usefulness of research in this area to be selective in their support.

In determining what type of research should be promoted, the following criteria should be taken into account.

(1) Relevance for public policy decisions. Admittedly, what is relevant for policy decisions may, in itself, raise considerable disagreement among both academics and policy makers. Whereas for some relevance implies an immediate, practical applicability, others would claim that it is the long range, basic considerations of the problem that are more important. Undoubtedly, fundamental issues, such as moral limitations in the application of force and citizen rights versus state needs, are highly relevant to combatting terrorism. Indeed, these are subjects whose importance reaches far beyond the problem of terrorism and they merit study for their own sake. However, in the context of this study, it seems to me that in order to meet the criterion of relevance, studies should at least deal specifically with the problem of terrorism on the basis of solid factual knowledge.

(2) Relative advantage of academia over government in the particular type and area of research. Academic advantage is in the ability to conduct research more leisurely and, therefore, more thoroughly. Within their expertise, academics' knowledge exceeds at least in depth – if not in breadth – that of public servants charged with responsibility for almost any particular area. Academics also have specialized research methods and techniques that are usually not a part of the arsenal of government officials. Studies that exploit these advantages should be encouraged, rather than those that resemble Op-Ed type personal beliefs that happen to come from academics.

(3) Accessibility of data. There is no use in supporting research that is faulty from the start because it cannot reach much of the data which it is supposed to analyze. This requirement poses a special problem with regard to academic independence, at least concerning the study of terrorists and terrorist groups, since much of the raw data are not accessible to the public.

In my opinion, research areas which merit encouragement are of two main kinds:

(1) In-depth studies of the specific terrorist groups, describing ideology, motivations, structure, decision-making processes, demographic and personality characteristics, etc. The importance of studies of this kind is obvious. It should be noted, however, that due to constraints inherent in the clandestine nature of the subject matter, psychological studies in this category (for example, on terrorist personality, group dynamics, leadership patterns, etc.)

may rarely be done in accordance with the usual standards of social science methodologies and techniques. Sociological and political science studies, on the other hand, are less dependent on direct access to individual terrorists and may, therefore, be conducted utilizing mostly publicly available information.

(2) Problem-oriented studies cutting across times and places. These are basically comparative studies looking into issues such as conditions leading to escalation in the level of terrorist violence, antiterrorism legislation, the utility of deterrence as applied to terrorist groups and to terrorism-sponsoring states, factors influencing the success of amnesty programs for terrorists, political negotiations with terrorist groups, hostage negotiations, etc. Because of the comparative nature of this kind of work, it may be advantageous to encourage the establishment of joint international data bases and international study groups. It is probably in this kind of study that the relative advantage of academic research can be brought to bear.

Modes of Academic Influence

Another conclusion concerns the effective modes of academic influence, regardless of the substance of the contribution. In this regard, a differentiation should be made between two types of academic impact: indirect and direct.

It seems to me that only marginal influence can be achieved through the traditional indirect ways of conveying the results of academic research. These ways are almost exclusively limited to publications, often written in academic jargon which is incomprehensible for the public at large, in scholarly journals or books whose readership is rather small (an Israeli politician has allegedly noted that in electoral weight, one poor neighborhood is worth ten universities). Occasionally, academic experts get some exposure in the mass media. I know of no study that measured the impact of media interviews with academic experts on decision-makers and on the public at large, but I doubt that they have a crucial influence even when they whistle the same tune (which they rarely do). In my opinion, the most effective way by which academics may attain a significant influence on government policy is through direct contact with government officials. There have been cases in which influence was gained merely on the basis of personal acquaintance, but this kind of impact cannot be expected to be an institutionalized avenue. A more systematic way is to encourage joint seminars, conferences, simulations, committees etc. Even these, however, do not provide for a sustained influence. As much as I can generalize, government attenders of such events usually listen attentively and then return to their offices where they have to cope with a terrible flow of urgent problems. They do not have the time for experimenting with new ideas and their natural tendency is to sink back to the comfortable bosom of old conceptions and routines.

It seems to me that influence from within the system is, generally, more effective and sustained than from the outside. Bilateral movement from academia to government service is, therefore, a process I would recommend as the best way to maximize academic influence on policy decisions. It is, perhaps, also the best way to keep academics in touch with reality. However, considering the broader role of the academic in society, this recommendation has certain disadvantages. For one, in democratic societies it is one of the academic's duties to function as Pinocchio's cricket, that is to say, to criticize government actions and policies, especially on issues where specialized knowledge is necessary for passing judgment. In a more general way, academic contribution can not be assessed only in terms of specialized knowledge. The multiplicity of ideas, intellectual competition of thoughts, the ceaseless reexamination of old concepts are all parts of academia's role in a free, liberal society. Clearly, government service is not the best way for encouraging academic independence, which is a vital prerequisite for fulfilling these broader – albeit less tangible – social roles, although it seems to be the best way to utilize academic qualities in the service of immediate policy needs. Academia as a whole, should and can serve both needs.

Terrorism, Research and Public Policy:
An Experience, Some Thoughts

Gustavo Gorriti

This paper argues that academic researchers may be able to learn something about the practical and ethical problems of studying terrorism from the experience of journalists who have faced similar problems in trying to report on war and insurrection.

Both academics and journalists must try to get beyond the self-serving statements of the terrorists and their government opposition. Both face the difficulty and danger of trying to talk with insiders in a clandestine organization. Most importantly, both academics and journalists face complex moral issues in conducting research under conditions where the value of information can sometimes be measured in political power and human life. Under these conditions, a close relation between researcher and government represents a problematic political judgment and a practical impediment to research.

The author examines the difficulties of studing terrorism by reviewing his own experience in covering the conflict between the Shining Path insurrection and the struggling democracy of Peru. He argues that it is precisely the government most deserving of support that deserves the value of objective and critical reporting. His conclusion is that terrorism researchers should beware of any contact with government and policy makers that goes beyond teaching and publication.

This study was prepared to try to answer specific questions about the possible contributions of independent (academic and journalistic) research to policy-makers on the subject of terrorism. The questions covered the general as well as the particular level. What should be the ideal relationship between academic research and policy-making as far as terrorism is concerned? And how could or would my own research contribute in that respect?

The concerns that were first elaborated in some papers were further discussed during the seminar in Santa Fe. A number of markedly different approaches were the subject of sometimes intense but very illuminating discussions. This study reflects my attempt to address those questions.

Ethical and Practical Problems in Studying Terrorism

The besieged or beleaguered rulers call on their wise men for enlightened help. That has seldom led to the ruler's disappointment, although it is hard to say the same for the wise ones.

Then why not call the learned people to help shape public policy toward terrorism? After all, few problems would seem more in need of a close co-operation between the practical concerns of policy-making and the presumably broader and deeper interests of academic research. As in every situation in which a society feels itself under certain peril, answers and practical solutions are demanded of its thinkers. The terrorism problem, however ambiguous or abused the term may be, is no exception.

There are many fields of academic research from which policy-makers could hope for additional knowledge, advice or both. Such fields might range from psychological profiles of individual terrorists within a given violent organization to thorough research of the organization's group dynamics and/or history, to comparative research about different terrorist groups. The causes of social violence, and the circumstances that tend to diminish or smother the violent response would be of interest as would comparative studies on the effectiveness of terrorist actions as the main strategy or as part of a wider one. And much might be learned about better approaches to counter-terrorism or insurgency.

All of the above would benefit from further research. And most, if not all of them, address very concrete concerns of governments. It seems obvious to me that, in so far as terrorism is concerned, most governments that confront its threat need the fresher and deeper approach that independent academic research can provide.

There are, of course, specific forms of research which governments tend to prefer. As a rule, the more concrete and action-oriented, the better. That kind of research – from a government's perspective – is probably well illustrated by the ideal picture of, say psychologists probing the hidden spiritual injuries of captured terrorists in order to find a pattern which would allow predicting, pinpointing, and preempting. But government officials also know that any well done research in matters related to their concerns will ultimately be of help both to immediate decision-making and to longer-range policy planning. From this standpoint, government pressure on research may be felt as legitimate. To try to comply with this pressure may also be felt to be in society's best interest, especially if not doing so may mean a far greater evil than infringing on the propriety of research methods.

But I think that the important questions come the other way around: is academic research on terrorism helped or harmed by a close working relationship with a given government? In my opinion, the problem lies here: in the relationship between governments and academics on terrorism-related problems, the policy-makers have everything to gain, unless they have unrealistic expectations about the immediate application of most of the research. But social scientists, historians and otherwise bona fide intellectuals need to be wary of the potential damage of such a relationship.

If ethical and methodological problems are important issues in social research in general, particular attention should be paid to them in research that deals with insurgency and terrorism. Besides moral reasoning, these issues have to do with the quality of scholarship on terrorism, with preserving intellectual freedom, and with maintaining and, if possible, increasing a wide and varied range of sources uncontaminated by suspicions about the state security endeavors of the researcher.

The problems of government-academic relationship in this field have different forms, dimensions and relevance according to the specific type of research on terrorism. One approach is focused, individualized, in-depth research on an existing terrorist organization using essentially primary sources; the other approach is comparative historical research that relies on available bibliography. Each approach poses different problems, but it is evident that the focused, contemporary, primary source approach is where the terms of the relation of the independent researcher with a given government become a critical issue. It has several points in common with the work of a certain kind of investigative journalism, and partakes of its problems too. I will try to identify some of them, stemming from my own journalistic experience in the concrete circumstance of covering and doing simultaneous research on an ongoing insurrection.

I would like to say from the beginning that I do not pretend to have a definitive answer to several of the questions I pose. Some of them have been a permanent worry to me in my work as a journalist, and their relevance, I felt, grew in direct proportion to the depth of the specific, sensitive information which a journalist, rather than an academic, is apt to obtain. But most concerns cover ground that is, I think, common to both.

Serious research on contemporary terrorist organizations has several specific problems. It seems to be mixed – at least from the perspective of an interested journalist – with a larger output of hurried, poorly researched, or slightly disguised pamphleteer work. Probably some of the reasons are that the subject is hazardous in itself, that good reliable data are very hard to obtain, at least through standard research methods, and that the boundaries between such investigation and state security work are ill-defined. Serious research has to tread in a rather undefined and often ambiguous area, one of the most important aspects of which is the definition of terrorism itself.

Dozens of governments, with many different ways of addressing opposition, dissension, and human rights, confront some form of rebellious violence or disobedience which is often labelled as 'terrorism'. Several, if not most, of these governments have been able to enlist the help of a certain number of their psychologists, psychiatrists, social scientists, and journalists – and seldom in high-minded ways.

The participation of physicians, for instance, in investigations using torture has been documented in many countries and is one of the gravest concerns of human rights organizations and of concerned physicians too [*Amnesty International, 1984; Kirschner, 1986*]. The use of physicians has been more specialized in the USSR, at least in the *glasnost* era, with psychiatry pre-eminent as a weapon against dissent insofar as state security assumed that dissent was itself a sickness [*Jydi, 1986; Jonsen and Sagan, 1985; Reich, 1985*]. Solzhenitsyn's 'First Circle' is another account of a certain specific relationship between scientific research and state security.

Under certain circumstances, therefore, the co-operation between academic knowledge and state security (rather than public policy) is liable to become the kind of nightmare amoral science portrayed in the film 'Marathon Man'.

If we are ready to turn our attention from communist governments, that still leaves the West. The West gets a better press, at least in the West, but many Western governments are not so nice either.

Take the Argentinian generals, for instance. If we are to believe Jacobo Timerman's testimony about his imprisonment and torture at the height of the so-called 'Dirty War' (1974–79), the generals had an almost obsessive hostility toward psychologists and psychiatrists. As Timmerman [*1981*] describes, scores were brutally arrested by the then familiar heavily armed men moving about in the Ford Falcons without plates. Then the endless torture. Although paranoiac rulers tend to have lethal phobias and obsessions, there were a number of professionals (including psychologists and priests) helping to keep prisoners alive and minimally articulate, so that interrogation could go on [*Argentine National Commission on the Disappeared, 1986*]. These examples may be thought of as extreme, but they point out a relation between state security concerns and expert knowledge that is relevant when discussing the possible ways whereby academic research may contribute to policy-making options on terrorism. So, probably one of the first concerns in this field should be the ways in which academic research on terrorism might be related to expert help on the mechanisms of state security.

There are other, less harmful cases, when the interaction between a government and academics may be used as an instrument to achieve other purposes such as helping a given government to legitimize itself, or trying to influence tacitly the accepted working definition of 'terrorism'. An example may be helpful: at the end of August 1987, the Chilean Ministry of the Interior and one Chilean university organized an international conference on 'terrorism'. Among the participants was Juan Maria Bordaberry, former president of Uruguay, who handed over power to the military at the beginning of 1970, just before the height of the counter-insurgency drive against the Tupamaros. For several years after the Tupamaros had ceased to be the slightest threat, Uruguay's democracy – the longest lived in South America – was a casualty of the military. Another participant was the Peruvian retired general Luis Cisneros, an important military politician whose continuous notoriety stems from his role as outspoken advocate of the use of indiscriminate violence as the main counter-insurgency tool. He has affirmed in an interview [*Gonzalez, 1983*] that in order to defeat the Shining Path insurgency, it is not only acceptable, but probably necessary, to kill 57 innocent people among every 60 dead in order to eliminate three Shining Path cadre.

It is clear that the not too subtle purpose of the organizers of such an event was to influence the working definition of 'terrorism', stressing it as a form of warfare in the East–West confrontation, in such a way as to help legitimize at least some of the policies of the host government, which in that case meant the dictatorial rule of the Pinochet regime. They have, certainly, their own ideas about 'how the West can win', and also their own peculiar interpretation of what Western values are. Among those who think of terrorism as a shadowy and violent expression in the confrontation between communism and anti-communism, they consider themselves the pragmatic and clear-headed lot. It is also clear, however, that when they refer to state-sponsored terrorism, they are not prepared to speak about the Orlando Letelier assassination.

Moral aspects aside, there is a conceptual problem too: whether the working definition of terrorism includes state terrorism or not. If it does, the contribution of academic research on terrorism to a state that uses terrorism on its internal or external front – or co-operates with states or groups that do – becomes problematic, to say the least. To co-operate or even interact on terrorism matters with governments that themselves resort to state terrorism would mean to make an artificial distinction between the object of study (terrorism) and some of the actual policies of the government, thereby risking an almost inevitable distortion of the disciplinary approach to the subject. Intellectual perspective, distance and objectivity become compromised, and the scientific approach to the study of terrorism may well suffer in a substantial way.

As most academics and intellectuals in general regret the existence of unsavory governments – although some may consider them a necessary evil – they would probably feel the need to avoid cooperation with governments with unacceptable policies on human rights, especially governments employing terror as state policy. But even if a rough agreement is possible on what acceptable governments are (probably governments that do not torture on a systematic basis, that do not kill people without at least a previous trial, and whose rulers are elected and somehow accountable), I am afraid several problems of the government-scholar relationship still linger on.

Most of the general ethical problems of social research are relevant to research on terrorism, even under the best of circumstances. This applies especially to research on existing organizations, more than to comparative or historical research. Herbert Kelman [*1972*], who has examined at length 'the ethical problems surrounding social research with their direct implications for human freedom' points out that one of the potential sources of ethical trouble arises from the fact that 'those who produce social research – both the research sponsors and the investigators – are in a position to gain some relative advantage from it'. Government-sponsored research on terrorism is sure to try to get every possible advantage from it, or to try to make it fit specific needs. That will probably affect the research itself, especially certain aspects of it, for example interviews with members of clandestine organizations, who are unlikely to place themselves willingly at a disadvantage. Or such research may simply be hazardous to the researcher.

The problem of research on existing clandestine organizations – which is a great part of the research on terrorism – is that at some point they must be asked to open up to give information. If that request is backed by the sponsorship of a certain government, it is likely that the subjects will find it hard to make the distinction between academic and police or intelligence work. The outcome can be, at its best, a distortion of the data or the availability of information for present or future research. As this is almost self-evident, research tied to policy-making aims in the sphere of terrorism, guerrilla war and insurgency has sometimes opted to conceal totally or partially the identity of the sponsor or the aim of the research.

That kind of research means a form of involvement which departs from normal practice of social science. As Kelman [*1972*] points out, 'such involvements, however, are by no means the norm among social scientists; in some fundamental respects, they go against the norms of the social science community, particularly if they involve secrecy, misrepresentation, and violation of confidentiality'.

Another problem that pertains to both the specific and comparative approach arises from research whose methodology remains within the framework of social science, and whose findings are open, but which is formulated under the sponsorship and within the framework of concrete points of interest of a governmental agency. The ill-fated 'Project Camelot' is perhaps the classic example [*Horowitz, 1967*]. Although it may be open to discussion whether this US Army sponsored project set out to answer legitimate social science concerns, the fact is that it was perceived as a tool in the counter-insurgency efforts of the US in Latin America during the 1960s. Obviously, the outcry that ensued did not help subsequent anthropological research.

A slightly different problem arises when legitimate and open academic research carried out within an academic environment is partially or totally funded by certain government agencies. An example that comes to mind is that of Harvard professor Nadav Safran who was at the center of a controversy in late 1985, when it was disclosed that a conference on Middle Eastern Affairs he had organized was funded in part by the CIA. At that time, it was felt that not only future research in the Middle East could be harmed, but also that some of the participants of the conference would be in rather uncomfortable positions in their home countries.

The above are, to my mind, some of the problems, ethical and practical, that may accrue from the relationship between academic research and governments in terrorism-related fields. The fact that any academic research on existing organizations is bound to be conducted in proximity to other kinds of investigation, such as police or intelligence work, should be another reason to draw a careful distinction between them.[1]

It may be that in open democratic societies where the potential leverage of the government over individuals is usually limited, intellectual freedom is likely to suffer less when consulting or working for the government on terrorism-related matters, and here perhaps a case can be made that the relationships between independent researchers and governmental agencies can be more flexible. But even here the ideal of free scientific inquiry is, in general terms, much better served by maintaining a distance from policy makers and by interacting with them preferentially through the open vehicles of communication: published material, open seminars and conferences.

Reporting Terrorism: The Shining Path

I find, especially in the data gathering stages of research that involves a fair amount of fieldwork, that researchers experience many of the same problems that journalists face in a more acute and obvious form. For journalists, it is all too obvious that journalistic work and intelligence gathering have much in common. This is one of the reasons why journalism makes an excellent cover for espionage. With some kinds of journalism, such as investigative reporting, the distinction becomes even more difficult. Because of that, ethical and methodological problems of journalism have been subject to extensive elaboration, and perhaps a closer look at them could help to clarify some of the same difficulties facing academic research on terrorism *vis-à-vis* policy-making.

To maintain the crucial distinctions between journalistic and intelligence endeavors, in as clear cut a way as possible, has long been recognized by journalists as critical, not only for the profession itself but also to democratic society as a whole. Indeed, one of the ways to measure democracy in a given society is to assess the independence of journalism from government-related concerns. The ideal relationship between a democratic government and journalism should be one of creative tension, even at the risk of promoting some cases of adversary relationship. However natural this tension seems now, especially in the post-Watergate era, it should be noted that this has been more often the exception than the rule; all too often journalism has surrendered its independence in favor of interest group or government-related goals. Even the most prestigious journalism, practiced by war correspondents, has rarely had objectivity as one of its distinctions [*Knightley, 1975*].

At this point I turn to a closer examination of the Peruvian insurrection, which exemplifies many of the concerns raised in this study.

It is not necessary to look too closely at the Shining Path insurrection to realize that the Peruvian state is in great need of any help it can get. From its modest and rather incongruous beginning, the Senderista insurrection has grown, year after year, in number of actions, and in the territory and population affected by these actions. What seemed at first a crazy little war has evolved, within a relatively short span of time, into a conflict that may destroy democracy and possibly plunge the country into civil war.

Violence has already done much structural damage. The trivialization of death has been one of the consequences. The threshold of outrage, horror and shock has been raised. People are not moved anymore by single deaths, unless it is the death of a prominent individual. But, at the same time, assassinations and other forms of terror continue to fulfill their specific role; they do not scandalize anymore, but they do scare in a more personal way. Callousness and fear co-exist well together.

Still, it continues to be a peculiar war. One of its most striking aspects is the very clouded understanding of it on the part of the Peruvian state, including the military and also the non-governing Peruvian elites. Part of this difficulty is owed to the fact that the strategic horizon is much more difficult to discern in guerrilla warfare than in conventional armed conflicts; but it is more than that.

The lack of understanding of the insurrection covers both facts and concepts. There is no agreement even on who or what the insurgents are. There is widespread ignorance about the Shining Path's strategic and tactical aims, as well as about its strength, numbers, and organization – not to mention the lack of knowledge about the internal dynamics of the organization and the identities of the second and third-tier leadership. As most of this information was relatively available, it appears that at least part of the intelligence failure may have been due to honest incompetence.

So, in practical terms, the Peruvian government is in dire need of useful advice to stem the growth of the insurgency and to defeat it. As a struggling democracy, with clear credentials in that respect, groping to find a way to survive in a part of the world where democracy has generally been the exception rather than the rule, it would seem that Peru's government has indeed a moral right to ask for help, and all the more so if the alternatives seem to be nothing short of social disaster: a bloody coup and/or civil war.

There are, however, problematic aspects of the way the Peruvian State has waged counter-insurrectionary war, and practical, as well as moral and legal implications. The investigative efforts of the police, for instance, have been largely based on interrogation of captured suspects. Usually interrogations have been based on physical torture.

Some police officers have, when talking off-the-record, readily admitted the use of torture, but at the same time, they have hotly contended that in comparison to what other police forces elsewhere in the world do, they are almost philanthropic. They also affirm that there is no other way of obtaining information, and some have a standard mimicry about what an interrogation of a captured terrorist by a human rights activist would sound like. It never fails to provoke laughter among their colleagues.

On a more important level, the military's counter-insurgency doctrine has, as one of its main tenets, the physical elimination of 'subversives'. This is not written in the largely exoteric handbooks; it belongs to the esoteric part of the doctrine. Some military officers, talking very much off-the-record, defend the practice of killing captured 'subversives' as a regrettable need. According to them, a 'crystalized' communist is beyond hope of redemption.

As Peruvian law forbids capital punishment, the whole legal process was bypassed in the emergency areas, in Peru's south-central Andes, especially since the military took charge in December 1982. A military dictatorship within a democratic government was 'de facto' established. As the number of those who disappeared mounted, there were tensions and clashes between the military and some branches of the judiciary. But these were not enough to put a definitive end to the abductions and executions.[2] Because of the human rights situation, not only have the two democratic governments that Peru has had since 1980 suffered political attrition, but among a considerable number of people there is the conviction that the cause of much of the violence and suffering is the military rather than the Shining Path.

There is little doubt that the military have been the source of a great amount of gratuitous suffering, especially in the countryside, where their overall approach to counter-insurgency has been to punish rather than to protect. With civilian life so easily expendable, no great effort was made to protect even populations that had sided with the government or were relatively neutral. A comparison of the number of casualties among civilian population and security troops shows that quite clearly.[3]

So, in short, the case of Peru is that of a democracy fighting back a thinly understood insurrection by means which might have been expected to be used by a rather brutal and largely incompetent dictatorship.

That does not mean that democracy has ceased to exist. On the contrary, it remains a lively, varied, somehow chaotic and definitely confused process. The coexistence between these two incompatible ways of government frequently lends a surreal face to the nation's reality and to the insurrection too. On one hand, people have been tortured, kidnapped or killed, but on the other, the Shining Path is able (since mid-1986) to control, almost openly, a Lima daily, *El Diario*, where not only Senderista propaganda is printed, but where terrorist or guerrilla actions are described in almost a war-communique style. Gross human rights violations are perpetrated, but often an imprisoned Senderista is set free – if he or she has managed to be brought to court – by judges or tribunals, on flimsy legal technicalities or loopholes. The Shining Path's semi-legal structure has an organization of committed, full-time lawyers, who represent all their captured cadre. They are fast, well organized and feared by the judges. To put it briefly, in the countryside, an innocent villager may be killed on vague suspicion only, while in Lima an important cadre may be freed through a legal loophole. As there is everything but a common-sensical, pragmatic middle ground, democracy is eroded as much by the unthinking, brutal ways of military as by the gross ineptness of most civilian authorities.

Covering this war, clear in principle, chaotic in practice, was a very difficult task for Peruvian journalism, including the magazine I worked for, the newsweekly *Caretas*. *Caretas* is a liberal magazine, usually centrist in politics, eclectic and irreverent. It has a strong commitment to democracy, and has been closed down several times during military governments, especially during the reformist Velasco regime (1968–75). All of us who worked there knew first-hand what it was to live under a dictatorship, and felt that every effort had to be made in order to nurture democracy and make it endure. Those were not nice feelings, but very real worries.

The need to maintain certain standards of objectivity was very clear, too, even if it would mean harm to the prestige or authority of the government. So we tried in principle to divide, as much as possible, the editorial from the news reporting – never an easy thing for magazines. At the same time, when writing the news about the insurrection, we tried at every possible point to make clear who had the responsibility for beginning the insurrection, for committing the aggression against society as a whole: the Shining Path. Probably in trying to do so, we over-stepped objectivity (especially until late 1982) in the sense that we may have leaned too heavily on adjectives to the detriment of a clear analytical picture.

But even then we reported on human rights abuses, and in such a way as to leave the government no choice but to act (making inquiries, naming investigative commissions) against the perpetrators. Our pressure stepped up after the military took charge in the Ayacucho region, and it became clear that their counter-insurgency doctrine and practice was incompatible with the rule of law. We did our best to keep the pressure on the human rights issue while at the same time reporting Senderista atrocities. We also tried to help find a way out of the vicious circle of guerrilla and state terrorism.

In order to do so, we researched and wrote at length about those cases (not too many, to be sure) of successful counter-insurgencies where intelligent, democratic-inspired methods prevailed against powerful guerrilla insurrections. We tried to make both the cases of Malaysia and the Philippines (under Magsaysay) well known. The results were not very good. The military already had its own set of ideas, and had been much influenced by the Argentinian experience. Even when the Argentinian generals lost face in the Malvinas/Falklands war, they still retained influence on counter-insurgency matters.

At any rate, the killing by the military went on, especially in 1984.[4] And, as the numbers of dead piled up, we had no choice but to become much tougher in denouncing the atrocities. It became clear by then that, step by big step, the counter-insurrectionary war had lost most of the elements it had at the beginning of an embattled democracy striving to defend itself. In the multitude of small clashes, ambushes, persecutions, dragnets, interrogation rooms and killing places that constituted the war, the security forces were almost indistinguishable from those of a military presidency. Jose Maria De La Jara had said in 1981 that, no matter how many people advised him to quell the insurrection using 'wood pajamas and dynamite suppositories', he'd never do that. By 1984, De La Jara was long gone and both the sleeping garb and the medicine were the order of the day.

At any rate, the campaign against tortures, disappearance and assassinations yielded some results; from the peak of 1984, human rights abuses fell considerably by 1985.[5] I believe that the main extent of our influence was in that field. It was, as it is, a restraining influence rather than a positive one. Experience taught us to take strong and uncompromising positions towards the military on human rights and the way they discharged their duties. We didn't subscribe to their assertion that they had a specialized wisdom, with only one possible way of doing things. On the contrary, we came to the conclusion that, with few exceptions, their professional handling of the insurgency was rather inept.

In retrospect, I think that we should probably have been more critical from the beginning, not letting some tough talk and posturing pass off as convincing strategy, as effective and constitutional direction of the war effort. If we had only been better prepared at that time! Then, as a matter of principle, we probably should have made more clear the separation of our reporting from our editorial point of view and both from our preaching efforts. But then remembering how fragile we felt our fledgling democracy to be – and the great need to make it endure long enough to become an essential part of the nation's life – I can hardly see a different approach. And, of course, suggestions and preaching were done openly in our magazine's pages, as was the reporting and research, with every effort being made to gather and use it strictly on a journalistic basis. Which is , I think, as it should be.

What would have happened if the government had been able to put together a counterinsurgency strategy that was both efficient and remained within the bounds of democratic legality? I think that in that case, the government would have not deserved editorial praise but objective, independent reporting. Not even in that circumstance should the specific quality of journalism be adulterated by non-journalistic co-operation with the government's policies. Briefing government authorities, giving them the identity of sources or sensitive information not yet published, disguising propaganda as news, or using the appearance of coverage for disinformation campaigns – all of that, no matter how well intentioned, goes against the very essence of what a free press is and should be, and therefore does a disservice to democracy in the long run.

There are, of course, several cases in which a degree of cooperation between government and journalism in terrorism-related cases in necessary. It generally has to do with withholding information from publication for a period of time (usually short) because of life-threatening considerations. This holds especially true in hostage-taking situations. Moreover, I believe that a government has a limited but real right to ask journalists not to disseminate specific information which may endanger the security of its forces or the lives of individual employees. The same considerations that apply to the protection of individual sources are relevant in this case. The problem is, of course, to have clear guidelines, which in several cases – as in Israel until December 1987 – were worked out on a fairly rational and just basis.

Conclusion

As a sort of conclusion, I would say that the perceived disadvantages of maintaining a clear distance between independent (academic, journalistic) research on terrorism and government are the same disadvantages that, in a wider perspective, are thought to be the disadvantages of democracy in relation to authoritarian or totalitarian regimes. The authoritarian regime promises better social control and discipline. But the distinct advantages of a democratic approach – an independent plurality of views, a fresh look from different perspectives, the freedom of inquiry and criticism within a discipline – all add up to greater creativity and original thought that ultimately benefit the whole of society. This benefit extends to governmental organizations – who, I believe, should prize original intelligent thought, insofar as the bureaucratic milieu is not the ideal one to produce it. Open communication with independent researchers – through the accepted vehicles of publications, seminars, conferences – are bound to produce much richer overall results for policy makers than repetitive and – to borrow the expression one government official used in Santa Fe – slightly incestuous echo-talk with trusty in-house academics.

NOTES

1. A caveat here: During the Sante Fe Conference two high ranking government officials from the United States government had some rather unexpected arguments to offer from the government's point of view, in favor of academic independence. Mr David Long from the State Department argued that the result from a too close relationship with certain academic experts on terrorism had been the unforeseen institution of an 'old boys' network' of experts, where original thoughts had become the exception and predictability the rule. It was, in his perception, a rather incestuous situation.

   Mr Larry Ropka, from the Defense Department was more emphatic. He stressed that in his opinion the best way for academics to relate with government would be to maintain 'independence and distance'. That way, he added, a fresh perspective, laden with original thought would more likely emerge.

   Mr Long, however – himself an academic – had not a very high opinion of what he called the academic 'virgins', who wouldn't come closer to government than a ten-foot pole. His metaphors made it clear that if he didn't favor the intellectual equivalent of promiscuity – much less incestuous promiscuity – he wouldn't agree either with stalwart chastity. His could perhaps be called the 'once in a while' approach. Mr Ropka's position, on the other hand, held that it was a good thing for academics to keep their flower.

2. On 20 June 1984 for instance, Peru's General Attorney, Alvaro Rey de Castro, sent a very tough letter to Army General Adrian Huaman, Emergency Area Chief in

Ayacucho. Rey de Castro reminded Huaman that any excess was punishable by law. A week later, Huaman sent a personal letter to his direct chief, Army general Sinesion Jarama, complaining that Rey de Castro made his work difficult. Apparently he got additional support, in so far as most mass graves in the area were discovered in July/ August. On 28 August Huaman was removed from his command post in Ayacucho for reasons unrelated to human rights.

3. According to official figures, the number of deaths until April 1987 is as follows:

   * Armed Forces: 106
   * Police: 363
   * Civilian Authorities: 169
   * Civilians: 3,852
   * Alleged Shining Path and MRTA guerillas: 4,620

   That amounts to 9,110 violent, insurgency-related deaths. The Shining Path claims that, for the same period, the number was around 30,000. I believe that a better estimate would be of around 15,000. It has to be added, though, that most of the casualties listed as alleged Shining Path, were in fact civilians. Even the most obtuse military agree that if most of them had been Shining Path members, the rebel organization would have, for most practical purposes, ceased to exist.

4. The number of 'disappearances' (usually abductions followed by assassination) that are denounced and registered in the Generals Attorney's Office for Human Rights adds up to 2,195 until October 1986. Most of the cases occurred in 1983 and 1984.

5. For an overall appraisal of human rights in Peru, see 'Abdicating Democratic Authority'. *Americas Watch Report*. October 1984. Also, 'Peru ...'. Amnesty International Document, 1984: 'Una Nueva oportunidad para la Autoridad Democratica'. 'America Watch Report'. September 1985; and 'Informe del grupo de trabajo sobre desapariciones forzadas o involuntarias', UN Human Rights Commission, December 1986.

Worlds in Collision, Worlds in Collusion: The Uneasy Relationship Between the Policy Community and the Academic Community

Raphael S. Ezekiel and Jerrold M. Post

Both the government national security policy community and the academic community are concerned with problems of political terrorism. A major gap exists, however, between these two communities in terms of cooperation and information flow. This gap reflects differences in primary mission, role definition, professional training, and career considerations. The government practitioner's requirement for dealing with crises and producing immediate results leads to a truncated time frame which insufficiently considers long-term causes and consequences. Moreover, he tends to place overly great reliance on classified information, insufficiently attending to understandings which may derive from open sources. This is a function of role, not training, for the academic who moves from the university to the government quickly adopts the government practitioner's orientation. The academic, on the other hand, may be inhibited by career considerations from cooperating with the government, for in some institutions this would reflect negatively on tenure considerations. Moreover, he may not convey his knowledge in a manner which is responsive to the time frame and practical requirements of the government. Each of the two communities can benefit from knowledge and perspective of the other, and from an enhanced understanding of the mutual institutional constraints. Internships, government-academic exchanges, joint workshops and seminars can assist in briding the gap. Moreover, academics can make important indirect contributions by re-framing problematic questions through public commentary in print and electronic media.

Understanding the complexities of political terrorism would seem to provide a natural opportunity for fruitful collaboration between government practitioners and academics. Yet both sides of this potential partnership acknowledge there is a significant gap between government and the academy. Differences in values, knowledge, and perspective complicate the relationship. Neither community is homogeneous, of course: there is diversity of positions and attitudes among academicians and government

117

practitioners. But at the same time there are central values within each community which create tension and contribute to the gap.

Two Cultures

Tension between government and academics has always been a hallmark of such policy-relevant fields as political science and international relations. Academic experts frequently believe that their specialized knowledge and perspective can contribute to the understanding and resolution of international conflicts. Some are frustrated by their perception of a general disinterest in their ideas by government 'bureaucrats', as well as by inability to find a channel to appropriate government consumers. Others assiduously avoid any contact with the government. Potential government consumers, on the other hand, often see academics as being insufficiently attuned to 'the real world' and not appreciating the constraints within which policy-makers operate.

When questions of co-operation between academics and government practitioners arise, central political and ethical values immediately come to the fore. The position of the scholar concerned with national security matters will, of course, depend to a great extent on the nature of the government. Some scholars clearly identify with the government and full cooperation is natural and desirable. Others, who are opposed to the government in power and its policies, cannot in conscience cooperate.

Time and place matter a great deal. American social scientists generally had no reservations about working for their government during the Second World War, but were deeply alienated during the Vietnam War. The national security researcher in Israel in recent years may be in a position akin to American scholars in the 1940s. Scholars who live under authoritarian regimes may have great difficulty in associating with their governments without violating their values, and may be forced to choose isolation. Yet, as Lifton's *The Nazi Doctors* makes frighteningly clear, insofar as the government represents sentiments held within the society, even authoritarian regimes will find some scientists and academics who do not experience conflict in using their specialized skills and knowledge to further government objectives.

A further barrier to cooperation concerns the radically different professional missions of academic scholars and government practitioners. During the 1930s, those concerned with the evolution of the social sciences suggested that social inquiry which was truth-driven could arise only within democratic societies. The succeeding years have only strengthened the importance of that line of reasoning. Free inquiry into the nature of reality is radically different from inquiry which aims to assess the effectiveness of different forms of behavior manipulation; the first aims at wisdom, the second at control. Scholars and practitioners are beholden to different masters, and many academics will look askance at government work on grounds that flow from these issues.

At a more mundane level, cooperation with the government can raise career issues. In many university settings, such cooperation can indeed have negative career consequences. Devoting significant professional time and energy to advising policy officials will be seen as 'applied work' by most academic review boards and will be valued less than classical scholarship. As a consequence, a shadow can be cast over the contributions of the academic's career which will be quite costly in terms of prestige, opportunity to carry out research, pay, rate of academic advancement, and tenure decisions. The scholar involved in applied work may see a need to protect his flanks at the academy. Moreover, conducting research in a field that does not have a long and recognized history may impose additional burdens. For example, excellent research in the relatively new field of women's studies has been discounted at tenure review because of the reviewers' lack of familiarity with and doubts about the legitimacy of this field. Somehow the research seems less legitimate than research on more traditional topics.

In the policy-relevant field of political terrorism, the gap between government and the academy reflects all of these general considerations, but unique aspects of political terrorism exaggerate the discontinuity.

Terrorism, by its very nature, is time urgent. Terrorists seek to create crises in order to call attention to their cause. Since violence or the threat of violence is the terrorists' basic tactic for creating crises, it is essentially impossible for the security forces of the concerned government to ignore the terrorists. As a terrorist group or organization mounts a campaign of terror, the security forces are inevitably drawn into countering terrorism. A primary function of government, after all, is maintaining public order and safety, and the government that cannot safeguard its citizens will not be long in power.

Accordingly, policy officials will require from their intelligence organizations and security forces the information, understanding and recommendations for action necessary to contain this threat. 'Our mission', according to a senior US government official, 'is to identify, locate and eliminate terrorists. Unless I can see a dead terrorist close at hand, I lose interest.' A man with a sophisticated understanding of the societal conditions that spawn terrorism, he went on to indicate that academic research was only of *professional* interest to him to the extent that it directly supported his primary mission: 'My time span is short – I'm impatient. I need a payoff.' Another government official who had devoted most of his career to counter-terrorism indicated, 'We simply don't have time to think about the big picture.' Wryly characterizing himself and his peers as 'members of the Silver Bullet Society', he indicated that they were 'seeking the magic bullet that will stop the terrorists'. Bemoaning the preoccupation with current events, he observed that, 'thinking three months ahead is long range planning'. While these words may seem to support the academic caricature of government practitioners as bureaucratic Neanderthals, in point of fact the officials quoted were highly sophisticated professionals, representing two government departments, whose truncated action-oriented perspectives are compelled by the requirements of their roles.

Reacting to terrorist-initiated crises is a major responsibility where lives are at stake. This perspective was captured by the remarks made by the commanding general at the initiation of a US government-sponsored conference on international terrorism several years ago. He indicated he would not be able to attend the conference because he had to fly off to a classified site on 'an important mission', and threw out as a parting shot, 'It's all well and good, all this intellectual philosophizing about the origins and psychology of terrorism, but in the final analysis, remember, we've got to get the bastards before they get us.' Incidents such as the suicide bombing of the Marine barracks in Lebanon, and the kidnapping of such senior military officials as General Dozier do not discourage this attitude.

The time perspective of the academic stands in vivid contrast. The academic's form of understanding is understanding within a long-term perspective. For the academic, a given event has *meaning* only in relation to its earlier history or in relation to other events. The academic perspective is not a function of greater wisdom or heightened intellectual understanding. It is a function of role; 'where one sits is where one stands'. Indeed, when academics make the journey to the corridors of government, they quickly find themselves with a foreshortened time perspective, needing to get results, to 'solve' the terrorist problem. The pressures to get results become magnified to the extent that the terrorists are successful. Moreover, it is a truism of American politics that the longest a policy can be operative is four years, and as a presidential term winds down, and the next election approaches, the sense of time urgency increases and the need to show tangible results becomes magnified. That major arms control agreements were consummated in the last two years of the Reagan presidency is not an accident.

This difference in time perspective is a major contribution to the gap between the academic and government practitioners and bedevils attempts at working together. The policy officials, as exemplified by the government officials quoted earlier, are dealing in an extremely short – for the most part current – time span. They want short precise answers to often urgent questions. They require practical answers: Who is the responsible group? What is their motivation? Will a given action produce a favorable result? What will be the cost? What is the down side?

But the academic *can not* give a short answer to a policy maker's question – not because the academic is long-winded or pretentious, but because the short answer is in fact not an answer; as noted earlier, a given event has *meaning* only in relation to its earlier history and its political and cultural context, and the academic has not given an answer until he conveys the meaning of the event in the fullness of its context. But to interpret an act of Middle Eastern terrorism in relationship to the Assassins of the eleventh century is apt to be perceived as an act of academic terrorism by the pragmatic policy-maker.

Another special feature of political terrorism which contributes to the gap between government and academia is the sensitivity of highly classified information about terrorists, their organizations, and their decision-making. An attitude frequently encountered in government organizations is, 'If it isn't classified, it isn't worth reading'. Further widening the gap, those who hold the above attitude will often believe that since only they have access to the sensitive classified cables, only they know what is really going on, and anyone who does not have access to the same information does not really understand, and hence is not worth listening to or reading.

A mirror image of this attitude exists in the academic community. In the United States, for example, many academics believe that the government, with its vast information gathering resources, surely must have detailed information concerning the personalities, decisionmaking, goals and strategies of the broad spectrum of terrorist groups. These academics are likely to believe that if only they had access to such high quality information, their own analyses would be immeasurably enriched.

There is a major difference between the relationship of academy and government in the United States and in countries with a domestic terrorism problem. In these countries the gap is often even wider, and it is not difficult to see why. With the notable exception of the activities of the Weatherman during the 'days of rage', the concern of the United States government is almost entirely directed toward terrorism abroad. While the targets may be American, the groups of concern, be they Shi'ite fundamentalists or the Red Army Faction, are foreign.

In contrast, in countries such as Spain or Peru, the scholar may share the expressed grievances of the terrorists even if disagreeing with their method. The Basque academician, for example, may well be a strong supporter of Basque autonomy. Indeed, in so far as the grievances of the terrorist group have a basis in political reality, as the terrorism scholar absorbs himself in the world of his objects of inquiry, he may become sympathetic to his subjects, may share a degree of their adversarial antipathy to the regime. Some of these scholars may come to feel that the government, if it is not a more dangerous entity than the political group that has turned to terror, is at least an equally dangerous force. They may come to feel, 'A plague on both your houses'.

In such circumstances, the government may see the terrorism scholar as too close or too sympathetic to his subject of inquiry. A special problem can arise if the scholar's methodology relies heavily on personal contact and interviews, for in that circumstance the government may see the scholar as a potential source of information who is withholding critical security information.

Narrowing the Gap

In the above discussion, we have attempted to portray differences in missions, role requirements and attitudes within the academy and the government policy community which contribute to the barriers to fruitful collaboration in understanding and dealing with problems of political terrorism. The extremities of the attitudes portrayed are likely to per-sist and contribute to continuing tension between the communites. Thus there will always be some government practitioners who consider academics as woolly-headed intellectuals who do not understand the real world; and there will always be some academics who look down upon government practitioners as expedient *apparatchiks* who do not really understand and are not interested in understanding the complexity of the problem. Some scholars will not only refuse all conversation with the government, but in their published work will write as though the govern-ment did not exist. Nevertheless, within each community there is a diversity of views and a perceived need for closer cooperation with the other, for steps to narrow the gap.

Exchanges between the academic and policy communities can contri-bute to narrowing the gap. Some academics may choose to enter the policy community, either temporarily or permanently. If they are able to enter government at a sufficiently senior level, their insights can then contribute to policy deliberations. Moreover, they will gain a depth of acquaintance with the system which will sharpen their perspective on their return to their universities. They run the risk, however, of losing the very difference in perspective that made them potentially valuable to the policy com-munity in the first place, for a long-term sojourn in the world of crisis makes short-term thinking all too natural. Indeed, the longer the sojourn, the more indistinguishable from his government brethren the pilgrim from academe is likely to be. But the sojourn in the corridors of govern-ment for the national security policy scholar can be an extremely valuable experience. He will not only learn the constraints of the policy world, but will also become schooled in the discourse of government. For the academic to bring to government the capacity for responding to a current need while relating the immediate crisis to a more comprehensive perspective is of immeasurable value to all parties. A number of US government agencies have scholar-in-residence programs for this very purpose.

For the government practitioner to have an academic sabbatical is equally valuable. It permits him to expand his horizons and broaden his perspective, to escape the constraints previously demanded by his fire-fighting role.

Ongoing programs can facilitate the same cross fertilization advocated in the exchange of individuals between government and the academy. All too often conferences on particular policy-relevant themes are hermetically sealed. Thus Middle Eastern scholars may discuss Islamic fundamentalism in one academic center while an 'in-house' conference of government experts may discuss the very same topic in a government conference center. While to be sure there are efforts to promote conferences that facilitate exchanges between academicians and the government, the general problems addressed in this contribution as well as the particular considerations applying to terrorism interfere with fully open exchanges. For example, the problem of access to sensitive classified information contributes in no small way to the persistence of barriers to such mutual exchanges. On the one hand, a large measure of enhanced understanding and useful exchange could occur between the academic and government communities on the basis of open information. This is particularly true of contextual understanding and mid-range and long-range trend analysis. Yet current intelligence will often crucially depend upon sensitive information which must, by its nature, be restricted in its dissemination. The need to place current evaluations in a more comprehensive perspective argues for increasing the pool of academic experts with security clearances as a further way of narrowing the gap.

In particular, there is a need for the academic consultant who remains clearly anchored in the academy but is able to draw on his expertise to assist the policy maker confronting crises as well as long-range problems. The greater the degree to which this is an ongoing relationship rather than only crisis-oriented, the more useful the consultant role will be. This requires learning on both sides. The academic consultant must be able to respond in such a way as to assist the policy-maker in his dealing with his real-world problems. He must be able to demonstrate an understanding of the policy-makers' needs and be able to see the world through his eyes. The manner in which he gives counsel can carry an educational message. Even more important than the answers given may be the questions asked in clarifying the nature of the problem, for these may help the policy official reformulate his problem. And the consultant must be able to be discreet in the conduct of his role with relation to his own colleagues in the academy.

The government official, on the other hand, cannot expect the consultant to be fully useful without providing him with a context of substantive information and the policy constraints. All too often answers are sought without a thorough examination of the complexity of the question. This kind of communication requires an atmosphere of trust which can only develop over time. Some government organizations have developed interdisciplinary panels of academic experts with security clearances who can provide ongoing counsel. They will meet periodically as a group and be available as individuals to respond to particular problems in their areas of specialized expertise.

There is a spectrum of roles which can usefully contribute to narrowing the gap between the academy and the government. An important role within this spectrum is that of writer/commentator. This is a step removed from policy, but is a role to be considered for academics who do not wish to have a direct involvement with the policy community. To influence the public's or the government's perception of a problem by one's writings is a traditional academic role. It is not glamorous and the probability that a particular book or article will have impact is quite low – most disappear without a trace. The rare exception, however, can catalyze extraordinary shifts in perspective and provide a new paradigm: Kennan's article on containment, Rachel Carson's *Silent Spring*, Michael Harrington's *The Other America*. The writings of serious students of social reality can, over time, lead members of a society – at all levels – to see an issue that was not seen before or to see an issue in a new fashion. Members of the policy community who have never met the writer in question will find themselves crafting policy answers to fit a situation that has been defined for them by the author. In effect, the policy community will absorb from the culture the definitions and interpretations that now have become 'obvious', 'self-evident', and 'matter of fact'. Thus, if the academic does have an impact, it can be significant. One will be framing the question and building the context in which the policy choices are made. No one is more powerful than the person who frames the question and – over time – academic scholars who make their thinking accessible can create the lenses through which the public and the government construe reality.

This intellectual task can be carried out by writing books and articles, by lecturing and by appearing in the media. Especially for the young scholar without a national reputation, gaining access to the written and electronic media channels is difficult, and it will usually be necessary first to develop a reputation in the academic community and a corpus of policy-relevant writing in scholarly journals.

A related form of influence derives from working with non-governmental groups. Social scientists can and have contributed to non-governmental constituencies which in turn have influenced the political agenda. The civil rights movement and the anti-war movement come at once to mind.

The last two roles we have mentioned – working with non-governmental organizations and working as a writer/intellectual – particularly fit the orientation of what we may term the anarcho-skeptical wing of the academy. The anarcho-skeptics may suspect that government by its nature can not translate intention to outcome effectively. (Recall Tolstoy's musings in *War and Peace* on the lack of connection between the intentions of generals and what occurred on the field of battle. A more recent statement of the same point is Tuchman's *The March of Folly*.) History, for the anarcho-skeptic, has little to do with the direct intentions of policy-makers, so that it does not seem profitable to devote inordinate energy to fine tuning their efforts.

A related set of perceptions can make the academic both pessimistic and wary of the attempt to influence policy through personal contact. It can seem unlikely that the individual academic can influence the course of government, with its considerable organizational history and momentum; the skeptic may pardonably suspect that rather more influence, however subtle, is likely to flow in the opposite direction.

Concluding Thoughts

While there will always be a gap between the academy and government, steps can be taken to narrow the gap. A major contribution to the magnitude of the gap is the lack of knowledge in both government and academy about each other's worlds. The roles sketched out above can contribute to a mutual education process.

Any initiatives that increase the knowledge of one another's worlds will be useful and all forums which contribute to interchanges between these worlds are to be encouraged. Government and foundation support for workshops and symposia which facilitate such exchange should be given high priority. In such forums personal links develop which in the long run play a major role in breaking down barriers between these communities. It is at least as important to transmit extant knowledge in both directions across the government–academic gap as it is to sponsor new research.

A final note: policy actions in this area affect human lives, and choices will have ethical implications. Sober consideration is appropriate as individuals consider their roles, the nature of their involvement and the extent of their co-operation. At an institutional level, wisdom must be the goal, and this goal calls for the fullest possible interchange of perspective and knowledge between the academic and policy communities.

Terrorism, Research and Public Policy: An Overview

Clark McCauley

Two major problems involved in defining *terrorism* are reviewed: the degree to which the term conveys a negative evaluation rather than an objective description of behavior, and the possibility that the range of behaviors referred to under this term is so diverse as to make the category useless for research purposes. It is argued that a tight definition of terrorism is not necessary in order to begin to learn from prototypic examples of the category. Then a number of generalizations from recent research are considered; these are relatively simple but have not always been obvious. Together these generalizations indicate that policy-makers might usefully consider the potential value of a 'no-response response' to terrorist challenge. Finally, a number of suggestions for future terrorism research are offered.

As noted in the introduction, there are two major issues addressed in this volume: whether terrorism represents a coherent research topic and how researchers may best contribute to policy-making in dealing with terrorism. Seminar discussion of the proper relation between terrorism researchers and policy-makers is well represented by Ezekiel and Post (this volume). There remains the question of the problematic status of *terrorism* as a research category, and I begin with an overview of seminar discussions of this issue. I also bring together from the seminar a number of generalizations from recent research that can inform policies aimed at fighting terrorism, and I end with some suggestions for future research on terrorism. This overview is of course my own interpretation of the seminar papers and discussions; any value in this interpretation depends upon the contributions to the seminar, but the seminar participants are not responsible for what is made of their work here.

Terrorism as Category

The issue of definition arose almost immediately in discussion of the study by Joseba Zuleika, a study that protests vigorously against the experts who sought to understand Basque violence as an example of terrorism. It is worth being clear about the nature of this protest, which reflects two concerns that may usefully be distinguished. One is a matter of evaluation:

to call an act of violence terrorism is unavoidably an evaluation of the act as unacceptable, unjustified, and wrong. Correspondingly, to call a person a terrorist is to evaluate the person as unacceptable, unjustified, and bad. I understand Zulaika to be protesting that this kind of evaluation gets in the way of useful understanding of both the behavior and the person. The second concern is the usefulness of the category of terrorism as a social science construct: does it assert a unity that does not exist, as did the now-debunked category of witchcraft?

Terrorism as Illegitimate Violence

Consider first the negative evaluation tied to the label of terrorist. It is rare that a group called terrorist has been proud to call itself terrorist; the last to do so may have been the Zionist Stern Gang of the late 1940s. Those who perform acts of violence for political ends prefer to call themselves liberators, guerrillas, freedom-fighters, or an army. If the term terrorist implies a negative evaluation, a summary judgment of illegitimate use of violence, then it can be argued that any study of terrorists must fail that begins from the use of this term. Whatever else it might do, such a study cannot let us understand the world as the terrorist sees it; the legitimacy of their cause is the premise of the terrorists' world and the justification of their violence.

Experienced terrorism researchers at the conference were confident that they could and did use the word terrorist without evaluation. Israeli Professor Ariel Merari, for instance, pointed out that his catalog of terrorist incidents around the world includes the incidents in which Israeli agents in Europe attempted to retaliate against Palestinians for the massacre of Israeli athletes in Munich in 1972. He also noted that Israeli and American scholars with no sympathy for the Palestinian Liberation Organization did not shrink from recognizing recent Israeli leaders Menachem Begin and Yitzak Shamir as former anti-British and anti-Arab terrorists. Similarly Martha Crenshaw, an American who wrote her Ph.D. thesis on the terror with which the Arabs of Algeria finally evicted the French, makes no judgment against their political legitimacy in calling the Algerians terrorists.

The issue of evaluation became more cómplicated, however, when the visitors from Washington joined the discussion. From the Pentagon, the State Department and the FBI, these men were confidently and deliberately making a value judgment in describing people as terrorists. Fighting and killing terrorists was the business of one (Larry Ropka), negotiating international agreements that will make terrorists international outlaws was the business of another (David Long), and forestalling and apprehending terrorists in the US was the business of the third (Richard Marquize).

It is interesting that the State Department is charged with determining which groups are and are not terrorists, in the everyday application of the trade statute that forbids most-favored nation status to nations supporting terrorism. Someone in the State Department is responsible for sitting down with a pencil and a list of all the world's nations, and putting x's next to the bad guys. This unenviable responsibility is linked to another: to determine a definition of terrorism that can be internationally agreed to, such that as many nations as possible will agree to prosecute and deny haven or support to individuals who are members of terrorist groups.

The model for international agreements, as David Long explained at the conference, is the agreement among civilized nations against chemical and biological warfare (CBW). Just as certain kinds of means are not acceptable in war, certain kinds of means are not acceptable political protest. This model encounters two notable problems.

The first is that conventions against chemical and biological warfare have not been conspicuously successful, at least not with regard to wars in and between less developed nations. Iraq evidently used chemical warfare against Iran and against Kurdish dissidents within its own borders, and has threatened Israel with a chemical attack should Israel strike against Iraqi nuclear facilities. Libya has been accused of building, with German assistance, a large plant to manufacture chemical weapons. The Angolan government and its Soviet allies have been accused of using chemical weapons against the UNITA rebels [*Bernstein, 1989*]. It appears, then, that restraint in the use of chemical and biological weapons tends to fail in conflicts where smaller nations see themselves as fighting a war for survival against a stronger enemy. But desperate war against a stronger enemy is precisely the outlook of the terrorist group fighting against established authority.

The second problem with international agreements against CBW as a model for agreements against terrorism is that, whatever the problems of the CBW agreements, they do at least admit of an objective definition of what it means to use a chemical or biological weapon. Evidence of a particular chemical, for instance, can be controversial – as illustrated by the difficulty of distinguishing residue of chemical weapons from 'bee droppings' in Vietnam – but at least the chemical sought has an objective existence and the possibility of objective demonstration. Terrorism may be as much in the chemistry of the perceiver as in the behavior of the perceived.

Attempts to provide objective definition usually focus on the use of violence against non-combatants, especially women and children. The definition offered by the US State Department is 'premeditated, politically motivated violence perpetrated against non-combatant targets by subnational groups or clandestine state agents, usually intended to influence an audience'. Except for the attribution to subnational groups or secret agents, this is a definition that fits much of conventional warfare. War in populated areas, strategic bombing, city bombing such as the Second World War attacks on London, Hamburg and Tokyo – all of these unavoidably kill non-combatants. Guerrilla war is unavoidably terrorism in the same sense – men, women, and children with no interest beyond personal and family survival will be killed in a test of wills. The State Department was not eager to label the Contras' war against the Sandinistas as terrorism, but it did kill non-combatants. So does the African National Congress in its conflict with both white and black enemies in South Africa.

Nor does the intention to influence a wider audience discriminate war from terrorism. War is 'politics by other means' for which the primary audience is the enemy. The goal of war is not simply inflicting casualties – US generals from Grant onward have been criticized for having no strategy beyond attrition – but to break the enemy's will to resist. The Tet offensive, for example, was a disaster for the National Liberation Front in terms of casualties – the Vietcong were broken as a fighting force and had to be replaced with North Vietnamese regulars – but Tet nevertheless succeeded in undermining US willingness to fight further in Vietnam.

In short, the trouble with the State Department's definition of terrorism is that, taken seriously, it makes much of modern nation-state war into terrorism. Whatever the success of terrorism researchers in making terrorism an objective and analytic category without moral implication, policy makers for nation states must judge violence as a means in relation to a particular end, since they will not judge violence as categorically unacceptable. Not only policy-makers but most major religions have some theory of what constitutes a just war [*Dugard, 1982*].

It follows that researchers and policy makers will often use the same word to talk past one other as their two cultures collide (Ezekiel and Post, this volume). The researchers will use the term terrorist as a research category while the policy makers use it to express evaluation; each side is likely to forget that the other attaches a different meaning to the word. The cost of this failure of communication will be, at a minimum, that the policy makers will be less able to see terrorists as terrorists see themselves and less likely to profit by research on non-criminal behavior that can help understanding of terrorist behavior. Several research directions that may have been thus under-attended to are suggested in the third section of this overview. In addition to research forgone, there may be more dramatic costs. As Wheeler (this volume) points out, one cost of seeing terrorism as illegitimate violence is that a military schooled for conventional violence can remain dangerously innocent about the threat of unconventional violence. US casualties in the suicide bombing of the Marine barracks in

Beirut called forth no courtmartials for negligence, but only an attribution that denied any military responsibility – the attack was not war but *terrorism*.

Terrorism as Research Category

Consider now the value of terrorism as an analytic category for terrorism researchers. The goal of any category for purposes of theory building is to put together instances of behavior that are similar in some way that permits order and understanding. Quarks are postulated to interpret patterns of cause and effect in high energy physics. Measles is a category that makes sense of a common pathogen and pattern of illness. It is the success of theory, especially understanding in terms of cause and effect, that is the warrant and validation of a scientific category.

From this point of view, debate about how to define terrorism is debate about how best to get to useful theory. At the simplest level of description, terrorism is group violence against another group. Conventional warfare, guerrilla war, gang war, and riots are all terrorism by this definition, which will be useful to the extent that the origins and explanations of all these kinds of behavior are the same. A narrower definition would require that the group violence be against non-combatants of another group. Now the bombing of Hamburg is terrorism, but trench warfare is not; gang war, guerrilla war and riots may or may not be terrorism. Still narrower would be a definition that requires that the violence be aimed against or in defiance of the authority of the state: terrorism from below, rather than terrorism from above. Now the bombing of Hamburg is not terrorism; gang war and riots may still be terrorism. To move in the other direction, toward a more liberal definition, terrorism may be defined without violence, as group behavior that consciously violates and challenges the larger political culture in which the terrorists operate. Now some cults are terrorist groups.

Each of the definitions above corresponds to a hypothesis about what concatenation of instances will prove to have useful similarities in terms of understanding behavior. There is no need to choose among these definitions until there is rather more evidence than now available concerning the quality of theory to emerge from each.

Another way of thinking about the problem of definition is to recognize that arguments over definition tend to be based on a classical view of categories as defined by necessary and sufficient conditions. Research in cognitive psychology [*Rosch, 1975*] suggests that human beings do not represent categories as sharp-boundaried and sufficiently defined, but rather have 'fuzzy' categories represented as a prototype or exemplar against which instances are compared as better or worse examples of the category. This perspective argues against debating the exact location of category boundaries. Probably all researchers can agree that violence by a small group against non-combatants associated with the authority of the state is terrorism; no one, for instance, seems to deny that West Germany's Red Army Fraction are terrorists. The narrower definitions of terrorism can be recognized as efforts to specify the prototype of terrorism while yet recognizing that the boundaries of terrorism as research category can only be argued on the basis of competing theories.

As noted in the Introduction, the evolutionary perspective shared by Sprinzak (this volume) and Crenshaw (this volume) offers at least the beginning of an answer to the doubts raised about terrorism as a research category. Sprinzak's is a theory of the psychological trajectory from conventional political opposition to terrorist behavior, whereas Crenshaw's is a theory of the life-cycle dynamics of groups that have reached the extremity of terrorism. At the individual level, then, it may be the common experience of individuals moving to conscious violation of social norms about aggression – the trajectory that ends with using atrocity as a means – that makes sense of studying terrorists as a category. And at the group level, it may be the common pressures of competition within and without the group – competition for sympathizers, for supporters, and for recruits in interaction with government response – that makes sense of studying diverse groups as species of the genus *terrorism*. Both theories may need further specification and more explicit comparison with the detailed histories of terrorist individuals and groups, but they have at least the advantage of speaking to Zulaika's concern that *terrorism* is an empty category.

Policy Implications of Research on Terrorism

Recent research on terrorism, as represented in this volume, leads to a number of generalizations with implications for anti-terrorist policy. Although the generalizations are relatively simple, they have not always been obvious. As presented here, the first few are relatively non-controversial reporting from the seminar whereas the later ones reflect more editorial interpretation and conclusion.

Anti-terrorist policies are aimed at enemies who are normal human beings. The easiest reaction to behavior that we do not understand is to call it crazy. The next easiest is to call it fanatic. These were the initial reactions to people who would risk their own lives to highjack planes, plant bombs and kill women and children without remorse. Psychiatrists in particular were called upon to provide understanding of these crazed criminals. Recent research however, is turning away from attempts to understand terrorism as the product of individual pathology. This is not to say that there is no pathology among terrorists, but the rate of diagnosable pathology, at least, does not differ significantly from control groups of the same age and background [*McCauley and Segal, 1987*]. Certainly there are terrorists who like the thrill of violence or actively enjoy hurting people, and these may even be specifically recruited for some kinds of terrorist act. But if these disturbed individuals were the sole or even major support of terrorism, terrorism would not be a problem.

Rather it is the case that terrorism is the work of normal persons [*Sederberg, 1989; Taylor, 1988*]. Terrorism has appeared often in recorded history – Jewish *sicarii* of the first century, Shi'ite Assassins of the twelfth century, Russian Narodnaya Volya of the late nineteenth century – and may usefully be considered as the warfare of the weak (Wheeler, this volume) and an outgrowth of normal opposition politics (Sprinzak, this volume). Still, there are centuries of history without report of terrorism, a record that gives hope that terrorism is episodic and situational rather than continuous and inevitable. It is to the social and organizational situation of terrorists, perhaps especially their intense small group dynamics, that research is turning now to understand how normal human beings become capable of terrorist violence. Most of us are capable of acts of violence in the right situation, or armies could not function.

Anti-terrorist policies are coping strategies, not solutions: The evidence of centuries (Wheeler, this volume) and of recent decades (Crenshaw, this volume) combine to indicate that terrorism is a problem with no solution. Threatening and killing noncombatants by groups too small to fight conventionally has been going on for a long time, goes on today, and will no doubt go on tomorrow. There is no vaccination that will prevent terrorism. There is no magic bullet or smart bomb that will kill only terrorists. Realistically the most that can be hoped for from an anti-terrorist policy is a decrement in terrorist activities and a decrease in losses to terrorism.

This ameliorist perspective is important in arguing against heroic policies to control terrorism, in particular against policies of great expense or large interference with personal liberties. Whatever it might be worth to put an end to terrorist threat, the likelihood is that no government policy can achieve this end. To take a recent example, there is little likelihood that the security of air travel can be significantly increased by the thermal neutron analysis machines that the Federal Aviation Administration (FAA) directed US carriers to install at airports. These machines are to detect plastic explosives of the kind that brought down Pan Am 103 in Scotland in 1988. Initial testing suggests 95 per cent detection probability with less than five per cent false alarms. If there are 100 bombs among the ten billion bags that pass through US airports annually, then there will be about five million false alarms each year for every bomb detected [*Speer, 1989*]. The costs of the system and its false alarms must be weighed against the size of the problem – 2,015 dead worldwide from terrorist attacks on commercial aviation in the last 20 years, 700 in the last four years [*Pletka, 1989*] – and against the likelihood that the technology of the terrorists can also be upgraded.

The ameliorist perspective is not only negative, however. The history of terrorism since the Second World War (Crenshaw, this volume) indicates that terrorists seldom succeed in overturning a government, unless they are part of a broad-based struggle for independence that enjoys some outside support (as happened in Algeria, Israel, and Vietnam). Terrorists occasionally can provoke a reaction that amounts to replacing civilian government with military government; the Tupamaros in Uruguay and the Montoneros in Argentina were destroyed after successes of this kind. Perhaps most important is the recognition that there are life-cycle dynamics for terrorist organizations just as for any human organization. Terrorist groups decline as much by disintegration from organizational problems and loss of outside support as by any government action. From this point of view it is indeed a major success if a terrorist group simply survives. The great majority apparently do survive, for five years or more (Crenshaw, this volume). In worldwide perspective, however, in the scale of threats to government and to the lives and welfare of citizens, terrorism is more persistent than dangerous – more like a cold virus than an AIDS epidemic.

Anti-terrorist policies can be more dangerous to government than to terrorists: Additional support for the ameliorist perspective comes from consideration of the costs of anti-terrorist policies. Whereas the success of such policies is problematic, the costs are frequently all too clear and certain. In the example above, the hundreds of millions of dollars to be spent for new bomb detectors ($750,000 to $1 million apiece) are dollars not spent addressing other problems, including pressing problems of health and welfare.

Beyond the dollar costs of the detectors, however, are what Dror [*1983*] calls 'second-order consequences' of terrorism that can be higher yet. An example is the division between the US carriers and the Federal Aviation Commission over who should pay for the detectors, the taxpayer or the airline [*Pletka, 1989*]. The FAA maintains that security is a cost of business for the airlines, to be passed on to the passenger. The airlines maintain that if, as US corporations, they are subject to terrorist threat that their foreign competitors are not, then the US government must pay the cost of the extra security or else pressure foreign airlines to install the same machines. Otherwise the US carriers will suffer a competitive disadvantage in the costs of doing business. The division of interest between the airlines and the FAA on this issue, or perhaps between US diplomacy and the diplomacy of other states on the same issue, is a second-order consequence of the downing of Pan Am 103.

Second-order consequences of terrorism, as the example illustrates, are the political consequences for the government of its own response to terrorism. These will typically include increased friction and division within the nation, distraction from other problems pushed lower on the agenda of public issues, and conflict of interest with other nations affected by the policy. Policies that increase the surveillance and police powers of the government undermine individual freedom, democratic institutions and the legitimacy of government. Policies of violent retribution against terrorists undermine restraints against the use of violence both nationally and internationally, and are likely to contribute to a tit-for-tat upward spiral in the level and indiscriminateness of violence. A recent study by Thompson [1989] has shown just this kind of pattern in the year by year record of political killings in Northern Ireland from 1922 to 1985.

Taken together, the financial, social, political, and moral costs of response to terrorism constitute a challenge to the democratic capacity to govern [Dror, 1983]. Especially for the more fragile democracies of the world, these costs can lead to crisis. Peru faces this crisis now in responding to the terrorism of the Shining Path; the danger is that the erosion of civil rights in fighting a well-organized rebellion will leave no Peruvian government worth fighting for (Gorriti, this volume). Even for more robust democracies, the indirect consequences of responding to terrorism may be more costly than the direct costs.

Anti-terrorist policies are communications to diverse audiences, with diverse effects: A terrorist act can be understood as a form of communication and much has been made of the symbiosis of modern terrorism and the mass media. Clutterbuck [1981], for instance, describes the television camera as a weapon waiting to be picked up. It is surely too much to say that terrorism depends on the mass media: terrorism existed before the mass media (Wheeler, this volume) and there are modern instances of terrorist successes without access to the mass media (Vietnam, early years of the Shining Path in Peru). But there can be little doubt that terrorists often seek to use the mass media to multiply the impact of their bombings, highjackings, or assassinations.

Concern over terrorists' successes in using the mass media has led to suggestions that governments need to learn how to turn the camera as a weapon against terrorists. Britain has controlled what can be seen of the

IRA on British television [*Bering-Jensen, 1988*], for instance, but this kind of policy cannot go very far if a free press is to be maintained.

Perhaps a better way to use the mass media against terrorism begins where the terrorists do: with action. Anti-terrorist policies are actions that are in a formal sense parallel to terrorist acts. They are communications to the same audiences: competing terrorist groups, the sympathizers from whom terrorists need support and recruits, the victims of terrorist acts and their relatives and sympathizers, and the governments and citizens of other nations supporting, ignoring, or combatting terrorism [*McCauley and Segal, 1987*].

A terrorist group is only the apex of a pyramid of supporters and sympathizers. The relatively few terrorists depend on the much larger numbers below them in the pyramid in many ways – for information, refuge, money, silence – and most particularly for recruits. The Red Army Fraction of West Germany was and is a very small group, but thousands turned out for the funeral of RAF leader Ulrika Meinhof. Most sympathizers are at a low level of commitment at the base of the pyramid, with increasing levels of commitment associated with smaller numbers higher up.

The pyramid of terrorists and their sympathizers stands in opposition to another (and usually much larger) pyramid composed of the policy makers and their supporters and sympathizers. The two pyramids – the terrorists' and the policy-makers' – are competing for the allegience or at least the recognition of a third group of people who have no particular sympathy for either; these non-aligned are the neutral ground on which the two competing pyramids are raised. The more robust the legitimacy of the state, the fewer will be found in this neutral ground and the more will be found in the pyramid headed by the policy-makers.

Even this picture is too simple. There are often multiple terrorist groups competing for the same sympathizers, that is, more than one apex of the same pyramid. Terrorist groups are often in conflict with one another for the same sympathizers, as for instance in Northern Ireland and among Palestinians. Policy-makers of a single government are often divided into factions in conflict for political power, as for instance in the US with Democrats and Republicans or in Israel with parties who would or would not transport all Palestinians out of Israel. Further, the competition of terrorists and policy makers takes place in an environment that includes the policy makers, supporters and neutrals of other nations, whose policies and outcomes are to greater or lesser extent bound up with those of the nation challenged by terrorism.

These different pyramids and even the different levels of the same pyramid represent importantly different audiences in that they will have diverse reactions to a particular policy. Different audiences will attend to different parts of the same communication, whether that communication is terrorist act or government response. Even when attending to the same communication, different audiences will have diverse interpretations and evaluations. The meaning of either terrorist act or government response is therefore not one but manifold, depending on the audience.

For policy-makers, evaluation of a proposed anti-terrorist policy requires predicting and weighing the reaction of each audience. In comparing possible responses to terrorist challenge, it is the integration of effects over the relevant audiences, perhaps weighting each effect by the importance of its audience, that indexes the expected value of each policy.

Determining this expected value is anything but easy. Consider the decision to send US fighter-bombers to Libya in what was designed as a 'surgical strike' against Khaddafi in retaliation for his support for terrorist groups striking at US citizens. In the event, Khaddafi was not killed but a stray bomb killed about a hundred residents – including women and children – of a residential area near Khaddafi's home. Without trying to decide whether this was a net gain for US security, it is clear that the effect of this strike was different for different audiences. The strike appears to have been popular with the American public, but probably strengthened Khaddafi's hand in Libya – and perhaps in other Arab nations – by providing local confirmation of the US as the international terrorist bandit Khadddafi had been inveighing against. It would be hard to tell a relative of the dead children that Khaddaffi is wrong and the US is right. The reaction of the European nations appears to have been a bit of a surprise to US policy-makers: European governments were encouraged by the US strike to move toward increased international cooperation in tracking and arresting terrorists. The point of this example is not that US policy-makers should have been able to predict who would be killed, or the reaction of each of the diverse audiences. Rather the point is the difficulty of this sort of prediction, a difficulty that can at least be recognized by trying to identify all the relevant audiences for an anti-terrorist policy.

Whatever the difficulty of comparing the expected value of different policies, once policy-makers have come to a decision they can legitimately ask for mass media coverage of the announcement of the policy and the rationale for it. The government reaction is news in the same sense that a terrorist act is news; against the terrorists' 'propaganda of the deed' can be opposed a 'propaganda of response to the deed'. Of course anti-terrorist policy will not usually generate the suspense or the striking visual images of death and destruction that terrorist acts can provide, but policy-makers can call on journalists and broadcasters to represent the public's need to know in a way that is not reducible to entertainment value.

In order to pursue this kind of anti-terrorist policy-making to maximum effect, a program of extensive public opinion research would be needed to predict the diverse reaction of diverse groups to a proposed policy. Policy makers are likely to think they can guess the response of the constituencies they represent, and these may indeed be the most important to political survival. But an anti-terrorist policy aimed at more than domestic political success must be determined and communicated with an eye to many other constitutencies, including the terrorists' sympathizers. Thanks to superior resources for conducting opinion research, policy-makers should be better able than terrorists to gauge the effects of both terrorist acts and anti-terrorist policies.

The no-response response to terrorism can be an active and effective anti-terrorist policy: A question that re-appeared a number of times during the seminar, in the midst of discussions of a variety of issues, was whether or when doing nothing in response to a terrorist challenge might actually be the best policy. This issue came to be referred to in shorthand as the question of the no-response response, and there was some argument that this alternative should be taken more seriously.

The no-response response that is to be taken seriously is one that is an active and public decision that is announced with the same status and attention to diplomacy that would be associated with a decision to strike back at a terrorist threat. A long political wrangle over how to respond, ending in failure of leadership to reach any agreement or decision, is a lack of response but is not the no-response response of interest here. Rather than being a failure of leadership, doing nothing can be an active accomplishment of successful leadership, in the same way that avoiding the promotional leadership that conduces to groupthink is an active accomplishment of successful leadership [*Janis, 1982; McCauley, 1989*]. Doing nothing also does not mean giving up on regular police and intelligence work under existing laws; it means doing nothing new, nothing different from what the same threat or violence would provoke if perpetrated by criminals without political purpose.

The obvious advantage of the no-response response is that it does not have the direct costs of some major initiative against terrorism, whether that initiative be a retaliatory strike, a new military or police force, new law, or new technology. The resources of time, effort, and money that such intiatives require are saved. Perhaps more important, much of the second-order consequences of a government response to terrorism can be avoided. Opportunity costs are avoided. The friction, division, and distraction from other issues that are introduced when attempting to divert limited resources to an anti-terrorism initiative – these are avoided. By comparison with any increase in police powers, the loss of individual liberty and the undermining of democratic institutions are avoided. By comparison with any kind of violent retribution, a further undermining of restraints against violence is avoided. This last savings looms particularly large in the light of the possibility that violence of any kind is one important cause of subsequent violence [*Thompson, 1989*].

Note that the argument is that *much* of the second-order cost of a government initiative against terrorism is avoided. Not all of the indirect cost can be avoided because an active prosecution of the no-response response does require the attention and effort of policy-makers in communicating their decision as an expression of confidence rather than an admission of weakness. In addition there are pressures for better security measures and for retribution from grieved and outraged relatives and friends of terrorist victims; these must be heard and acknowledged, but without permitting them to become the determinants of policy.

One way to do this requires policy-makers to admit frankly that the power of the US is not now and perhaps never has been great enough to guarantee all noncombatant citizens from risk of political violence. The doctrine of mutual assured destruction, for instance, makes every American citizen a hostage to the restraint of the US and the USSR in use of nuclear weapons. Furthermore it can be pointed out that political violence is only one of the costs of a free society: drugs, prostitution, gambling, AIDS, and even traffic fatalities are all part of this cost [*Horowitz, 1983*]. Traffic accidents offer a particularly striking comparison: statistically, the riskiest part of air travel – including the risk of terrorist attack – is the ride to the airport. Government policy could cut auto deaths to near vanishing, by requiring auto manufacturers to produce cars that cannot exceed 25 miles per hour, for instance, or by enforcing speed limits of 25 miles per hour. There is no danger of such a speed limit, because the costs are large and obvious. The argument for the no-response response is that the costs of trying to guarantee citizens against terrorist violence are less obvious but potentially much larger.

In short, there are significant second-order costs to non-response; it would be a long term and serious challenge to policy makers to communicate the case for the no-response response to their citizens. To maximize effectiveness, the communication would have to begin long before the terrorist challenge for which the no-response response is appropriate. And the nature of this communication would need to be informed by opinion research, as noted above, that can predict the reactions of the diverse audiences who will evaluate the no-response response to terrorism.

In addition to avoiding direct and indirect costs at home, the no-response response has a number of significant advantages as a weapon against terrorists. It cannot miscarry to bring violence against terrorist sympathizers or the uncommitted, who will react with increased support for the terrorists. It seizes the moral high ground by recognizing that noncombatant victims of terrorist violence are martyrs for the legitimacy of the state in the same way that terrorists are martyrs against the state. This advantage may be more powerful than the attention usually accorded it; the legitimacy and popularity of the IRA were re-invigorated – some would say resuscitated – a few years ago by IRA men whose hunger strike became a fast to the death in a British prison [*Beresford, 1988*]. More generally, there is research to show that minorities are most persuasive to majorities when they persevere in a position that goes against immediate self-interest [*Moscovici, 1985*]. Even without research, it seems likely that majority positions too are more persuasive to the extent that they are seen to serve principle rather than self-interest.

Another important advantage of the no-response response is that it deprives the terrorists of recognition as an enemy, a recognition that Post [*1986*] emphasizes as an important source of identity and self esteem for the individual terrorist. At the group level as well, government reaction confers status on the terrorist group. This status can be important in competition with other groups for the allegience of the less-active supporters and sympathizers on which the terrorists depend. Both individual and group status can in large measure be denied to a terrorist group by the no-response response.

In sum, the importance of the no-response response flows from the previous four generalizations. If terrorists are normal people in abnormal groups, if terrorists are unlikely to be decisively defeated by government forces, if attempts to defeat terrorism can be more dangerous to the government than to the terrorists, if in any case anti-terrorist initiatives are communications with diverse and difficult to predict effects on diverse audiences – then the no-response response merits attention as potentially the best available reaction to terrorist challenge. At very least, as Crenshaw [*1983*] suggests, any other proposed reaction to terrorism can usefully be measured against the no-response response.

Indeed the value of the no-response response might be multiplied if policy-makers were willing to adopt a no-policy policy (Rapoport, personal communication)! Rather than declaring a national policy toward terrorists – no negotiation, or negotiation but no concession, or retribution, or pro-active defense – policy-makers might content themselves with declaring their intention to safeguard national interests as best they can, under whatever circumstances they face. Terrorists would find it more difficult to predict the reactions of policy makers and more difficult to embarass them for the inevitable departure from stated policy. Thus a no-policy policy may be valuable in maximizing the alternatives available to policy makers facing a particular terrorist threat, and may be even more valuable in legitimating the no-response response.

Future Research Toward Understanding Terrorism

I move now to more explicit consideration of some of the directions of research suggested in the five generalizations above, and to some other directions for research suggested by the contributions to this volume.

The communications model advanced above leads directly to audience research aimed at understanding the perceptions of both terrorists and policy-makers. Every act of either terrorist or government is a message that goes out at the same time to the pyramid of sympathizers below them, to rivals for the same supporters, to opposition policy-makers and their pyramids, and to the non-aligned or neutral grounds of the opposing pyramids. The same act can convey a different message to these different audiences. Even the different degrees of sympathy and commitment at the different levels of a single pyramid can constitute very different audiences, for whom the same act is interpreted and evaluated differently. An example is the tension between the Irish Republican Army and their supporters that is described by Thompson [*1985*]: the IRA presses for expansion of the definition of legitimate targets of violence but IRA supporters occasionally mobilize to protest a new expansion as barbaric.

The model of competing pyramids suggests that it would be helpful to know how the dialog of terrorist act and government response is received, interpreted, and evaluated. This is a kind of segmented audience research more familiar in advertising than in academic social science. Still, a notable example of this kind of research is the very extensive polling done for President Reagan, which evidently exceeded anything similar accomplished for any preceding US president [*Honomichl, 1989*]. At any given moment Reagan was in a position to know what issues were most important to Americans and what their evaluation of each issue was. Presumably this information made it possible for him to know better how to direct the agenda of policy-making. The point is that, to the extent that terrorism and anti-terrorist policy are interacting communications, it is desirable to know more about the impact of this dialog on relevant audiences.

One way of thinking about the kind of audience research suggested is that terrorism is a challenge to the legitimacy of government and anti-terrorist policy is an answer to that challenge. The political science literature may suggest how to measure the legitimacy of both government and terrorist group such that changes in each can be tracked by polling research or focus-group research.

In addition to audience research, the seminar contributions and discussions suggest more academic kinds of research that may be of help in understanding terrorism and its effects.

First is the question of how people react to rare but highly salient events. Research in cognitive psychology has recognized that some rare events, such as nuclear accidents and natural disaster, are systematically over-estimated in terms of their perceived probability and the attention given them. Some more common events, such as death by accident at home, are systematically underattended to [*Slovik, Fischoff and Lichtenstein, 1982*]. It seems possible that basic research on perceived risk could illuminate how terrorist acts, which are also are rare but salient events, may be overattended to.

A second line of research that might be helpful focuses on how minorities sometimes succeed in influencing majorities. As mentioned earlier, Moscovici [*1985*] has initiated research on this question and suggests that the dynamics of minority influence are qualitatively different from the dynamics of majority influence. In particular this research suggests that minorities can influence the private opinions of the majority even when the public expressions of the majority remain unchanged. The degree of influence exercised by minority on majority has been found to depend on the consistency of the minority position and the degree to which it is seen as contrary to the self-interest or security of the minority. There does appear to be a useful parallel here, to the extent that terrorists are consistent and risk-taking in their commitment to violence. Thus the research on minority influence may prove to be useful in understanding how a terrorist minority can produce real sympathy for their cause, at least among those not already hostile toward them.

A related direction of research is more historical. What makes a martyr? Not every individual who dies for a cause stimulates greater devotion to that cause in others. Some sacrifice themselves without being noticed, or are noticed but labeled as incomprehensible or crazy. There could be something useful to be learned by considering the history of the concept of martyrdom and looking for differences across times and cultures in the social construction of martyrdom.

Third, terrorism research might find it useful to distinguish between *internalization* or private acceptance of persuasion, on the one hand, and *compliance* or public agreement without private acceptance, on the other hand. This distinction has been useful in understanding attitude change [*Kelman, 1961*], group dynamics [*Jones and Gerard, 1967*], and group-think [*Janis, 1982; McCauley, 1989*], and would seem therefore to have some potential for understanding the dynamics of terrorist groups. Of course it can be difficult to determine whether group agreement reflects internalization, compliance, or some combination of these, especially in a small and cohesive group. Nevertheless the evidence of conflict over strategy, tactics, and especially leadership within terrorist groups is evidence that failures of private acceptance do often occur in these groups. Sometimes the result of conflict is a fissioning into new groups, or even death for some members of the group [*McCauley and Segal, 1987*].

The importance of the distinction between internalization and compliance in combatting terrorism is suggested by the experience of dealing with Chinese soldiers captured by UN forces in the Korean War [*Bradbury, Meyers and Biderman, 1968*]. In combat the Chinese fought very well, seldom surrendering unless in very adverse conditions; as POWs, however, the same soldiers divided into pro- and anti-Communist factions and fought battles within the camps that left many dead. Over half the Chinese POWs refused repatriation to China after the war (they were sent back anyway, to speed return of US POWs from China). Evidently the social control exercised in the Red Army was more successful in terms of compliance than in terms of internalization, and it could be useful to know to what degree this might be true of some terrorist groups as well.

A fourth direction of research would be to apply what has been learned about the motivation and behavior of men in combat to understanding the behavior of terrorists. In war, normal men are brought to behaviors of extreme violence, and, without denying the importance of the rules of war that distinguish the soldier from the terrorist, it seems likely that there are important aspects of individual and group psychology that are common to both. The classic work of Stouffer *et al. [1949]* on the American soldier in WWII provides a convenient starting point for this kind of inquiry, but research from the Vietnam War may be more relevant. That is, the experience of fighting a guerrilla war – small groups fighting isolated battles in difficult terrain controlled, at least at night, by the enemy – may be more like the experience of terrorist groups than like the experience of large-force battles in the Second World War.

Fifth, there is a distinction between *instrumental* and *expressive* aggression [*Krebs and Miller, 1985*] that might be of use in the study of a terrorist violence. Instrumental aggression is behavior aimed at hurting another in the service of some other goal, for instance for money, self-preservation, justice, or correction. Spanking a child is instrumental aggression, if done without anger; so is pulling a tooth. Expressive aggression is behavior for which the primary goal is hurting another, and this kind of aggression is usually associated with emotions of anger, hate, or revenge. In dealing with terrorists it would seem helpful to know whether their violence is, as they usually say it is, strictly instrumental in the service of their political cause. If so, negotiation is a realistic policy response, and terrorists can be led to renouncing terrorist tactics as Arafat recently did for the PLO. But there may be dynamics of personal commitment, including revenge for dead or tortured comrades, that push terrorists from violence as a strategy to violence as an identity and a way of life [*Post, 1986*]. Similarly, the trajectory from protest to terrorism

(Sprinzak, this volume) may include at the extreme a stage of conflict with the state that extends to the reversal of every social norm and a real hatred for every person associated with the society against which the terrorists have set themselves. Here negotiation is probably useless.

As with the distinction between compliance and internalization, the distinction between instrumental and expressive aggression can be difficult to make in practice. It is probably safe to say that many acts of violence are committed with some combination of instrumental and expressive motives. Nevertheless, the distinction may be important at the extremes, where some terrorists act coldly ('nothing personal' says the IRA – Thompson and Quets [*1990*]) and others kill with excess and emotion ('Dig it', says Bernadine Dohrin about the Manson Family rampage, 'First they killed those pigs, then they ate dinner in the same room with them, they even shoved a fork into a victim's stomach! Wild!' – Collier and Horowitz [*1989*]). Killing without emotion may seem worse in being somehow less human than killing with emotion, but the prospect for negotiation may be better with those who kill coldly.

Sixth is the possibility of finding something useful about the anti-social extremism of terrorism by looking at research on the pro-social extremism of those who risk their lives to help others. In particular there is recent research with those Europeans who helped hide Jews from the Nazis during the Second World War that seems to show that there was some kind of identifiable social marginality about many of those who helped in this fashion [*Oliner and Oliner, 1988*]. The idea here is that terrorism and extreme altruism are alike in being anti-normative behavior of clinically normal persons.

Seventh and last is a research implication of Sprinzak's theory of the individual trajectory to terrorism (this volume). Sprinzak suggests that government could learn enough about political opposition groups to provide early warning of the transition to terrorism. There may be problems with this degree of surveillance in a democratic environment, but Sprinzak's theory does focus attention on the transitions from one stage or level of opposition to another. If only groups that have completed the trajectory to terrorism are studied, the transitions will tend to seem inevitable. But Sprinzak is at pains to suggest that the transition to terrorism is not inevitable, and the implication of his suggestion is that opposition groups should be studied who have not made a commitment to terrorism. That is, understanding of terrorism might be advanced by study of political opposition groups that moved toward but stopped short of or retreated from terrorism. The goal is to learn what determines the transition from normal opposition to terrorism.

The common denominator of these suggestions for research on terrorism is the recognition that terrorists are normal people behaving abnormally.

The premise of cognitive psychology is that people respond, not to the world as it is, but to the world as perceived. The premise of anthropology, history, political science, social psychology, and sociology is that the world perceived is not the product only of individual cognition, but is rather a social construction anchored in group norms. Those who would enter the mind of the terrorist will need everything that cognitive and social science can contribute toward understanding how men will kill to advance a vision of reality worth living for.

Consolidated Bibliography

AbuKhalil, As'ad, 1987, 'Internal Contradictions in the PFLP: Decision Making and Policy Orientation'. *Middle East Journal* 41, 361–7.

Amnesty International (AI), 1984, 'Peru: Human Rights Violations'. London (AI pamphlet).

Amnesty International (AI), 1986, 'Human Rights in Chile: The Role of the Medical Profession'. London (AI pamphlet).

Amon, Moshe, 1982, 'The Unraveling of the Myth of Progress', D. C. Rapoport and Y. Alexander (eds.), *Morality of Terrorism: Religious and Secular Justifications*, New York: Pergamon Press, pp. 62–76.

Aran, Gideon, 1985, *Eretz Yisrael: Between Politics and Religion* (Hebrew), Jerusalem: The Jerusalem Institute for the Study of Israel.

Arnon-Ohanna, Yuval, 1981, *The Internal Struggle Within The Palestinian Movement 1929–1939* (Hebrew), Tel Aviv: Yariv-Hadar.

Argentine National Commission on the Disappeared, 1986, *Nuncas Mas: The Report of the Argentine National Commission on the Disappeared*, New York: Farrar, Straus, Giroux.

Aron, Raymond, 1959, *On War*, New York: Doubleday Anchor Books.

Bandura, Albert, 1973, 'Social Learning Theory of Aggression', in J. F. Knutson (ed.), *The Control of Aggression: Implications from Basic Research*, New York: Hawthorn.

Bandura, Albert, (in press), 'Mechanisms of Moral Disengagement', in W. Reich (ed.), *The Psychology of Terrorism*, Washington, DC: The Wilson Center Press.

Bass, Gail, Jenkins, Brian M., Kellen, Konrad, and David Ronfeldt, 1981, *Options for U.S. Policy on Terrorism*, Santa Monica, CA: RAND Corporation.

Bateson, Gregory, 1972, *Steps to an Ecology of Mind*, New York: Ballantine Books.

Becker, Jilliaan, 1977, *Hitler's Children: The Story of the Baader–Meinhoff Gang*, New York: J.B. Lippincott.

Becket, J.C., 1971, 'Northern Ireland', *Journal of Contemporary History*, Vol. 6, No. 1.

Beidelman, Thomas, 1970, 'Towards More Open Theoretical Interpretations', in M. Douglas (ed.), *Witchcraft Confessions and Accusations*, London: Tavistock.

Bell, J. Bowyer, 1978, 'Terror: An Overview', in M. H. Livingston, L. B. Kress and M. G. Wanek (eds.), *International Terrorism in the Contemporary World*, Westport, CT: Greenwood Press, pp. 36–43.

Beresford, David, 1988, *Ten Men Dead*, New York: *Atlantic Monthly Press*.

Bering-Jensen, Henrik, 1988, 'The Silent Treatment for Terrorists', *Insight*, 21 Nov., 34–5.

Bernstein, Jonas, 1989, 'Marks of Chemical Warfare Bear Distinct Soviet Shape', *Insight*, 26 June, 28–30.

Bhagwan, Vishnoo, 1954, *Constitutional History of India and Its National Movement*, 4th ed., Delhi: Atma Ram.

Billington, James H., 1958, *Michailovsky and Russian Populism*, London: Oxford University Press.

Bittman, Ladislav, 1972, *The Deception Game: Czechoslovak Intelligence in Soviet Political Warfare*, Syracuse, NY: Syracuse University Research Corporation.

Bond, Brian, 1977, *Liddell Hart: A Study of His Military Thought*, New Brunswick,

NJ: Rutgers University Press.

Bowyer, J. Barton, 1982, *Cheating*, New York: St. Martin's Press.

Bradbury, William C., Meyers, Samuel M. and Albert D. Biderman, 1968, *Mass Behavior in Battle and Captivity*, Chicago, IL: University of Chicago Press.

Burgess, William H., III, 1986, 'Special Operations Forces and the Challenge of Transnational Terrorism', *Military Intelligence*, 12.2, 8–15, 48.

Callwell, Charles E., 1906, *Small Wars: Their Principles and Practice*, 3rd. ed., London: Harrison and Sons.

Caselli, Gian Carlo, 1986, 'Comment nous avons vaincu les Brigades rouges', *Le Nouvel Observateur*, 21–27 Nov, 30.

Chaliand, Gérard, 1985, *Terrorismes et guerillas: techinques actuelles de la violence*, Paris: Flammarion.

Chesnais, Jean-Claude, 1981, *Histoire de la violence en Occident de 1800 a nos jours*, Paris: Robert Laffont.

Chomsky, Noam, 1986, 'Middle East Terrorism and the American Ideological System', *Race & Class* 28, 1–28.

Christides, Vassilios, 1984, 'Naval Warfare in the Eastern Mediterranean (6th–14th Centuries): An Arabic Translation of Leo VI's Naumachia', *Graeco-Arabica* 3, 137–48.

Clark, Ramsey, 1988, 'The Dimensions of Terrorism', in H. Köchler (ed.), *Terrorism and National Liberation*, Frankfurt a.M.: Verlag Peter Lang, pp. 41–8.

Clausewitz, Carl von, 1976, *On War*, trans. M. Howard and P. Paret, Princeton, NJ: Princeton University Press.

Clauss, Manfred, 1979, 'Die Rezeption der Antike bei Francois-Noel (Camille-Gracchus) Babeuf', *Gymnasium* 86, 81–94.

Cline, Ray S., and Yonah Alexander, 1984, *Terrorism: The Soviet Connection*, New York: Crane, Russak.

Clutterbuck, Richard, 1977, *Guerrillas and Terrorists*, London: Faber.

Clutterbuck, Richard L., 1981, *The Media and Political Violence*, New York: Macmillan.

Collier, Peter and David Horowitz, 1989, *Destructive Generation: Second Thoughts about the '60s*, . New York: Summit Books.

Cooper, H.H.A., 1978, 'Terrorism and the Intelligence Function', in M.H. Livingston, L.K. Kress and M.G. Wanek (eds.), *International Terrorism in the Contemporary World*, Westport, CT: Greenwood Press, pp. 287–96.

Cordes, Bonnie, 1988, 'When Terrorists Do the Talking: Reflections on Terrorist Literature', in D.C. Rapoport (ed.), *Inside Terrorist Organizations*, New York: Columbia University Press; London: Frank Cass, pp. 150–71.

Crenshaw, Martha, 1983, 'Conclusions', in M. Crenshaw (ed.), *Terrorism, Legitimacy, and Power*, Middletown, CT: Wesleyan University Press, pp. 143–9.

Crenshaw, Martha, 1986, 'Psychology of Terrorism', in M. Hermann (ed.), *Handbook of Political Psychology*, San Francisco, CA: Jossey-Bass, pp. 379–413.

Crenshaw, Martha, 1987, 'How Terrorism Ends', Paper presented to the American Political Science Association.

Crenshaw, Martha, 1988, 'Theories of Terrorism: Instrumental and Organzational Approaches', in D.C. Rapoport (ed.), *Inside Terrorist Organizations*, New York: Columbia University Press; London: Frank Cass, pp. 13–31.

Crenshaw, Nancy, 1978, *The Cyprus Revolt*, London: George Allen & Unwin.

Crick, Malcolm, 1976, *Explorations in Language and Meaning: Toward a Semantic Anthropology*, New York: John Wiley.

Dagron, G. and Mihăescu, H. (eds.), 1986, *Nicephorus Phocas, La traité sur la guérilla (de velitatione) de l'empereur Nicéphore Phocas (963–969)*, Paris: Centre national de la recherche scientique.

Davie, Maurice R., 1929, *The Evolution of War*, New Haven, CT: Yale University Press.

Demaris, David, 1977, *Brothers in Blood: The International Terrorist Network*. New York: Charles Scriber's.

Dennis, George T., 1985, *Three Byzantine Military Treatises*, Washington: Dumbarton Oaks.

Dowdling, Joseph A., 1978, 'Prolegomena to a Psychohistorical Study of Terrorism', in M. H. Livingston, L. B. Kress and M. G. Wanek (eds.), *International Terrorism in the Contemporary World*, Westport, CT: Greenwood Press, pp. 223–30.

Drake, Richard H., 1986, 'Julius Evola and the Ideological Origins of the Radical Right in Contemporary Italy', in Peter Merkl (ed.), *Political Violence and Terror: Motifs and Motivations*, Berkeley and Los Angeles, CA: University of California Press.

Dror, Yehezkel, 1983, 'Terrorism as a Challenge to the Democratic Capacity to Govern', in M. Crenshaw (ed.), *Terrorism, Legitimacy, and Power*, Middletown, CT: Wesleyan University Press, pp. 65–90.

Dugard, John, 1982, 'International Terrorism and Just War', in D. C. Rapoport and Y. Alexander (eds.), in *The Morality of Terrorism: Religious and Secular Justifications*, New York: Pergamon Press, pp. 77–98.

English, J. A., 1987, 'Kindergarten Soldier: The Military Thought of Lawrence of Arabia', *Military Affairs* 51, 7–11.

Evans-Pritchard, Edward E., 1951, *Social Anthropology*, New York: The Free Press.

Falk, Richard, 1988, 'The Overall Terrorist Challenge in International Political Life', in H. Köchler (ed.), *Terrorism and National Liberation*, Frankfurt a.M.: Verlag Peter Lang, pp. 15–22.

Farrell, William R., 1986, 'Organized to Combat Terrorism', in N. C. Livingstone and T. E. Arnold (eds.), *Fighting Back: Winning the War against Terrorism*, Lexington, MA: D. C. Heath, pp. 49–58.

Ferracuti, Franco, 1982, 'A Sociopsychiatric Interpretation of Terrorism', *The Annals of the American Academy of Sciences* 463, Sept.

Ferrill, Arthur, 1985, *The Origins of War: From the Stone Age to Alexander the Great*, London: Thames & Hudson.

Fields, Louis G., Jr., 1986, 'The Third Annual Waldemar A. Solf Lecture in International Law: Contemporary Terrorism and the Rule of Law', *Military Law Review* 113, 1–15.

Finn, John E., 1987, 'Public Support for Emergency (Anti-Terrorist) Legislation in Northern Ireland: A Preliminary Analysis', *Terrorism* 10, 113–124.

Ford, Franklin L., 1985, *Political Murder: From Tyrannicide to Terrorism*, Cambridge, MA: Harvard University Press.

Fournier, Louis, 1982, *FLQ: Histoire d'un Mouvement Clandestin*, Montreal: Quebec-Amerique.

Franzius, Enno, 1969, *History of the Order of the Assassins*, New York: Funk & Wagnalls.

Frazer, James G., 1922, 'The Golden Bough', 3rd ed., 2 vols. New York: Macmillan.

Freud, Sigmund, 1950, *Totem and Taboo*, New York: W. W. Norton.

Fuller, John F. C., 1923, *The Reformation of War*. London: Hutchinson.

Furlong, Paul, 1983, 'Political Terrorism in Italy: Responses, Relations and Immobilism', in *Terrorism – A Challenge to the State*, London: Frances Pinter.

Gaddis, John Lewis, 1987, 'Expanding the Data Base: Historians, Political Scientists, and the Enrichment of Security Studies', *International Security* 12, 3–21.

Gentili, Alberico, 1933, *De iure belli*, trans. J.C. Rolfe (Classics of International Law, No. 16, 2 vols.), Oxford: Clarendon Press.

Gonzalez, 1983, *QueHacer*, #20.

Gros, Bernard, 1978, 'Terrorism and Literature', in M.H. Livingstone, L.B. Kress and M.G. Wanek (eds.), *International Terrorism in the Contemporary World*, Westport, CT: Greenwood Press, pp. 447–53.

Guelke, Adrian, 1986, 'Loyalist and Republican Perceptions of the Northern Ireland Conflict: The UDA and Provisional IRA', in P.H. Merkl (ed.), *Political Violence and Terror: Motifs and Motivations*, Berkeley, CA: University of California Press, pp. 91–122.

Guevara, Che, 1961, *Guerilla Warfare*, New York: Vintage Books.

Gurr, Ted Robert, 1970, *Why Men Rebel*, Princeton, NJ: Princeton University Press.

Gurr, Ted Robert, 1980, 'On the Outcomes of Violence Conflict', in T.R. Gurr (ed.), *Handbook of Political Conflict*, New York: Free Press, pp. 238–94.

Hacker, Frederick J., 1976, *Crusaders, Criminals, Crazies*, New York: Norton.

Hahlweg, Werner, 1977, 'Moderner Guerilakrieg und Terrorismus: Probleme und Aspekte ihrer theoretische Grundlagen als Widerspiegelung der Praxis', in M. Funke (ed.), *Terrorismus: Untersuchungen zur Struktur und Strategie revolutionarer Gewaltpolitik*, Dusseldorf: Athenaum Verlag, pp. 118–39.

Hanle, Donald J., 1989, *Terrorism: The Newest Face of Warfare*, Washington: Pergamon-Brassey's International Defense Publishers.

Hardman, J.B.S., 1978, 'Terrorism', in W. Laqueur (ed.), *The Terrorism Reader*, New York: New American Library, pp. 223–30 (= '1933 Terrorism', *Encyclopedia of the Social Sciences* 14, 575–9).

Herman, Charles F. (ed.), 1972, *International Crises: Insights from Behavioral Research*, New York: Free Press.

Honomichl, Jack, 1989, 'How Reagan Took America's Pulse', *Advertising Age*, 23 Jan., 1, 23, 25.

Horne, Alistaire, 1977, *A Savage War of Peace: Algeria 1954–1962*, London: Macmillan.

Horowitz, Irving L., 1967, 'The Routinization of Terrorism and Its Unanticipated Consequences', in M. Crenshaw (ed.), *Terrorism, Legitimacy, and Power*, Middleton, CT: Wesleyan University Press, pp. 38–51.

Hubbard, David G., 1971, *The Skyjacker: His Flight of Fantasy*, New York: Macmillan.

Hutchinson, Martha Crenshaw, 1978, *Revolutionary Terrorism: The FLN in Algeria 1954–1962*, Stanford, CA: Hoover Institution Press.

Ibn, Khaldun, 1958, *The Muqaddimah: An Introduction to History*, tr. F. Rosenthal. 3 vols., New York: Pantheon books.

Ivianski, Zeev, 1988, 'The Terrorist Revolution: Roots of Modern Terrorism', in D.C. Rapoport (ed.), *Inside Terrorist Organizations*, New York: Columbia University Press; London: Frank Cass, pp. 129–49.

Jacobs, Harold (ed.), 1970, *Weatherman*, Berkeley, CA: Ramparts Press.

Jaffee Center for Strategic Studies, 1986, 'Inter 85: A Review of International Terrorism in 1985'. Jerusalem: The Jerusalem Post.

Jaffee Center for Strategic Studies, 1987, 'Inter 86: A Review of International Terrorism in 1986'. Jerusalem: The Jerusalem Post.

Janis, Irving, 1982, *Groupthink*, Boston, MA: Houghton, Mifflin.

Janis, Irving L. and Leon Mann, 1977, *Decision making*, New york: Free Press.

Janke, Peter, 1983, *Guerrilla and Terrorist Organizations: A World Directory and Bibliography*, London: Macmillan.

Jenkins, Brian M., 1975, 'International Terrorism: A New Mode of Conflict', in D. Carlton and C. Schaerf (eds.), *International Terrorism and World Security*, London: Croom Helm.

Jenkins, Brian M., 1980, *The Study of Terrorism: Definitional Problems*, Santa Monica, CA: The RAND Corporation.

Jenkins, Brian M., 1983, *Some Reflections on Recent Trends in Terrorism*, Santa Monica, CA: The RAND Corporation (RAND Paper P-6897).

Jones, Edward E. and Harold B. Gerard, 1967, *Foundations of Social Psychology*, New York: Wiley.

Jousen, Albert and Leonard Sagan, 1985, 'Torture and the Ethics of Medicine', in E. Stover and E. Nightingale (eds.), *The Breaking of Minds and Bodies*, New York: W. A. Freeman.

Jydi, Charles, 1986, 'Psychiatry: A New Form of Repression', *S.O.S. Torture*, June.

Kaplan, Abraham, 1978, 'The Psychodynamics of Terrorism', *Terrorism: An International Journal* 1, 237–54.

Karsten, Rafael, 1967, 'Blood Revenge and War Among the Jibaro Indians of Eastern Ecuador', in P. Bohannon (ed.), *Law and Warfare: Studies in the Anthropology of Conflict*, Garden City, NY: Natural History Press, pp. 303–25.

Keegan, John, 1976, *The Face of Battle*, New York: Vintage Books.

Kelman, Herbert C., 1961, 'Processes of Opinion Change', *Public Opinion Quarterly* 25, 57–78.

Khawam, René R., 1976, *Le livre des ruses: la strategie politique des Arabes*, Paris: Phébus.

Kirschner, Robert, 1984, 'The Use of Drugs in Torture and Human Rights Abuses', *The American Journal of Forensic Medicine and Pathology* 5.

Knightley, Phillip, 1975, *The First Casualty*, New York: Harcourt Brace.

Kolias, Taxiarchis G., 1984, 'The Taktika of Leo the Wise and the Arabs', *Graeco-Arabica* 3, 129–35.

Knutson, Jeanne N., 1980, 'The Terrorist's Dilemmas: Some Implicit Rules of the Game', *Terrorism: An International Journal*, Vol. 4.

Krauss, Ellis E., 1974, *Japanese Radicals Revisited: Student Protest in Post-War Japan*, Berkeley, CA: University of Calfornia Press.

Krebs, Dennis L. and Dale T. Miller, 1985, 'Altruism and Aggression', in G. Lindzey and E. Aronson (eds.), *Handbook of Social Psychology*, Vol. II, 3rd ed., New York: Random House, pp. 1–72.

Kuhfus, Peter M., 1985, 'Die Anfänge der Volkskriegsdoktrin in China', in G. Schulz (ed.), *Partisanen und Volkskrieg: zur Revolutionierung des Krieges im 20. Jahrhundert*, Gottingen: Vandenhoeck und Ruprecht, pp. 57–91.

Laqueur, Walter, 1977a, *Guerilla: A Historical and Critical Study*, London: Weidenfeld & Nicolson.

Laqueur, Walter, 1977b, *The Guerilla Reader: An Historical Anthology*, New York: New American Library.

Laqueur, Walter, 1977c, *Terrorism*, Boston, MA: Little, Brown.

Laqueur, Walter, 1978, *The Terrorism Reader: A Historical Anthology*, New York: New American Library.

Laqueur, Walter, 1986, 'Reflections on Terrorism', *Foreign Affairs* 65, 86–100.

Laqueur, Walter, 1987, *The Age of Terrorism*, London: Weidenfeld and Nicolson.

Lawrence, Thomas E., 1939, 'The Evolution of a Revolt', in A. W. Lawrence (ed.),

Oriental Assembly, (= *1920 Army Quarterly* 1, 55–69), London: Williams and Norgate, pp. 99–134.

Leach, Edmund, 1975, *Culture and Communication*, Cambridge: Cambridge University Press.

Leach, Edmund, 1977, *Custom, Law, and Terrorist Violence*, Edinburgh: Edinburgh University Press.

Leaf, Murray J., 1985, 'The Punjab Crisis', *Asian Survey* 25, 475–98.

Legault, Albert, 1983, 'La dynamique du terrorisme: le cas des Brigades Rouges', *Revue Etudes Internationales* 14, 639–81.

Levi-Strauss, Claude, 1962, *Totemism*, Boston, MA: Beacon Press.

Lewis, Bernard, 1967, *The Assassins: A Radical Sect in Islam*, London: Weidenfeld & Nicolson.

Lider, Julian, 1982, *Military Theory: Concept, Structure, Problems*, (*Swedish Studies in International Relations*, No. 12), New York: St. Martin's Press.

Liddell Hart, B.H., 1950, *Defence of the West*, London: Cassell.

Liddell Hart, B.H., 1967, *Strategy*, 2nd ed., New York: New American Library.

Lipset, Seymour Martin and Earl Raab, 1970, *The Politics of Unreason: Right Wing Extremism in America 1790–1970*, New York: Harper & Row.

Livingston, Marius H., Kress, Lee Bruce and Marie G. Wanek (eds.), 1978, *International Terrorism in the Contemporary World* (Contributions in Political Science, No. 3), Westport, CT: Greenwood Press.

Lopez-Alves, Fernando, 1985, 'Urban guerrillas and the Rise of Bureaucratic Authoritarianism in Uruguay: 1959–1972', Paper presented to the American Political Science Association.

Luttwak, Edward N., 1976, *The Grand Strategy of the Roman Empire*, Baltimore, MD: Johns Hopkins University Press.

Luttwak, Edward N., 1987, *Strategy: The Logic of War and Peace*, Cambridge, MA: Harvard University Press.

McCauley, Clark, 1989, 'The Nature of Social Influence in Groupthink: Compliance and Internalization', *Journal of Personality and Social Psychology* 57, 250–60.

McCauley, Clark R. and Mary R. Segal, 1987, 'Social Psychology of Terrorist Groups', in *Review of Personality and Social Psychology* 9, ed. by C Hendrick. Beverly Hills: Sage, pp. 231–56.

McCormick, Gordon H., 1988, 'The Shining Path and Peruvian Terrorism', in D. C. Rapoport (ed.), *Inside Terrorist Organizations*, New York: Columbia University Press; London: Frank Cass, pp. 109–26.

MacDonald, Brian R., 1984, 'Leisteia and Leizomai in Thucydides and in *IG* I^3 41, 67, and 75', *American Journal of Philology* 105, 77–84.

MacMullen, Ramsey, 1966, *Enemies of the Roman Order*, Cambridge, MA: Harvard University Press.

Madelin, Philippe, 1986, *La galaxie terroriste*, Paris: Plon.

Malinowski, Bronislaw, 1926, *Crime and Custom in Savage Society*, New York: Harcourt Brace.

Mallin, Jay, 1978, 'Terrorism as a Military Weapon', in M.H. Livingston, L.B. Kress and M.G. Wanek (ed.), *International Terrorism in the Contemporary World*, Westport, CT: Greenwood Press, pp. 389–401 (1977 *Air University Review* 28, 54–64).

Merari, Ariel (ed.), 1979, *Kingfisher Game: Summary of Procedure and Analysis*, Tel Aviv: The Center for Strategic Studies and the Office of the Prime Minister's Adviser on Combatting Terrorism.

Merari, Ariel and Shlomi Elad, 1986, *The International Dimension of Palestinian*

Terrorism, Boulder, CO: Westview Press.

Merari, Ariel and Nehemia Friedland, 1980, *Israeli Public Attitudes Toward Terrorism*, Tel Aviv: The Center for Strategic Studies.

Merari, Ariel and Nehemia Friedland, 1985, 'Social Psychological Aspects of Political Terrorism', in Stewart Oskamp (ed.), *International Conflict and National Public Policy Issues* (Applied Social Psychology Annual, Vol. 6), Beverly Hills, CA: Sage, pp. 185–205.

Merkl, Peter, 1986, 'Rollerball or Neo-Nazi Violence', in P. Merkle (ed.), *Political Violence and Terror: Motifs and Motivations*, Berkeley, CA: University of California Press.

Mickolus, Edward, 1978, 'Trends in Transnational Terrorism', in M.H. Livingston, L.B. Kress and M.G. Wanek (ed.), *International Terrorism in the Contemporary World*, Westport, CT: Greenwood Press, pp. 44–73.

Milan, Alessandro, 1979–80, 'Ricerche sul latrocinium in Livio I: Iatro nelle fonti preaugustee', *Atti dell' Instituto Veneto di Scienze, Lettere ed Arti* 138, 171–97.

Morf, Gustav, 1970, *Terror in Quebec*, Toronto: Clark, Irwin.

Moscovici, Serge, 1985, 'Social Influence and Conformity', in G. Lindzey and E. Aronson (eds.), *Handbook of Social Psychology*, Vol. II, 3rd ed., New York: Random House, pp. 347–412.

Most, Johann, 1885, *Revolutionäre Kriegswissenschaft*, New York: Internationaler Zeitungs-Verein.

Nef, Jorge, 1978, 'Some Thoughts on Contemporary Terrorism: Domestic and International Perspectives', in J. Carson (ed.), *Terrorism in Theory and Practice*, Toronto: The Atlantic Council of Canada, pp. 3–30.

Newfield, Jack, 1970, *A Prophetic Minority*, New York: Signet Books.

Niv, Cavid, 1975, *Battle for Freedom: The Irgun Zvai Leumi (Hebrew)*, Part Two, Tel Aviv: Lausner Institute.

Oliner, Samuel P. and Pearl M. Oliner, 1988, *The Altruistic Personality*, New York: Free Press.

Otterbein, Keith F., 1973, 'The Anthropology of war', in J.J. Honigman (ed.), *Handbook of Social and Cultural Anthropology*, Chicago, IL: Rand McNally, pp. 923–58.

Parker, Harold T., 1937, *The Cult of Antiquity and the French Revolutionaries*, Chicago, IL: University of Chicago Press.

Picard, Robert G., 1987 'News Coverage as the Contagion of Terrorism: Dangerous Charges Backed by Dubious Science', *TVI Report* 7, 39–45.

Pletka, Danielle, 1989, 'Who Should Pay for Air Security?' *Insight*, 15 May, 20–21.

The Port Huron Statement, 1964, SDS pamphlet, New York.

Post, Jerrold M., 1984, 'Notes on a Psychodynamic Theory of Terrorist Behavior', *Terrorism: An International Journal*, Vol. 7, No. 3.

Post, Jerrold M., 1986 'Hostilite, Conformite, Fraternite: The Group Dynamics of Terrorist Behavior', *International Journal of Group Psychotherapy* 36 (2).

Powell, William, 1971, *The Anarchist Cookbook*, New York: L.Stuart.

Quester, George H., 1982, 'Eliminating the Terrorist Opportunity', in D.C. Rapoport and Y. Alexander (eds.), *The Morality of Terrorism: Religious and Secular Justifications*, New York: Pergamon Press, pp. 325–46.

Radcliffe-Brown, A.R., 1937, in *Encyclopedia of the Social Sciences*, Vols. IX–X (ed. by E.R. Seligman), New York: Macmillan, pp. 202–6.

Rapoport, David C., 1971, *Assassination and Terrorism*, Toronto: Canadian Broadcasting Corporation.

Rapoport, David C., 1982, 'Terror and the Messiah: An Ancient Experience and

Some Modern Parallels', in D.C. Rapoport and Y. Alexander (eds.), *The Morality of Terrorism: Religious and Secular Justifications*, New York: Pergamon Press, pp.12–42.

Rapoport, David C., 1984, 'Fear and Trembling: Terrorism in Three Religious Traditions', *American Political Science Review*, 78, 658–77.

Rapoport, David C., 1985, 'Why Does Messianism Produce Terror?' Paper presented at the annual meeting of the American Political Science Association (Aug.), New Orleans.

Rapoport, David C., 1987, 'Why Does Religious Messianism Produce Terror?' in P. Wilkinson and A.M. Stewart *Contemporary Research on Terrorism*, Aberdeen: Aberdeen University Press.

Rapoport, David C., 1988, 'The International World as Some Terrorists Have Seen It: A Look at a Century of Memoirs', in D.C. Rapoport (ed.), *Inside Terrorist Organizations*, New York: Columbia University Press; London: Frank Cass, pp.32–58.

Rapoport, David C., 1990, 'Sacred Terror: A Contemporary Example from Islam', in W. Reich (ed.), *The Origins of Terrorism: Psychologies, Ideologies, Theologies, States of Mind*, New York: Cambridge University Press, pp.103–30.

Rapoport, David C. and Yonah Alexander (eds.), 1982, *The Morality of Terrorism: Religious and Secular Justifications*, New York: Pergamon Press.

Reich, Walter, 1985, 'The World of Soviet Psychiatry', in E. Stover and E. Nightingale (eds.), *The Breaking of Minds and Bodies*, New York: W.A. Freeman.

Rivers, Gayle, 1986, *The War Against the Terrorists: How to Win It*, New York: Stein & Day.

Röllig, Wolfgang, 1986, 'Assur – Geissel der Völker: zur Typologie aggressiver Gesellschaften', *Saeculum* 37, 116–28.

Romano, Anne T., 1984, 'Terrorism: An Analysis of the Literature', dissertation, Fordham University.

Rosch, Eleanor, 1975, 'Cognitive Representations of Semantic Categories', *Journal of Experimental Psychology: General* 104, 192–233.

Rose, R.B., 1978, *Gracchus Babeuf: The First Revolutionary Communist*, Palo Alto, CA: Stanford University Press.

Ross, Jeffrey Ian and Ted Robert Gurr, 1989, 'Why Terrorism Subsides: A Comparative Study of Trends and Groups in Terrorism in Canada and the United States', *Comparative Politics* 21, 405–26.

Rubenstein, Richard E., 1987, *Alchemists of Revolution: Terrorism in the Modern World*, New York: Basic Books.

Rumpf, Helmut, 1985, 'International Legal Problems of Terrorism', *Aussenpolitik* (English ed.) 35, 388–404.

Russell, Charles A. and Bowman H. Miller, 1977, 'Profile of a Terrorist', *Terrorism* 1, 17–34.

Saxe, Maurice de, 1971, *Reveries of Memoirs upon the Art of War*, Westport, CT: Greenwood Press.

Schelling, Thomas C., 1966, *Arms and Influence*, New Haven, CT: Yale University Press.

Schindler, Dietrich, 1979, 'State of War, Belligerency, Armed Conflict', in A. Cassese (ed.), *The New Humanitarian Law of Armed Conflict*, Vol. 1, Naples: Editoriale Scientifica, pp.3–20.

Schmid, Alex P., 1983, *Political Terrorism: A Research Guide to Concepts, Theories, Data Vases and Literature*, New Brunswick, NJ: Transaction Books.

Schmid, Alex and Janny de Graaf, 1982, *Violence as Communication: Insurgent Terrorism and the Western News Media*, Beverly Hills, CA: Sage.

Schmid, Alex P. and A.J. Jongman, 1988, *Political Terrorism: A New Guide to Actors and Authors, Data Bases, and Literature*, 2nd ed. Amsterdam/New Brunswick, NJ: Transaction Publishers.

Schnapp, Alain and Pierre Vidall-Naquet, 1969, *Journal de la commune etudiante*, Paris: Editions de Seuil.

Sederberg, Peter C., 1989, *Terrorist Myths: Illusion, Rhetoric, and Reality*, Englewood Cliffs, NJ: Prentice Hall.

Service, Elman R., 1971, *Primitive Social Organization*, 2nd ed. New York: Random House.

Slovik, Paul, Fischoff, Baruch and Sarah Lichtenstein, 1982, 'Facts versus Fears: Understanding Perceived Risk', in D. Kahneman, P. Slovik and A. Tversky (eds.), *Judgement under Uncertainty: Heuristics and Biases*, New York: Cambridge, pp. 463–89.

Speer, James R., 1989, 'Detection of Plastic Explosives', *Science*, 31 March, 1651.

Sprinzak, Ehud, 1976, 'France: The Radicalization of the New Left', in M. Kolinsky and W.E. Paterson (eds.), *Social and Political Movements in Western Europe*, London: Croom Helm.

Sprinzak, Ehud, 1977, 'Marxism as a Symbolic Action', in S. Aviner (ed.), *Varieties of Marxism*, The Hague: Martinus Neijhof.

Sprinzak, Ehud, 1985, 'Kach and Rabbi Meir Kahane: The Emergence of Jewish Quasi Fascism', *Patterns of Prejudice*, Vol. 19, Nos. 3–4.

Sprinzak, Ehud, 1987a, 'From Messanic Pioneering to Vigilante Terrorism: The Case of the Gush Emunim Underground', *Journal of Strategic Studies*, Vol. 10, No. 4, Dec. (Special Issue: 'Inside Terrorist Organizations' edited by D.C. Rapoport).

Sprinzak, Ehud, 1987b, 'The Psychopolitical Formation of Extreme Left Terrorism in a Democracy: The Case of the Weatherman', Paper presented at the Conference on the Psychology of Terrorism, Woodrow Wilson International Center for Scholars, Washington, DC, 16–18 March and in press in W. Reich (ed.), *The Psychology of Terrorism*, Washington, DC: The Wilson Center Press.

Steiner, Franz, 1967, *Taboo*, Hardmondsworth: Penguin Books.

Sterling, Claire, 1981, *The Terror Network*, New York: Holt, Rinehart and Winston.

Stouffer, Samuel A. *et al.*, 1949, *The American Soldier, Vol. 2: Combat and Its Aftermath*, Princeton, NJ: Princeton University Press.

Strauss, Eric, 1951, *Irish Nationalism and British Democracy*, New York: Columbia University Press.

Taheri, Amir, 1987, *Holy Terror: The Inside Story of Islamic Terrorism*, London: Hutchinson.

Tantum, Geoffrey, 1979, 'Muslim Warfare: A Study of a Medieval Muslim Treatise on the Art of War', in R. Elgood (ed.), *Islamic Arms and Armour*, Scholar Press, pp. 187–201.

Targ, Harry R., 1979, 'Societal Structure and Revolutionary Terrorism: A Preliminary Investigation', in M. Stohl (ed.), *The Politics of Terrorism*, New York: Marcel Dekker, pp. 119–43.

Tarrow, Sidney and Donatella della Porta, 1986, 'Unwanted Children: Political Violence and the Cycle of Protest in Italy, 1966–1972', *European Journal of Political Research* 14, 607–32.

Taylor, Maxwell, 1988, *The Terrorist*, London: Brassey's.

Teodori, Massimo (ed.), 1969, *The New Left: A Documentary History*, New York:

Bobbs Merrill.

Terry, James P., 1986, 'An Appraisal of Lawful Military Response to State-Sponsored Terrorism', *Naval War College Review* 39, 59–68.

Thompson, John L.P., 1985, 'Crime, Social Control, and Trends in Political Killing', Paper presented at the Annual Meetings of the Sociological Association of Ireland, Belfast.

Thompson, John L.P. and Gail A. Quets, 1990, 'Genocide and Social Conflict: A Partial Theory and a Comparison', *Research in Social Movements, Conflicts, and Change* 12, 243–64.

Thompson, L.P., 1989, 'Deprivation and Political Violence in Northern Ireland, 1922–1985: A Time-Series Analysis', *Journal of Conflict Resolution* 33, 676–99.

Timmerman, Jacobo, 1981, *Prisoner Without a Name, Cell Without a Number*, New York: Knopf.

Tololyan, Khachig, 1986, 'Conflict and Decline in Armenian Terrorism', Paper presented to the American Political Science Association.

Tololyan, Khachig, 1988, 'Cultural Narrative and the Motivation of the Terrorist', in D.C. Rapoport (ed.), *Inside Terrorist Organizations*, New York: Columbia University Press; London: Frank Cass, pp. 217–33.

Trelease, A.W., 1971, *White Terror: The Ku Klux Klan Conspiracy and the Southern Reconstruction*, New York: Harper Torchbooks.

Turney-High, Harry Holbert, 1971, *Primitive Warfare: Its Practice and Concepts*, 2nd ed., Columbia, SC: University of South Carolina Press.

Turney-High, Harry Holbert, 1981, *The Military: The Theory of Land Warfare as Behavioral Science*, West Hanover, MA: Christopher Publishing House.

U.S. Department of State, 1986, 'Patterns of Global Terrorism: 1985', Washington, D.C.: Office of the Ambassador at Large for Counter-Terrorism.

U.S. Department of State, 1988, 'Patterns of Global Terrorism: 1986', Washington, D.C.: Office of the Ambassador at Large for Counter-Terrorism.

Van Creveld, Martin, 1990, *The Training of Officers: From Military Professionalism to Irrelevance*, New York: The Free Press.

Venturi, Franco, 1960, *The Roots of Revolution*, London: Weidenfeld & Nicolson.

Vought, Donald B. and James H. Fraser, 1986, 'Terrorism: The Search for Working Definitions', *Military Review* (July), 70–76.

Walter, E.V., 1969, *Terror and Resistance: A Study of Political Violence*, New York: Oxford University Press.

Wardlaw, Grant, 1988, 'Terror as an Instrument of Foreign Policy', in D.C. Rapoport (ed.), *Inside Terrorist Organizations*, New York: Columbia University Press; London: Frank Cass, pp. 237–59.

Weber, Max., 1949, *The Methodology of Social Sciences*, New York: The Free Press.

Wheeler, Everett L., 1981, 'The Origins of Military Theory in Ancient Greece and China', in *International Commission of Military History*, Acta 5, *Bucharest 1980*, Bucharest: Romanian Commission of Military History, pp. 74–9.

Wheeler, Everett L., 1988a, 'The Modern Legality of Frontinus' Stratagems', *Militärgeschichtliche Mitteilungen* 44. 1, 7–29.

Wheeler, Everett L., 1988b, 'Polla Kena Tou Polemou: The History of a Greek Proverb', *Greek, Roman and Byzantine Studies* 29, 153–84.

Wilkinson, Paul, 1979, 'Social Scientific Theory and Civil Violence', in Y. Alexander, D. Carlton and P. Wilkinson (eds.), *Terrorism: Theory and Practice*, Boulder, CO: Westview Press.

Wilkinson, Paul, 1986a, *Terrorism and the Liberal State*, revised edition. New York: New York University Press.

Wilkinson, Paul, 1986b, 'Trends in International Terrorism and the American Response', in L. Freedman, Ch. Hill *et al.* (eds.), *Terrorism and International Order*, London: Routledge & Kegan.

Wilkinson, Paul, 1981, *The New Fascists*, . London: Grant McIntyre.

Wilkinson, Paul, 1982, 'The Laws of War and Terrorism', in D. C. Rapoport and Y. Alexander (eds.), *The Morality of Terrorism: Religious and Secular Justifications*, New York: Pergamon Press, pp. 308–24.

Williams, John W., 1989, 'Carlos Marighela: The Father of Urban Guerrilla Warfare', *Terrorism* 12, 1–20.

Wittgenstein, Ludwig, 1971, 'Remarks on Frazer's "Golden Bough"', *The Human World* 3, 18–41.

Wolf, John B., 1978, 'Terrorist Manipulation in the Democratic Process', in M. H. Livingston, L. B. Kress and M. G. Wanek (eds.), *International Terrorism in the Contemporary World*, Westport, CT: Greenwood Press, pp. 297–306.

Wright, Fred and Phyllis Wright, 1962, 'Violent Groups', *Group* 6 (2).

Wright, Quincy, 1965, *A Study of War*, Chicago, IL: University of Chicago Press.

Zulaika, Joseba, 1988, *Basque Violence: Metaphor and Sacrament*, Reno, NV: University of Nevada Press.

Subject Index

Citation Index